Thunder in my Soul

Thunder in my Soul
A Mohawk Woman Speaks

Patricia Monture-Angus

Fernwood Publishing
Halifax

Editing: Brenda Conroy
Design and production: Beverley Rach
Cover Photo: Denis (Okanee) Angus
>   The photograph on the cover was taken in "The Bowl" at the University of
>   Saskatchewan during the Welcome Week Pow Wow hosted by the Indigenous
>   Students Council. The combination of "Indian" tradition and the university
>   is appropriate for the cover of this book.

Printed and bound in Canada by: Hignell Printing Limited

A publication of:
Fernwood Publishing
Box 9409, Station A
Halifax, Nova Scotia
B3K 5S3

Fernwood Publishing Company Limited gratefully acknowledges the financial support
of The Ministry of Canadian Heritage.

Canadian Cataloguing in Publication Data
Monture-Angus, Patricia
Thunder in my soul

Includes bibliographical references.
ISBN 1-895686-46-6

1. Native peoples -- Canada -- Women. *
2. Native peoples -- Canada -- Social conditions. *
3. Native peoples -- Canada -- Legal status, laws,
etc. * I. Title.

E78.C2M66 1995   323.1'197071   C95-950066-9

Contents

Flint Woman Speaks

Politics of Oppression
1. Education

Politics of Oppression
2. Women and Politics

Politics of Oppression
3. Justice

Dedications

To Denis:
for being helper and healer;
to Nadia, Brandon, Genine, Blake and Kate:
for being mommy's soul comfort
and being ever so patient with my many absences;
and especially to Yvonne:
for showing me the true meaning of courage.

This book is for you, sister-in-law.

Foreword

Thunder in my Soul is a landmark collection of essays and papers by Patricia Monture-Angus. This is the first collection of papers to be presented in book format by a First Nations woman scholar from a Canadian university which explicitly addresses Aboriginal peoples experiences with education, racism, reforming the criminal justice system and feminism.

Patricia Monture-Angus has collected her papers, many of which have been published elsewhere but which have been revised for this collection, along with new works. Her writing is riveting because she has incorporated into her work the traditional methodology of First Nations people—storytelling. She writes like she speaks; from her heart, using her own often painful experiences as a First Nations woman to illustrate how profoundly wronged Aboriginal people have been in Canadian society.

Patricia Monture-Angus provides a glimpse into her own heart in this collection. As an academic, her style is refreshing and engaging, beyond most of the work produced about Aboriginal peoples in the university setting. She freely shares with the reader her own personal experiences. This is a brave move as so often First Nations peoples have been forced to hide their identities and conceal the painful experiences we have had in Canadian society. Also, it is very difficult to write of your own personal experiences in a fashion which connects the academic work and the political context of Aboriginal people's lives. This Patricia Monture-Angus does remarkably well. Her writing is interesting, both for a non-Aboriginal audience as well as Aboriginal readers. It is also refreshing and accessible for universtiy and non-university audiences.

Patricia is a path breaker for all Aboriginal peoples, and especially for women. While she shares her experiences and reflects on the institutions of Canadian society which have wronged and continue to wrong Aboriginal peoples, her writings and recollections of her experiences do not leave a bitter taste. Patricia Monture-Angus is a visionary who has her eyes firmly fixed on a better future for all Aboriginal peoples. Her work is always reconstructive. She is diligently and creatively imagining a better future for all peoples, Aboriginal and non-Aboriginal. Because of her dedication to her writing, her honesty and openness in sharing her experiences, her work is clearly inspirational.

This collection just provides to a wider audience what Patricia Monture-Angus has given to many of us, and the universtiy community, for many years: a rock solid conscience and a clarion call for change. She is a truly remarkable woman, professor, writer, and last but in no ways least, a dedicated and loving mother. Her work has given me great personal strength over the years and I am delighted that it can now reach a broader audience who I am sure will also be moved by the thunder and the vision in Patricia Monture-Angus' soul.

Mary Ellen Turpel
June 1995
Asimakaniseekan Askiy Reserve
Saskatchewan

First Words

The Thunders are very important spirit beings to many First Nations people. Every winter they go away, and I miss them very much. Nearing the end of winter, I always find myself impatiently waiting for the return of the Thunder Beings. We know that spring is truly here when the Thunders return. These spirit people are tricksters. They tease us—just try talking to them sometime. Their strength and power envelopes me. They have always been a source of both strength and inspiration to me. It is not a sad thing to me that there is thunder in my soul.

The image of thunder is also a response to some of the labelling I have experienced in my travels in the non-Indian world. I have travelled this country from coast to coast more times that I can count. Much of this travelling has involved the conference circuit, including the participation at many "feminist" conferences. One of the experiences I have of this circuit is being called "angry." This labelling, and it is a form of silencing, always amazes me because I am not an angry woman. Calling someone angry has a lot of negative connotations. I suppose I have at least a million reasons to be angry when I reflect upon the history of oppression, racism and colonialism that my people and every other First Nation in this territory have survived. I have struggled very hard to grow through this anger of my youth, and thunder is the image I have replaced anger with.

I have dreamed about this book for a very long time. As a little girl, I can remember wanting to be a writer when I grew up. Sitting in front of my computer—which is much easier to relate to than a piece of square white paper—writing has always been soul comfort for me. It has allowed me to name the thunder and many other things I have felt. I have had the good fortune to have a number of articles published in academic journals over the years. Although I am proud of this as an accomplishment (and recognize

1

that it is also a privilege), it has always felt bittersweet to me. Most First Nations people do not have access to so-called learned journals, even though the rates of our involvement in post-secondary institutions has dramatically increased since I began my university education in 1979. I do not know of one Indian reserve that has installed a law library. As I have always written for my people, it seems ironic that they have the least access to what I have published. This book fulfills my dream to share my thoughts with those people I wrote them down for, Aboriginal people.

I have learned a lot about myself through the preparation of this book. I have spent a lot of time with my ideas, reading and re-reading drafts. Editing this volume has meant that I have had to examine carefully many personal experiences, and some of those experiences I would like to not to have to remember. I have muddled through my pain and anger until it has turned again to thunder. It has been a rewarding experience. It has also been a troubling experience.

I have been troubled by my ability to share my Aboriginal ideas only in the English language. Every time I edited the papers in this volume, I hesitated when I saw the word Aboriginal or Native or First Nations or Indian. These were words I had used in the original text. I was not comfortable with them but I used them. Every draft, I changed my mind about which word I would use. None of these words feel right or fit right (like shoes a size too small).

I am more comfortable with the word Indian than I am with the words Native or Aboriginal Peoples. Perhaps it is because it is the word I grew up with. Familiarity is comfortable. I know that others are more critical of the use of the word Indian, a word forced on our people because explorers got themselves lost. I used to like the phrase First Nations best. But, in recent years it has come to be used in an exclusionary way referring only to status Indians. I also believe that some consistency in the terminology chosen (Aboriginal, Native, Indian, First Nation and so on) is of assistance to people just beginning to learn about Aboriginal people and issues. I have settled, somewhat arbitrarily, on using the term Aboriginal except for when I mean to refer to Indians (or First Nations—and these terms are interchangeable in my work).

Aboriginal people (or Peoples) is the phrase most in "vogue," at least in legal circles (and owes its origins to the 1982 constitutional amendments). There is another exception. In this paper, I talk about my personal experiences and there the word Aboriginal did not feel right. I am comfortable with the word "Indian" even though I know many other Aboriginal people will cringe when I use this word. I want to re-claim that word, Indian, once forced upon us and make it feel mine. As this book is my soul comfort, I have decided to set aside my concerns with the inappropriate labels that have been forced on Indian people. After all, this labelling is not the responsibility of those who carry the false names. It is also why I refer to myself as Mohawk whenever possble.

I tell this story about naming because it is symbolic. Growing up "Indian" in this country is very much about not having the power to define yourself or your own reality. It is being denied the right to say, "I am!"—instead, always finding yourself saying, "I am not!" In some places in the book, I have chosen to use the word Indian or First Nations, even recognizing that they can be viewed as excluding others. My experience is the experience of a person entitled to be registered under the *Indian Act*. Further, I have never been denied that right. These facts shape how I understand life, law and politics.

There is another important story about naming to tell. In 1991 when I got married, I assumed my husband's surname. This decision was about respecting the Cree family I married into. I use the two last names so that everyone knows how I am related to both the Crees and the Mohawks. My husband's name was Okanee. However, my husband is not by birth an Okanee. This happened to many Indian people. Our last names got all mixed up because of the application of Canadian laws about naming. Okanee was his mother's married name and my husband has two brothers from this relationship, Kenny and Jim. His mother and father were never married but stayed together for many years after her marriage broke up. Donald Angus and Louisa Okanee (my husband's parents) raised five children together. They are Gordon, Leonard, Larry, Yvonne and Denis. My husband's father asked (although he would not admit this) my husband to assume his name. Denis agreed to begin carrying the name Angus. I have become an Angus too. This will be confusing to many people, but it feels very right to correct that mistake made after my husband's birth. This explanation is also meant to curtail the gossip—no, I have not divorced and re-married. I have been too busy writing for those kinds of adventures.

The first step on the road you and I will walk together in this book is the first article that I published. This article changed my life. The response of the academic community to it came as a large surprise, even though I was sufficiently warned about the change that would come. Suddenly, many people I had never met knew of me. They felt they knew me in a personal way. In a sense I became "Flint Woman." The birth of "Flint Woman" allowed me to access an image of myself that I am comfortable with. Even after six years of university teaching, it is hard to image myself as the professor. "Flint Woman" is, therefore, an article that means very much to me. Even though I do not necessarily think in the same way any more, I still believe it is important to share this part of myself and my own intellectual evolution. There have been three other articles published in the "Flint

3

Woman" series, and they are in fact grouped together as Part One in this text. This is the first time they have been published together. They were written so that they should be read together and it is fulfilling for me to see them like this.

The second "Flint Woman" piece, "Reflecting on Flint Woman," was written when a friend and colleague, Richard Devlin, asked to republish "Flint Woman." I balked. By that time, I had gone through several more transitions (including becoming a law professor). I did not want that article republished. It seemed that such a republication would only freeze me in a moment in time, a moment I had passed in my personal development. In the way I was taught, we are always responsible for learning. Knowledge is not static. I offered to write a second piece, one that reflected my current thinking—hence the name, "Reflecting on Flint Woman." In a sense, I was talking back to myself.

At the completion of the second "Flint Woman" piece, although I did feel a certain satisfaction on reaching another deadline, I was still not satisfied. The article was technical, formal and legal. There was a side of "Flint Woman," the personal side, I had not yet shared. When asked to write for another publication, I took the opportunity to write the third story about "Flint Woman." It is very much about the woman who stands behind the other two. Only when the three pieces are read together do I have any sense of personal completeness.

In this collection, an article appears which has never been published under the auspices of the "Flint Woman" label. It does, however, clearly belong in this series. It is the fourth and final article of the series (maybe). "Flint Woman" feels complete to me now. Four is an important number in the Indian world. There are four seasons and four directions. Four is the number that ends a cycle. A friend, Nin Thomas, suggested a cycle has now been completed and I agree with her. I already feel like I have moved beyond the time I needed "Flint Woman." I have come to understand myself and feel easier about who I am.

The second part of this book is called "The Politics of Oppression." It is different from the first part of the book. The papers in this section are more academic and less personal. In this way, these papers fit together. There are also common themes which bring the papers in this section together. They reflect my thinking about law, politics, justice and change. It would be impossible for me to write about these topics without focusing my comments on women, our oppression and the abuse we have survived. I do not believe that our ideas can ever transcend our gender or our culture. As women, there is little doubt that we are abused and oppressed both within Canadian society but more sadly within our own First Nations communities. There is no doubt that this is the present reality. My dream is about the return to the tradition of great respect for women among First Nations. I celebrate my gender and the gifts I carry as woman. This is largely possible because I have escaped, for now, the individual abuse I once lived. I am also conscious that not all of my sisters and brothers have been so fortunate.

The papers in Part Two are organized around three separate headings. The first section, "Women, Politics and Law," has as a focus the last decade of constitutional wrangling in this country. This section also attempts to explain the structure of Canada's constitution (and especially the provisions regarding rights and government powers) in language that is accessible. There are other important understandings shared in this section about culture, gender and Aboriginal aspirations in the political sphere.

The second section of this part focuses on my ideas and experiences as both a student and an educator. Canada has yet to provide an opportunity for Aboriginal people to be educated in a meaningful way. The two papers in this section document some of the difficulties I have experienced, Aboriginal aspirations in this area and my own ideas for change. Education, and using non-Indian education, as a way to create change has been a central focus of my life over the last ten years. This focus has been the source of a lot of pain, confusion and frustration, with too few significant successes. When I decided I wanted to become a law professor, there was no one before me who had accomplished this goal. Quite often, when facing contradiction, I wish there was someone I could turn to who has answers. As a mother, I am particularly aware that there are many young people coming along behind me. I share these stories of pain, confusion and frustration in the hope that those who come behind me will not feel like they stand alone, looking into a deep mist. Although the belief in change through education of Aboriginal people in mainstream educational institutions is sometimes difficult to maintain on a daily basis, I still believe that in the long-term this education will at least partially equip us for the future. Traditional knowledge, the ability to know who we are as Indians, is more essential to our well-being and survival. This knowledge is best transmitted through those wise old people who reside in our communities.

The last section of this book focuses on justice. In some ways it is the section of the book that is most important to me. Often, justice (or the lack of justice) is the motivation in my life. The injustice Aboriginal people in Canada's system of criminal law and so-called correction is what took me to law school from the street. I have spent more than a decade of my life (my life has not yet reached four decades) going to visit Aboriginal men and women who are caged in Canada's prisons. Many of the people in the iron cages have touched my heart, inspired me or forced me to think. These pages are dedicated to the gifts you have given to me for I have received much more from my experiences behind the wall than I can ever imagine being able to give back. Justice remains illusive for Aboriginal people in Canada. It is a quest for justice that keeps the fire in my heart kindled.

There are a number of people that I must pay respects to. Unfortunately, there are so many people I would like to mention, I find it impossible to name them all. There are three women, without whose support and kindness, I would never have survived my first five years of law teaching. They are my Cree and Ojibway colleagues, professors Darlene Johnston, Irene Linklater and especially Mary Ellen Turpel. It is in their spirits and their courage that I often find my strength to carry on another day in the hallowed halls of legal education. Some days, those steps forward are the most painful steps I ever take. There are many Aboriginal law students who in their struggle and courage to succeed at law school continue to bring inspiration and strength. In particular I pay my respects to Joan Mercredi, Bonnie Pelletier and Catherine Rhinelander. I would also like to thank my colleagues at the University of Saskatchewan. Professors Winona Stevenson, Maria Campbell and Frank Tough have been especially kind and supportive. Native Studies is a marvellous discipline and has provided me with an opportunity to free my mind from the shackles of law. A constant source of both strength and peace in my life is James Youngblood "Sakej" Henderson. He is the director of the Native Law Centre at the University of Saskatchewan. He is my "uncle-at-law" and the trailblazing of the generation of Aboriginal lawyers before me have made my path possible and less rocky. There are also a number of women who have supported this work by trying to keep me organized over the last six years of my academic life and by puzzling over my handwriting when trying to enter these papers into the computer. These women are Molly Ross, Sandra Harnum (both at Dalhousie University), Barbara Main (University of Ottawa) and Cheryl Holst (University of Saskatchewan).

Perhaps the most important person to this book is left to thank and that is Errol Sharpe, the soul of Fernwood Publishing. He initiated the writing of this book when he approached me with the idea. Without his confidence in me this book would have likely only remained an idea in the back of my mind. I am also indebted to the staff at Fernwood. Brenda Conroy is a wonder with words and all the technical rules I like to ignore. She is a kind and patient editor, an experience I have infrequently had in the past. I am also grateful for the contributions of Beverley Rach who was responsible for design and layout.

The other side of my inspiration is drawn from my family. The children we raise—Nadia (Pelletier) Brandon, Genine, Blake and Kate—are the most treasured gifts I have ever received. I cannot describe the joy and wisdom they bring to my life every day. This book is dedicated to their little spirits and the mother's prayer that they will never have to walk the pain that my generation has walked. My husband, Denis Angus, has sacrificed a great deal in staying home and nurturing those little ones. His commitment has facilitated the writing of this book (and many other things). His photograph on the cover is my respect for his creativity, the gift that he carries and is nurturing. Dr. Michael Monture has spent many hours discussing issues of survival and contradiction in a professional world with me. I am grateful that when I hurt he can carry some of the burden with me. He has influenced many of the ideas in this book. My brother, David Monture, has also always been a source of comfort for me. There are several other friends who belong to my found family. Denise McConney and daughter Wynonah, Patti and Darrell Tait and daughter Tara, Penny Major and son Drew, Brad Seneca, Patti Doyle Bedwell, Shirley O'Connor, Bob Crawford and Leona Sparrow; your frendship creates a circle of support which had made it possible for me to chase my dreams. These are the people who walk beside me on my earth walk.

It is a sense of belonging with my people, the Mohawk (even when geographically removed from my home community) that has carried me through thus far. In the last four years, I have also had the support and nurturing of the Cree Nation, of Treaty Six. I married a man from the Thunderchild First Nation in northwestern Saskatchewan. His family and his community have also been supportive and nurturing of me, such that I now feel that I have two nation homes. I have had the good fortune to be nurtured by many traditional teachers—young and old. All of these traditional teachers have been so patient in their sharing with me and I am afraid teaching me has required the greatest amount of patience. I have for so long wanted to give back all that has been shared with me. Any errors or misunderstandings in the presentation of their teachings are my own.

This book is my prayer for my people and for all First Nations. It is shared with you in the spirit of gift giving. It is in part a reflection on my own journey down that healing road. It is also a reflection on my own struggle to shed the colonized shackles which bind my mind, my spirit and my heart.

My "Kookum" (grandmother in Cree) sits on my bed at night and watches me when I sleep in those times of my life when I struggle and my spirits are low. My "Mushum" sits outside my window and sings Indian songs on his hand drum. My parents long ago left their earth walks but never have I felt that they left me alone. Those first seven years of kindness, love and nurturing they gave me are my most important years. They are the solid years on which I have been able to build this life I now have. These are my remembrances of two generations of ancestors. Behind them stands a lineage that dates back to time immemorial. When my bare foot caresses the earth, I am connected to that long line of beings whose blood now flows in the earth of the territory I now call home. Their bodies and bones build the foundation that nurtures my life. I know that it is impossible for me to ever walk alone.

Patricia Monture-Angus
Thunderchild First Nation
in the March 1995 snowstorm.

Flint Woman Speaks

1

Ka-nin-geh-heh-gah-e-sa-nonh-yah-gah

CHAPTER ONE WAS ORIGINALLY WRITTEN *in 1987 and first published in* Canadian Journal of Women and the Law, *2, 1 (1986): 157-171. It is commonly referred to as "Flint Woman." Ka-nin-geh-heh-gah-e-sa-nonh-yah-gah translates roughly into English as "the way Flint Women do things." The way of Flint Women is a way of strength in which the fire of our nation shall be kept kindled. This is the responsibility of the women of the Mohawk nation (who are known as the "People of the Flint"). In this way, this comment follows the oral tradition of my people.*

I have come to realize the importance of the experiential because without human experience we will never achieve a true form of equality. In order to understand equality, people must understand caring. Without understanding caring, we cannot understand "peoplehood," be it in a community as small as a gathering of a few people or something as large as the global community. Each person must be respected for who and what they are. Only when we all understand caring will we have reached equality.

Aboriginal history is oral history. It is probably fortunate for Aboriginal people today that so many of our histories are oral histories. Information that was kept in peoples' heads was not available to Europeans, could not be changed and molded into pictures of "savagery" and "paganism." The tradition of oral history as a method of sharing the lessons of life with children and young people also had the advantage that the Elders told us stories. They did not tell us what to do or how to do it or figure out the world for us—they told us a story about their experience, about their life or their grandfather's or grandmother's or auntie's or uncle's life. It is in this manner that Indian people are taught independence as well as respect because you have to do your own figuring for yourself.

11

Following this tradition of oral history and storytelling, I want to share one of my experiences with you. Like most academics, I spend at least a little bit of time going to conferences, listening to other people, and learning and sharing what we are thinking. This is a story about a conference I attended, a legal conference, that I want to tell you. It is also a story about anger. My anger[1] is not unique to this conference; it is paralleled at many other conferences I have been to and the classes I have been to, most other days in my life, so it is an important story.

I arrived at the conference at supper time. That was no mistake. I wanted people to be busy doing something else when I arrived. You see, when you know you are going to be the only Indian in the place, it is not exactly a comfortable feeling. Although the drive from my home to the lodge where the conference was being held was only forty-five minutes, it seemed much longer.

I was scared. I was scared because I was going to be the only Indian person in pretty much a room full of White people. And it just was not any old bunch of White people; this was a gathering of university professors—law professors from elite and non-elite schools all across the continent; the kind of people I had held in awe and respect through these last eight years of university; people who are published and doing the things now that I am still dreaming of doing and working toward.

I was scared too because I know that those people do not think the same as I do. White people do not line up reality in the same way that I do. They do not understand life and creation the same as I do. They do not know things in the same way that I do. I guess what I am not saying, because I am trying to be polite, is that I know that racism exists in Canada. I know that, because I have lived it.

I planned well; everybody was busy when I arrived at the conference. I checked in and got unpacked and settled without incident and decided that I would go for a walk to stretch my legs. I was happy and relieved to be out in the woods again, near the water. As the earth is my mother, being close to her is always calming. As soon as I got outside of my room, I bumped into a couple of women friends, women that I went to school with at Queen's. They are students too, so that lessened the burden of feeling a little out of my element as a student in with all these professors. I started to unwind and feel much more comfortable.

It was not very long before it was time to go to the evening session. It was a large group session. It had been explained to me earlier that we would be breaking down into four small working groups first thing the next morning. In order to set the stage for that, the entire group (approximately fifty people) was meeting for a discussion that evening. The discussion was down the road and around the bend in a community hall in this small village where the lodge was located. It was kind of nostalgic and rustic, and I had managed to shake most of my fears before I got there.

I think the topic of discussion that evening was racism. I am finding that my memory is a little bit foggy after the events to follow. I know that I sat and listened. I wanted to know where people were coming from. I was not going to jump with both feet into a situation and gathering I knew very little about.

I know that I was not entirely happy about what I heard, that it did not sit well and I lost the comfortable feeling that I had carried with me into the room. I know that because I spoke, and if I remember right, I spoke about understanding and respect. I spoke about how it is that the position of Aboriginal people is so frequently described as a position of disadvantage. This is not true simply for Aboriginal people, but also for Black people and Chinese people and Chicano people and Mexican people and anybody else who does not fit into the norm of White and middle-class. Generically, I am speaking about racism and sexism and classism and all the other "isms" and of how the individuals who fit those stereotypical classifications get qualified as disadvantaged. We are only disadvantaged if you are using a White, middle-class yardstick. I quite frequently find that a White, middle-class yardstick is a yardstick of materialism. We will see how valued you are by the size of your bank account or the number of degrees you can write after your name.

Questioning the disadvantage?

I explained how I just could not understand how Aboriginal people are disadvantaged. Looking only at the materialistic yardstick, just about everybody in the country knows that we have less education and less income and more kids and less life expectancy than the majority of the other people in this country, but I still do not see, I said, how we are truly disadvantaged. You see, when non-Indian people are not satisfied with the world they see around them, and it seems to me that more and more of the people that I meet are in this position, well, those people do not have anywhere to turn. They have nowhere to run to. I have an entire community, or rather, pockets of community all over this land. Wherever you find Aboriginal people, things are done in a different way, against a different value system. And the measure is not materialism. It is not what you are that counts, it is _who_ you are. So when the world of the dominant culture hurts me and I cannot take it anymore, I have a place to go where things are different. I simply do not understand how that is disadvantaged.

I also do not understand that by having the teachings of the Elders available to me—different ways of learning, different ways of knowing, the ways of traditional spirituality—that I am more disadvantaged than White people. I have had the opportunity to learn Aboriginal teachings, to learn about body, mind and spirit, to learn about balance. Most of the time I am a happy and complete individual, but when I look around me at the people at university, this is not by and large what I see. I see a lot of people who are hurt, a lot of people who know how to live in their heads and do not know that anything else even exists. I have a hard time understanding again how my experience is an experience of disadvantage. Disadvantage is a nice, soft, comfortable word to describe dispossession, to describe a situation of force whereby our very existence, our histories, are erased continuously right before our eyes. Words like disadvantage conceal racism.

When I left the gathering, I remember I felt a little bewildered. Why was it my professor friend had so insisted that I go to this conference? I had spoken, but I did not feel like many people had listened. I know they did not listen. It did not seem that people wanted to hear what I was saying, it did not seem like most of the people in that room wanted to understand how it was that we are different. This bewildered me, but it did not surprise me. This refusal, this inability to accept difference and respect difference and rejoice in difference is the point at which my anger grows. Equality is really a celebration of difference.

There was a reception after the gathering back at another room at the lodge and I went to that. I really did not talk to anybody except for the two students that I had met earlier, and looking back, I think that was because I was looking for a safe place to be. A safe place to stand, one that was not threatening. My experience of the first evening at the conference set the stage for the following day. I did not stay at that reception for very long. I did not feel comfortable. Why should I stay? I was tired, so I went to sleep.

The next morning I got up and went over to breakfast. What a breakfast we had! The food was so good. Again, I stayed pretty close to the women I knew from Queen's. I had decided through breakfast that I just wanted to watch again for a while because I definitely was not feeling like I was in a safe place. This is pretty typical of an Indian person who is not feeling comfortable. We are taught that inaction is a better course than action because it is in that manner that we learn where it is we are and how to participate.

During breakfast, the professor friend who had invited me and who was involved in organizing the conference came over to me and asked me if I would mind changing small section groups because one group only had one "person of colour" in it. My friend did not want to leave that person all by themselves. On one hand I was really pleased that this professor was conscious enough to know that when you leave a minority person alone in a gathering of non-minority people, you are leaving that person in a vulnerable spot. But at the same time, the conscious shuffling of bodies from one group to another made me uneasy. Was I no more than a coloured face? This shuffling of bodies contrasts against the Indian way, in which things are allowed to happen as they should. This belief reflects the recognition that we cannot control our natural environment. We cannot master the universe. I have not been able to fully unpack the feeling of discomfort that the move from one group to another group caused. But it did serve to intensify the fact that I really just wanted to watch and that I really was not trusting the people that were around me. This should be understood as my fear and my difficulty and my problem. It has to be my problem as it is *my* daily reality. If what I am saying is going to be understood, it must be understood as what I, as one particular person, am feeling and am experiencing and what I think of it. I think it is of value in that it is the experience of a member of a dispossessed group within this society.

The morning session and lunch were rather uneventful for me. We had a good intellectual talk in my small section and made a good effort at getting to know one another. For the most part, I sat back and listened and did not have a whole lot to say. My friends will tell you that is somewhat unusual. I was starting to feel a little bit comfortable again. After lunch, we went back to our small session.

I should probably tell you a little bit about the woman who stepped forward as chair at this particular small section meeting. She was not the group facilitator. She is a White woman, I guess from a fairly privileged background. She teaches at an elite United States law school. She conveys herself in a caring manner.

She started the afternoon session by telling a story. That story was about a sixty-seven-year-old Black woman, whose name I forget, who lived in the Bronx or some place like that. She was poor. She was a month behind in her rent. Because she was a month behind in her rent, her landlord wanted to evict her. She was old and arthritic and had no place to move to, so she just decided that she was not going to go. The landlord contacted the police and the police came to her apartment door and told her she had to move. Well, if I remember right, they kicked in her door and found her with a knife—she was not going to leave her home. So the policeman, a Black man, shot her hand off. I am not too sure how or why or the details, I have lost them. Then he shot her in the head, dead. The police officer was eventually charged with murder or manslaughter, the point being that there were criminal charges laid. He was not convicted; I do not know if that means we are supposed to believe that this sixty-seven-year-old Black arthritic woman was a danger to society or what, but she is dead.

In the manner of good lawyering, we began to pick at this hypothetical. What if she had been a White woman and he had been a Black man, would he have been convicted? What if he had been a White man, would he have been convicted? And on and on and on in the method of legalism we went. I started squirming in my chair. I did not miss the fact that the Black woman in the room was not missing the fact that I was squirming in my chair. I could not identify why, but the conversation we were having hurt.

I suppose I sat and listened for about half an hour. I am not sure how much I really listened. I was thinking quite intensely on why is this hurting me. Why is this experience so brutal? Why do I want to get up and leave the room? I do not want to hear anymore of this.

By the time I spoke I was almost in tears. What it was that I had identified was that we were talking about my life. I do not know when I am going to pick up the phone and hear about the friend who committed suicide, the acquaintance that got shot by the police, the Aboriginal prison inmate that was killed in an alleged hostage taking, ironically two days after two Aboriginal inmates in Stoney Mountain had killed a White prison guard. *This is my life.* I do not have any control over the pain and brutality of living the life of a dispossessed person. I cannot control when that pain is going to enter into my life. I had gone away for this conference quite settled with having to deal with racism, pure and simple. But, I was not ready to have my pain appropriated. I am pretty possessive about my pain. I worked hard for it. Some days it is all I have. Some days it is the only thing I can feel. Do not try to take that away from me too. That was happening to me in that discussion. My pain was being taken away from me and put on the table and poked and prodded with these sticks, these hypotheticals. "Let's see what happened next?" I felt very, very much under a microscope, even if it was not my own personal experience that was being examined.

I explained this to the group and I know I cried a little bit, I do not hide my emotions and I guess that is difficult for some people to handle. I probably talked for five or so minutes trying to explain what it was that was troubling me, upsetting me. I put it all on the table. When I was done, like so many times before, everybody just kind of sat there and looked at me. I watched the Black woman in the room quite carefully. She seemed relieved, so I guessed what I had done was alright and I waited.

The woman who was facilitating the conversation said essentially, "What do we do next? I think what Trisha said is important and what do we do from here? Does this mean that we cannot discuss issues of racism because we are causing more hurt when we do?" I did not like the sound of that idea too much because I do not think that until racism is understood we are ever going to be rid of racism, that is the kind of beast it is. I thought about my criminal law class in first year. When we had to deal with the issue of rape, or whenever the issue of rape had to be dealt with, be it in the rules of evidence or whatever, people took great pains to make sure that they are not inflicting any harm on any of the women in the room. "You never know when one of the women in the room in the class that you are teaching has been a victim of rape." But as an Indian woman, I have never had the same courtesy extended to me when the issue was clearly racism.

In my first year criminal law, for example, I remember taking a case, a case about an Indian man. I think he was charged with breaking and entering. He was under the influence of alcohol at the time of the offence. I do not remember the point of the case or the legal issue at stake, but at sentencing the judge was describing this Aboriginal man and it kind of felt like this: "He is Indian and he is drunk and he is illiterate" and all of that belongs in one mouthful, so it is not a problem if we send him to jail for X number of years.[2] "After all, he can go and see the rest of the Indians in jail." This case was only about ten or fifteen years old at the time I studied it, which was four years ago. The professor certainly made no more note than in passing, if he did that much, that this was a stereotype of Indian people that was being portrayed and conveyed by the judge. I was hurt. I had felt very exposed at having my personhood and my reality laid bare on the table in front of the people in class without my consent. In that very same course the very same professor, at some length and with great caution, dealt with the issue of rape, explaining that he did not want to inflict any harm on any women in the class. He certainly hoped that this would not be the case. Yet, when we deal with the issue of racism, very much so do we allow ourselves to be blind to the further pain that we are inflicting.

I felt strong, although quite exhausted, at having put on the table the way I had been feeling as we talked hypothetically about the murder of this Black woman in the United States by the police officer. I felt that—and maybe this is self-congratulatory—my tears and my pain had brought us to a really good place. The rest of the discussion that afternoon focused on racism and how to deal with racism in a classroom. How do we talk about racism? When do we talk about racism? In what manner do we talk about racism? Several of the men brought up how they would identify with feeling invisible, as I had earlier mentioned, when the issue of gender was discussed. Men are seen as the perpetrator and never the victims of the social reality that we live in. I thought that was a good point and all in all we had a good discussion that afternoon.

I left and went back to my room to have a little bit of a rest before dinner and did not stay for the wine and cheese or before-dinner drinks that were going on after our small section. I needed some time and some space to be alone to let the rawness subside. At six o'clock I went to supper, I sat beside a law professor from California, a Chicano man I believe. We had an animated chat. During our conversation, I remember noticing that a very heated discussion was occurring at the dinner table behind me. It involved the woman who had headed up my small section that afternoon and the two women friends from Queen's who were attending the conference as students. It also involved at least several other White men. At the time, I had the feeling that something important was going on in that discussion, but I did not pay any attention to it. After supper there were no activities scheduled for the evening. It was just a rest and socializing time. I socialized a bit and chatted and then went back and crawled into my bed, still feeling quite exhausted.

The following morning, all the small sections were to meet to discuss what had gone on the previous day. I found it very, very difficult to get out of bed that morning. I was feeling very exposed and raw. I just did not feel up to walking into breakfast where I could possibly have to carry on a conversation, especially a conversation about yesterday's discussions. So I waited around for the general store to open so I could go in and get myself a cup of coffee. The plenary started before I got my coffee.

I arrived at the plenary to hear the woman who had introduced the story of the Black woman's murder in our small section quite emphatically, and almost to the point of being defensive, insist that the issue she was talking about was not an issue of gender. This puzzled me greatly, because the woman in question is a White woman, and by her own admission she does not know very much about racism. I sat through a lot of that conversation not knowing quite what to think, knowing I did not understand what I heard. The conversation kept returning to the woman's insistence that this is not a gender issue.

At some point during that conversation, I finally figured out what everyone was talking about when one of the women there described what had taken place at the dinner table behind me the night before. The dinner table conversation focused on the desire of many "minorities" to challenge the structure of knowledge in a way that is inclusive of our pain. This challenge also requires a critical assessment of the sources of knowledge and how they are sanctioned as legitimate.

During the discussion at the dinner table, a Hawaiian law professor, also a minority woman, offered this story. She was having dinner with a group of her legal colleagues. The topic of the conversation at that dinner was sports. As she told the story, the conversation began to centre around specific athletes, I believe football players, and what the people at the table thought of each of these superstar athletes. The woman who was telling the story was asked to comment on a certain individual and she said something like, "I used to really like him. I used to think this man was a great, great athlete. Then I saw him advertising beer or underwear or some such thing on television and I do not believe he is really interested in sports for the sake of sports.[3] With all these endorsements that he has been doing, I think he is interested in sports only for money." The unfortunate part of that comment, and the woman did definitely confess that she simply did not know what else to say and did not know an awful lot about football or sports, was that the athlete in question was Jewish. There was a Jewish man sitting at the table at the dinner, and he took offence at the woman's comments. To him it sounded like very much "those money grubbing Jews" stereotype again. This was definitely not the intent of the woman. Her point in telling this story was that intent does not excuse somebody from racism. Racism is racism, and racism stings. All the good intentions in the world do not take away the sting and do not take away the pain.

Shortly after the story was told, the session got very interesting. One of the men who had eaten dinner the night before with the woman who told that story identified himself. He was quite defensive. He took great pains to explain that he did not intend to harm anyone, that he was very concerned about "minority" issues and helped "minorities" whenever he could, but that he was seriously questioning whether the conference was accomplishing anything. I do not remember all that he said. What I do remember was getting angry. I said to one of the Queen's students next to me that I was getting very, very tired of hearing White men speaking for me, especially when I am in the room. I am quite capable of speaking for myself.

At this point, I began to notice that my friends were definitely uncomfortable. They were more uncomfortable than I was, and I could not figure out why. The whole morning I got the feeling that everybody else had a secret that excluded me. Something very important and very definite was going on here and I was somehow being excluded from it, and I could not quite grasp what it was. I was very shortly to find out.

After the man had finished speaking, the woman who had initiated the conversation that morning and he got into a definite back and forth—very argumentative, very quick, with each attacking the other's position—each stating how important the issue of racism was, both stating that racism had very much been dealt with. The man insisted that with all this experiential stuff we were definitely going overboard and that it was certainly time for us to begin dealing with important things like "mega-theory." "Let's make this academic and stop feeling for a while." He also took great pains to explain all he had done to help minority people and how long he had been there for minority people. I think he was questioned about how he knew he was helping if he did not know what minority people actually felt.

Anyway, this arguing match went back and forth and back and forth, with emotions getting higher and higher on both sides of it. All through it, the woman insisted, "No, we are talking about racism, not gender. The fact that I am a White woman and that two other women there were White women and that the three men that were there were White men did not make it an issue of gender. Yes, there were issues of gender involved in it, but that was not the important issue." I was getting very bewildered about how this was not an issue of gender.[4] White people were the only ones doing the talking.

Everything clicked into place when I realized *why* it was not an issue of gender: the comment that had gotten the entire conversation going the evening before had been made when one of the men and the woman were talking about whether this conference was too experiential. The woman from my small section had said, "No, it is not experiential. Let me show you the good stuff that can come out of the experiential, let me show you the good stuff that came out of the pain." Then she finished telling the story about the pain that I had laid on the table the previous afternoon, and the man had said, "The pain of minority people is like television, we can turn it on and off as we want to."[5] The woman who had brought this conversation to the meeting and put it on the table that morning finally let that comment slip into the conversation. There had been at least a covert agreement to keep this comment from me. No wonder I had felt awkward and excluded.

I was stunned. I was standing up speaking before I knew it. I cannot find the words to describe how brutalized I felt when those words came out. That was me that was being discussed all morning. Did the man intend to belittle my pain and my life? Did he know how deeply he had clawed into my essence? Did that woman intend to appropriate my pain for her own use, stealing my very existence, as so many other White, well-meaning, middle- and upper-class feminists have done?

It is difficult for me to remember what it was that I said. I know I cried. In many ways it was an emotional outburst and I was aware, I think, that the people there might discount my words on this ground. But I said what I thought needed to be thought about. It has been too long, I said, that we have not been listened to. Whenever something like this happens in discussion of gender and race, I cannot separate them. I do not know, when something like this happens to me, when it is happening to me because I am a woman, when it is happening to me because I am an Indian, or when it is happening to me because I am an Indian woman. The forum has not been set yet in which those issues can be discussed. There are a lot of teachings that Aboriginal people have about balance and harmony and tranquillity, about well-being. The modern education system is not aware of these things. They have not listened. They have not understood. They still believe that they are going to help us. Well, I do not want to be a White person. You cannot make me be a White person. You cannot help me be a White person. Look at this world, look at what is around you. The earth is my mother. She is being raped. She is being destroyed. There will not be anything left soon if we do not start taking care of the earth. And you, as a White man, and you, as a White woman, stand there and tell me that I do not know, I do not understand—because I feel.

I was angry all right, and I was hurt, I do not know how long I stood and spoke before exhaustion and numbness set in. I responded to what had been said that day as violence, for what had been done to me that day was violence. The White people there had already decided that I was not supposed to hear about that comment. That comment was what had been making the friend next to me so uncomfortable: she was afraid that comment would slip out and I would be hurt. Well, I am glad that it did slip out, even thought I was hurt. I do not deserve to have those things kept from me. As I said before, my pain is all I have some days. Do not take it away from me. It is mine. Understand it, understand where the pain comes from and why: I have to struggle with that. If we cannot understand this pain that women, that Aboriginal women, that Black women, that Hawaiian women, that Chicano women go through, we are never going to understand anything. All that mega-theory will not get us anywhere because without that understanding, mega-theory does not mean anything, does not reflect reality, does not reflect people's experience.

I remember speaking again about being labelled disadvantaged. Sure, Aboriginal people in this country are disadvantaged, everybody knows that. Everybody knows the statistics. But those are all social and economic variables. You cannot go out and measure how happy people are. You cannot count happiness. You cannot turn happiness into nice neat tidy statistics. Aboriginal people are only disadvantaged if you use that materialistic yardstick. If you accept those kinds of measures about who is good and who is not, Aboriginal people are not "good." But if you want to go to a community where you are cared about as an individual who is important, go to a traditional Aboriginal community. That is not disadvantaged. What I have had is a real and an important advantage. When that world out there has hurt me, when I grew up and I did not like what I found and did not like what I saw out there in the city, I had some place to run to. I had another alternative. Most people do not walk into an alternative lifestyle, an alternative value structure. They do not have the same kind of access to those things because they are not people of a "minority" culture. I do not want to be called disadvantaged anymore. Call me economically poor, call me uneducated, call me all of those things. The education I have achieved does not mean anything. Do not call me disadvantaged anymore.

I think I talked a long time. I do not know. I think I was in shock. I felt brutalized, violated, victimized—all of those things—but I was not silent. I knew I had to respond, I knew I could not sit there and let it continue. I could not consent to my own disappearance and my own death. I could not watch anymore, so I spoke. I was standing up speaking before I even realized that I was standing up speaking, at least thirty seconds went by before I realized I was on my feet addressing this group, I am saying something, *again*. When are those of you who inflict racism, who appropriate pain, who speak with no knowledge or respect when you ought to know to listen and accept, going to take hard looks at yourself instead of at me. How can you continue to look to me to carry what is your responsibility? And when I speak and the brutality of my experience hurts you, you hide behind your hurt. You point the finger at me and you claim I hurt you. I will not carry your responsibility any more. Your pain is unfortunate. But do not look to me to soften it. Look to yourself.

I wanted to sit down but I could not. I kept talking and trying to explain until I could not talk anymore. The words were all there in my head, my mind was fine, it was going ninety miles a minute and I wanted to keep on talking. Then I just shut down, there was nothing left, no strength left to keep trying to explain. I have explained this same thing so many times that I get exhausted. But, if one person in that room understood what I had to say, understood what it is that so many Aboriginal people I have listened to and spoken to have said, heard what the Elders have taught me, if one person understood it, it was worth that last ounce of energy. If I had to speak again tomorrow and the day after and the day after, it will be worth speaking again.

I reached a point where I just could not talk anymore, but I did not know how to stop. Everybody else just sat there. I looked at them and they looked and looked and looked at me and I felt as if I had been caught under a microscope: "What is she going to do next. Let's watch." I could not think how to sit down. I could not think how to finish what I had started saying. I did not know what to do. Finally, I looked some more and they looked back some more and I ended my talk the only way I knew how. That was in an Aboriginal way, and that was to say: "*Megwetch*,[6] I am glad you listened. I am glad that I stood up and talked, let these words I have spoken be good words." Then I sat down. After I sat down, I looked at them some more and they looked at me. My friend put her hand on my knee and gave it a squeeze. I wiped some more tears away and I felt at least as though I had a little bit of energy. A woman across the room very much wanted to break the silence. That is another difference between Aboriginal peoples and non-Aboriginals. Aboriginal people understand that silence is not a bad thing and silence can mean a lot of things. A lot of things can be said without opening your mouth. The silence itself did not make me uncomfortable, but the fact that everybody else in the room was uncomfortable with the silence made me uncomfortable.

Eventually, this woman spoke and she said: "What can I do to help?" Well, that pulled the rug right out from under my feet again, because I do not need you to help me. Helping is offensive; it buys into the, "I am better than you are" routine. I know the woman who spoke did not intend to inflict that fresh pain; I know she did not understand that, but all I could think of were some unpleasant things to say to her. I was to the point where I was defensive and I knew I could not speak in that manner because I knew she had spoken from a kind and sincere place, the only words that she knew how to speak. I was very grateful when one of the other minority women, the one who had earlier told the story of how intent does not excuse racism, spoke very eloquently indeed and addressed the issue in a good way. I was very grateful for that and it made me smile. It made me smile because when we women—we Indian women and Black women and Chinese women and Hispanic women—are together we take care of each other. She took care of me and she spoke when I could not speak anymore. She carried the ball for awhile, which is something you see all too rarely in this individualistic world that we live in. When will all peoples, all nations, all colours, respect the circle of life?

After that, the session got wrapped up and there was a lot of nervous energy in that air. People did not know what to do. Before I knew what happened, I was surrounded by the men and women of colour who sat in that room. In their physical proximity to me I felt safeness. I knew they understood, I knew they had been there too and they stayed there with me and it was good.

Another good thing happened. We (all the so-called "minorities"[7]) went to lunch together and we did something we oh-so-rarely do at a racism conference: we sat together and we talked about what racism means to us. What it means to go to a conference like this and never get a chance to be with each other and how we do not get a chance to hear each other.[8] We do not know what the differences are between a Black woman's experience and an Indian woman's experience because we have never had the chance to talk about it. This is one of the ways that racism and oppression are perpetuated. But we need to talk about it, so that is what we did. We talked about our need to talk about it and it was a start and it was a good lunch. The reason that we all went to lunch together was because we wanted to demonstrate to the White people there that we do stand together, that there is solidarity amongst us. You cannot attack the only Indian woman at a conference and think that the Black women are not going to be there standing beside her, because they will be there standing beside her.

This story does not have an end. It goes on and on and on. When I am done telling this one, I can tell you another one and another one and another one and another one. I want to know and I want to believe that it makes a difference. That what I have struggled with will make a difference to my son and to his children and to those who come after. We have an obligation to those children to see that there is something here for them, but I am scared that is not happening and it is not happening fast enough. How many hundreds and hundreds of years have we been doing this?

Notes

1. Looking back, it now seems unfortunate that I chose to describe so much of what I was feeling in the language of anger. This is more fully discussed in the fourth "Flint Woman" piece, Chapter Four, "Surviving the Contradictions."

2. I still have my old criminal law textbook [Don Stuart and Ron Delisle, *Learning Canadian Criminal Law* (Toronto: Carswell, 1982)] lying around. As I prepared to republish this paper I thought it would be interesting to go back and take a look at the case that had caused me so much anguish. The case, to my surprise, is not a sentencing case. It is a case about the accused "intent" to commit a crime. Students of law understand that intent is a very complex matter. The intent required to secure a conviction varies from offence to offence. In the case of *R.* v. *George* [1960] S.C.R. 871, Ritchie J. quotes the trial judge as follows:

    > A man of 84, was violently manhandled by *an Indian* on the date noted in the Indictment . . . as a result of which he was in hospital for a month. During this scuffle he was badly injured, dumped into a bathtub and pulled out again when he agreed to give *the Indian* what money he had, $22 (emphasis added; in Stuart and Delisle, 322).

    I have never seen a case where a "White person" has their race referred to in this kind of derogatory manner (and this is not a comment on the serious offence that was committed).

It is interesting to me that my memory is so different from the textbook. I cannot remember if what I recall reflects class discussions or my confusion in this class, a class which is a required part of the first year curriculum. I struggled with criminal law more than I struggled with my other first year classes. This is partly because I carried with me a certain bias (largely a result of what I had experienced on the streets growing up). My experiences were very different from the majority of my classmates. Part of the struggle I faced was based in my cultural background. I had no place to locate this complicated understanding of intent. Lacking intent does not excuse your behavior in "Aboriginal Law." There is no parallel concept. None of these considerations, however, excuse the intense pain I felt when we studied this case.

3.   There are also obvious gender implications in this re-told story.

4.   Looking back, it is very interesting to me to note how the conversation became diverted and focused very narrowly on a particular conversation among White people. I am not suggesting that we should have discussed "mega-theory" but the discussion could have focused on a substantive discussion of racism rather than degenerating into a "fight" about which "isms" had operated during the dinner table discussion. This is an important example of how difficult it is to discuss issues of race/culture in the conference format. It demonstrates one "tactic" that is used to avoid discussing racism in a manner that is responsible to those who suffer the consequences of racism.

5.   In some ways this is an accurate reflection of how I experience pain. I do have some control about whether or not I let it in (not whether or not a particular situation is harmful). I have learned to turn myself on and off to stop having to feel all the pain (and that is not always a conscious process). The resulting numbness is not a healthy way to experience life. Whether this (White male) law professor from an elite American university could (or knowingly) capture a portion of my experience, is not the point. His telling of my story is an appropriation of grave proportions not to mention the inappropriate way in which he chose to express it.

6.   This is the word in Ojibwe for thank you.

7.   I am disturbed by the language choices available to me to describe the experience of non-White people. Speaking of White versus non-White, coloured and not, does not accurately reflect my experience. I am not sure Aboriginal people are "people of colour." We are very different, at least in one way. We are the original people of this territory. We have no other "motherland" to return to. In this sense, we are not "minorities."

I am disturbed for another reason. White people are not all the same. They are of various racial/cultural backgrounds. White peoples are as diversified as Aboriginal peoples. By constructing this dichotomy, I am falsely feeding a conflict which is not real. The other extreme is to be silent and not try to describe racism (culturalism) and the effects that it has had on my life. It is interesting to me to note that when I use the term "White people" it often invokes a hostile response. This hostile response is a tool of silencing and I will not be forced into silence as a result.

The last concern I will mention here is what the colour dichotomy—White versus not—does to Aboriginal people who are fair skinned. It creates a hierarchy of experience based on a biologically determined trait. This is not to deny that White skinned privilege does operate to advantage certain people. It also operates to exclude the experiences of some fair skinned Aboriginal people as not legitimate.

8. Earlier I mentioned the discomfort I felt at having one of the coordinators shuffle the "coloured" bodies around so that there were at least two "minority" representatives in each group. Consider who that advantages. The People of Colour were there to accommodate the White experience of the conference. Our presence was not about speaking to each other. Our presence was an appropriation. Unfortunately, this is a common experience I have had at conferences.

2

Reflecting on Flint Woman

CHAPTER TWO WAS WRITTEN IN 1990 and first published in Canadian Perspectives on Legal Theory, *edited by Richard Devlin, Toronto: Emond Montgomery, 1991, pp. 351-366.*

The ways of my people teach that there is a special beauty in living life according to the old First Nations ways. These old ways teach us how to live in respect of creation. Part of this special beauty we have been given is our ability to learn about creation. A person is never so complete that he or she has a perfect understanding of creation. Learning is, therefore, a lifelong process. Because all living things—the animals, plants, humans, the wingeds, the water life—are a part of creation, we are all created equal. The life process is continuous. It exists independent to our individual human existence. What must be understood is that the circle of creation is the centre of the life way of First Nations Peoples.[1] It is the way in which our experiences are understood.

What I am concerned about is that the First Nations ways of understanding and learning are not the same as those that are accepted within the dominant institutions of learning in this land, especially within legal institutions, including law schools. The understanding and respect of these different ways must be recognized and respected if we are truly going to make any headway in "race relations."

We must stop and consider the preliminary assumptions underlying institutional beliefs and ideas. These assumptions shape the content of our thinking. This is necessary before we blindly make our way forward assuming we all think, learn and understand alike. In the words of Marlyn Kane (Osennontion):

> If the educators are going to teach anybody, and if their students are going to learn anything, then we have to try as much as possible to get them to at least realize that they are going to have to twist their minds a little bit (or a lot) to try to get into the same frame of mind as us, or to try to get on the same wave-length. They must realize that their own thinking cannot be applied to what we are going to say, so that what we say "fits"—there seems to be a tendency for that to happen. We must somehow get them to empty their heads of what they may think they know about us, so that they are prepared to begin to learn the truth. (Kane and Maracle 1989: 7)

It is necessary that we (all races)[2] must begin collectively to define our social relations, institutions, and values in an inclusive as opposed to exclusive way. Within law schools, it is the study of jurisprudence that is best suited to an analysis of this kind.[3]

It is not for the benefit of so-called minorities that this re-evaluation of assumptions and understandings is so necessary. The accepted and conventional academic process affirms that understanding. Complicity then characterizes what scholars have become by habitually clinging to the processes which establish traditional power. Not only is this dangerous, but it is also anti-democratic. Mari Matsudi (1988: 7) gives a number of examples of the traditional processes which are problematic, and the following is but one example:

> Citation counts are a standard measure of academic prestige. Scholars proceed in research and information-gathering by following a trail of footnotes. In addition to following footnotes, people cite what they have read and discussed with their academic friends. When their reading and their circle of friends are limited, their citations become limited. The citations then breed further self-reference. This process ignores a basic fact of human psychology: *human beings learn and grow through interaction with difference, not by reproducing what they already know.* A system of legal education that ignores outsiders perspectives artificially restricts and stultifies the scholarly imagination. (3, emphasis added)

My point is a simple one. My purpose in challenging the way academics think and process is *not* a benevolent one for the benefit of some disadvantaged group. It is necessary for the benefit of all people. The goal is to develop legal and educational institutions which are inclusive as opposed to exclusive and hierarchical.

I want to facilitate this purpose by continuing a discussion that I started

27

in an article written and published several years ago (printed as Chapter One in this volume). This article was named in Mohawk and is more commonly referred to as "Flint Woman." The concepts central in that first article—race, culture, women, law, education, disadvantage, silencing and exclusion—are concepts which continue to occupy a great deal of my thinking time. I now understand these concepts in a more complete, but not perfect, way. I am not recanting what I said. This is not the way I think or feel about that first piece. That piece is important for a number of reasons. It offers an important insight for those people who have never been silenced because of their race and culture.[4] It offers those individuals the opportunity to understand the cost to other individuals that they silence, willfully or not. Just as important, it offers the opportunity to consider the cost to themselves of silencing others. All that I am saying about that first piece, is that I now understand things in a different way. I have had several years to think, to live, to learn, to grow. Therefore, I should understand things in a different way if I have been fulfilling my traditional responsibility to learn.

The way I am using the concept of responsibility is unique to the First Nations way of ordering the world. It can be juxtaposed to the rights philosophy on which Euro-Canadian systems of law are based. The focus of First Nations society is not based solely on individual rights but also on collective rights.[5] Collective rights are greater than groups of individual rights. In my understanding of First Nations ways, both individual and collective rights are of utmost importance. They must be understood together. Responsibility as a basis for the structure of a culturally based discourse focuses attention not on what is mine, but on the relationships between people and creation (that is both the individual and the collective). Oren Lyons explains in this way:

> We human beings, however, have been given an added responsibility. We have been given an intellect—that is, the ability to decide for ourselves whether we will do a thing this way or that way. The human being has been given the gift to make choices, and he has been given guidelines, or what we call original instructions. This does not represent an advantage for the human being but rather a responsibility. All the four colours of mankind received those original instructions, but somewhere in time, in many places, they have been lost. It is a credit to us native people that we have retained those instructions. Many non-Indians have tried to destroy the original instructions because they view them as detrimental to progress. (1986: 6)

Obligations and duties are rights-based words and do not hold the same meaning that I give to responsibilities.

"Flint Woman" was written during a particularly frustrating period in my life. I was overwhelmed by the number of ways I was silenced and excluded during my university education (particularly during my legal education). Naturally then, this first article was shaped around silence and exclusion. What I have come to understand since that time, and now understand to be my responsibility, is the responsibility to be empowering and not merely reactionary. The experience of racism is one that is done to us. We react to racism. Even our pain and anger are reactions. It is objectification. We must begin to be subjects to the extent that we can be. Effectively, you then end your own silence and to a lesser degree, your exclusion. Exclusion is a different experience. It is what is done to you collectively as members of a distinct group. To end exclusion, we must do more than offer our pain, but we must also offer our visions on what must come.

This process of gaining control over your experience is essential. Therefore, what is just as important as the ways in which we are silenced, are the ways in which we receive and maintain our voices. We receive our voices when we become empowered and overcome the silencing. And there is an important connection between overcoming silencing and ending collective exclusion. It is much easier to exclude a silent so-called minority, than a vocal one. "Flint Woman" is important as an example of the way in which one voice, my voice, was re-claimed. My voice is the voice of a Mohawk woman, mother and law professor. My voice is all that I have experienced and can speak to. It is a mere glimpse in what was and remains a very long process, a very long struggle.

The relationship between race and gender is also an important aspect of the "Flint Woman" discussion about silencing and exclusion. I am particularly concerned with silencing along the lines of race (more appropriately culture) than gender. I do not mean to be constructing a hierarchy of "isms" nor do I intend this to be perceived as exclusionary. It merely reflects that my voice is the voice of a Mohawk woman (mother and law professor). It is *only* through my culture that my women's identity is shaped. It is the teachings of my people that demand we speak from our own personal experience. That is not necessarily knowledge which comes from academic study or from books.

The First Nations concept of learning is introduced in the "Flint Woman" article. It is a theme which runs through the entire article but this particular quotation is illustrative:

> Aboriginal history is oral history. It is probably fortunate for Aboriginal people today that so many of our histories are oral histories. Information that was kept in peoples' heads was not available to Europeans; could not be changed and molded into pictures of "savagery" and "paganism." The tradition of oral history as a method of sharing the lessons of life with children and young people also had the advantage that the Elders told us stories. They did not tell us what to do or how to do it or figure

29

out the world for us—they told us a story about their experience, about their life or their grandfather's or grandmother's or auntie's or uncle's life. It is in this manner that Indian people are taught independence as well as respect because you have to do your own figuring for yourself. (Chapter One, p. 11)

There are two points I wish to make here. The first is that the role experience plays in qualifying individuals is different in my culture. A personal example is that I have frequently been referred to as a "prison expert." It is always necessary for me to qualify this statement, as I am an academic expert only. My knowledge comes from books and volunteer experiences within the criminal justice system. Within my culture, this does not make me an expert. I have never spent any time in jail as a prisoner and I cannot speak to that experience. The second point is the importance of oral history. In order to communicate with others of my profession, I must rely upon a medium, the written word, which is historically a foreign way of communication given my cultural identity. The fact that my participation in academia goes through at least several stages of translation and accommodation (so that you can hear me) is an invisible edge in my participation. Effectively, it is a form of exclusion for the majority of First Nations.

Since the writing of "Flint Woman," I have made a political choice to adopt the term First Nations and not Native. Of the choices (Aboriginal, Native, Indian, etc.) this is the terminology I now am most comfortable with. Writing for a introductory text for women's studies, I discuss this difficulty of determining what to call myself:

> I am a member of the Ho-Dee-No-Sau-Nee Confederacy. The Confederacy is a "political" union which is a democracy in the truest sense of the word. For many years, our nations were known as the Iroquois. But, this is not how we call ourselves. There are six nations which make up the Ho-Dee-No-Sau-Nee Confederacy. We are the Seneca, Oneida, Onondaga, Cayuga, Mohawk, and Tuscarora. I do not like to say that I am a Mohawk woman. A friend recently told me that she had been taught that Mohawk means "man-eater" in one of the European languages. This is not a nice way to be known. That is not what being "Indian" means to me. I am a proud member of my nation and that is a good way to be. This is just one good example of how colonialism and oppression operate in the dominant society.

> When I was growing up, the word I learned to describe who I was, was "Indian." Since then, I have learned that it is not a good way to name myself. I have been learning how these constructs and processes support racism. The meaning of the word "Indian" is a purely legal

definition. An Indian is a person who is entitled to be registered under the definitions in the Indian Act. It is also not a good way to describe ourselves because it is a definition that has been forced on us by the federal government. (1993: 328)

Not being in control of the process of naming, that is, defining who you are, serves as one of the most express examples of silencing that I can think of.

This process of learning about creation that I was talking about earlier must encompass a reflection on and with the traditional gifts and responsibilities that we were given. I must strive to understand how I fit into creation. There are four guiding principles which illuminate the way in which we are expected to respect these traditional gifts and responsibilities. The guiding principles are kindness, sharing, truth (or respect) and strength. These principles are different aspects of the same whole (or circle). When you are kind the kindness is returned to you. When you share you reap the benefits of what you share. Perhaps you share a teaching and in this way the teachings are kept alive. Sometimes the truth is hard, but it may be the only way that we will learn. These three responsibilities—kindness, sharing and truth—will lead to the fourth, which is strength. One principle cannot exist without the other three. There is no changing them. They exist just as the north wind continues to blow.[6] And they shall continue to exist in this way for all the generations left to come.

These traditional concepts I have just shared with you are impossible to explain to you in a paragraph, chapter, or even a thousand books. These principals must be lived and shared to be understood. Oren Lyons, also a member of the Confederacy, explains these concepts in this way:

> Imagine a circle divided into four parts by directional arrows. This is the universal symbol that all indigenous peoples recognize and understand immediately. The centre of that circle is the family, and at the heart of it is the woman. Just as Mother Earth is the core of life, so the woman as mother is the core of her family.[7] The family sits in a circle, and that circle is called the clan. The clans in turn also sit in a circle, and that circle is called a nation. Then these nations sit in a circle, and that is called the world. Finally, there is the universe, which is the largest of the circles. The symbolism is meaningful, and it is important. (1986: 160)

There are two things that must be understood. The ways of First Nations cannot be understood or explained at a glance. And second, these ways are not the same as the ways known to the dominant society.

It is the ways of my people that are at the core of my being. It is from the teachings that I draw my strength, my hope and my vision for the future.

Becoming a law teacher has not shifted the traditional focus in my life. It remains the core of my being. But, becoming a law teacher has fundamentally shifted my thoughts as I now reflect on "Flint Woman." As I prepared myself to teach, I had to consider the many ways that I had been silenced and excluded. Now that I have a position of responsibility, how do I prevent the silencing of someone else? What I came to realize was that it is not the silencing that is so crucial. What is important is to give my students the opportunity to develop their own unique voices, specifically, their legal voices. A legal voice that also respects the fact that they may be women, or homosexual, or poor, or First Nations, or Black.

The empowerment that comes when we find our voices is so often what is missing in our education systems. Law school is merely a reflection of what is happening generally in education systems from primary to university. We take away people's voices and force them to conform to status quo values and norms. And in law, the norm was defined solely by the monolithic White (and male) voice. For me learning to teach was and is fundamentally learning how to respect different voices.

A monolithic legal voice developed in the law for a very long time. It was the voice of White men of at least a middle-class upbringing. This brings our focus back to what is central. As long as the monolithic voice remains sanctioned in law and education, these experiences will be silencing and exclusionary for those of us who speak in a different voice. Again, this means we all lose.

Participating in a system which does not reflect the basic value structures of my culture is a constant challenge on a number of different levels. Whenever I write or speak, I often complain that I feel like I am engaging in a long process of footnoting life. It sometimes feels like I never get out of the footnote and truly live. This process of language, which I am referring to, is definitional (or perhaps, more accurately, re-definitional) and structural. I do not believe that First Nations people use English words in the same way as people who do not share our culture with us. We all use the same words but they mean different things. An example should make this point clearer. In my language (Mohawk[8]), we have the Great Law. It is our constitution. A literal translation from Mohawk to English is "the great big nice." I am not sure about you, but this has not been my experience of the Canadian legal tradition.

It is very important to understand the relationship between language and silencing and exclusion. Remember, as I earlier pointed out to you, that the sanctioned form of discourse within my culture is oratory. The emphasis on oral as opposed to written culture is overlooked. The result is that First Nations people are often referred to as illiterate. And I do not deny that many of my people have not had the privilege of a long and/or meaningful formal education. Neither is my point that reading is not important. The dominant culture has

32

sanctioned the truth and importance of the written word. The dominant society largely believes that without the practice of writing things down, you cannot have law or knowledge. This is one of the reasons First Nations laws and legal orders were invisible to the first settlers, traders and explorers. It is another one of the difficulties that First Nations continue to confront. And again, this sanctioning is also silencing and exclusionary.

Oral history is also a concept that is not well understood. Having a culture based on oral history means something greater than valuing the spoken word over the written word. It is an entire process of accurately recording history. The courts have tended to simplify the process of oral history and treat it as something less advanced than recording history on paper. This fits very neatly with the "noble savage" stereotype. This is wrong. What you hold in your head cannot be taken from you and destroyed in the same way a book can. The institution of oral history also ensures the passing down of history from generation to generation. One example from a recent judgment should clarify this point:

> In addition to the findings that were *essential* to the issues before him, the trial judge paid counsel for the Temagami Band the *courtesy* of dealing extensively with matters of some historical and cultural interest but of little relevance to this case. As to the history of the band, the trial judge expressed disappointment that so little evidence was given by band members. Chief Potts was the principal Indian witness to give oral history *and his testimony was not oral history in the traditional sense.* His own family did not arrive in the Land Claim Area until 1901, and his principal source of information was not his parents and grandparents. Instead, he gave evidence that was the result of his research and that which he had learned from other members of the band who were not called as witnesses. His evidence was not, in any sense, the best evidence available, and there were available older band members who could recount oral tradition. Chief Potts' testimony was not similar in quality to the type presented in other cases where oral history has been admitted . . . [9] (emphasis added).

There are present in the courts' interpretation several fundamental misconceptions of First Nations. First, oral history is not only passed down from grandparents to parent to child. First Nations society is not structured around linear and nuclear family concepts. Second, by inference, Chief Potts' knowledge is characterized as childlike. This completely overlooks the fact that the man was selected by the community to represent them as Chief. Again, the "noble savage" imagery appears. Finally, oral history does not mean, "I was there!" "I saw." Clearly the rules of evidence operate to the disadvantage of oral history. It was not Chief Potts who misunderstood oral history, but the judges hearing this case.

What is also overlooked is what my people have done with language! We have taken a language that does not speak for us and given it a new life. Perhaps, we break all of the structural, style and grammatical rules. But we have learned to use a language which was forced upon us to create powerful messages which convey to you our experience.[10] I do not call this a problem. I call it creativity. It is time my people give themselves credit for the great things we have accomplished against great adversity, rather than continuing to accept and embrace our exclusion. I am proud of my people. We are a strong, creative people. This is witnessed by the fact that we are still here to share with you.

A second good example of the importance of language is found in one of many justice inquiries that are happening across Canada.[11] The Marshall Inquiry has already made public its final report. The report opens highlighting several findings including the recognition "that the fact that Marshall was a Native was a factor in his wrongful conviction and imprisonment" (Nova Scotia 1989: 15). Consider the language chosen for a moment. The report comes very close to embracing the notion that what happened to Mr. Marshall happened because of the racism inherent in the criminal justice system (and elsewhere) in this country. I am disappointed that the Commission did not embrace that "racism" word and instead chose soft language. Racism is a word which suggests the collective nature of actions against entire groups of people. However, the language of the Marshall Report by focusing only on one "Native" man suggests that the problem was merely an isolated incident. I know this is not the true nature of the problem. Language is powerful. Yet, in this important report, it was overlooked.

The study of law only confounds the exclusionary experience of language. Law is a very structured discipline with rules of style and language unique only to itself. It requires that we examine the way in which perception is subtly embraced in language. It then requires that we critically examine the way we load our perceptions and how each of our perceptions shape our realities. This is the same process I earlier referred to as examining our assumptions. The academic literature sometimes refers to this as reconstruction (for instance, see Scott 1988).

Law's rigid structure often forecloses the involvement of "outsiders" in our profession. Is that the purpose or intention of the rigid structural rules of the legal system? In any event, these rules do compound the First Nations or other dispossessed collectivities' sense of powerlessness. Our understanding of law is not represented within the structure of the Canadian legal system. We experience that system, particularly the criminal justice system, as racist and oppressive (from Sugar and Fox 1989). We, as individuals, did not participate in the process whereby the legal system was formed. We did not participate in the process of agreeing to the assumptions and values reflected in that system. Further, we have been excluded as Peoples in participating in the formation of that system. More importantly, First Nations Peoples have never consented to the application of the Canadian legal system to any aspect of our lives. It is important to note that the issue of consent is different from the issue of inclusion. These realities are continually ignored by the Canadian government, the legal profession and the judiciary. Only by understanding the history of the Canadian legal system can we then understand why the result of this system is not justice but exclusion and force (Monture 1987).

It seems a logical expectation to me that legal studies in Canada will begin to examine this critical area of exclusion. Jurisprudence courses seem to me a logical place to start. Jurisprudence is the formalized study of legal systems and the corresponding legal philosophy. This is frequently accomplished by the review of judicial decisions. This approach is too constraining and unnecessarily so. It separates form from content. As Mari Matsudi earlier described, it is an approach which allows the accepted practices to continue to define the future. At minimum, this is exclusionary, dangerous and anti-democratic.

Returning to the notion of footnoting life, there are a number of words which I will naturally understand in a different way. This is natural because my experience is different from the mainstream. These words or concepts are racism, anger and pain, intent, and discrimination. These concepts must be given meaning that is greater than the meaning which they have historically been given. The concepts have been defined by collectivities that have had "power over" the individuals lives which they are describing. If we *cannot* revisit these conceptual premises then any work we may accomplish to change social structures further down the line will become inverted or meaningless. This is a process which is complex and requires description in detail.

Anger and pain are the colourful prisms through which I experience and learn. Anger and pain are words for me which go together. Perhaps, they are feeling words, but they are essentially caught up in my learning process. Anger is largely external, in the sense that my anger is usually defined by someone outside of myself. It is common experience among so-called minorities to be labelled as angry. Most of the time, when I am so labelled, I am not feeling angry. My suspicion is that people use this label when they are having a difficult time hearing what it is that I am saying. I resent being forced to carry a negative label to convenience someone else who cannot cope with what they themselves are feeling. This is oppression at the individual level. Until now, I have not thought as much about the use of pain as a concept as I have about anger. I know that they are connected and that the connection is a descriptive version of racism. Anger and pain, perhaps, are the violence that grows out of racism.

35

In re-considering "Flint Woman," I discovered that pain is a re-occurring theme in that article. I describe:

> I do not have any control over the pain and brutality of living the life of a dispossessed person. I cannot control when that pain is going to enter into my life. . . . I am pretty possessive about my pain. It is my pain. I worked hard for it. Some days it is all I have. Do not try to take that away from me too (Chapter One, p. 16)

What was interesting for me to note in my review of this concept is that pain is externally sourced. It is not-resolved anger. It is not anger changed to pain. Pain is the instantaneous result of living racism, just as physical violence results in pain. When I pick up the telephone only to hear that yet another First Nations woman has committed suicide at the Prison for Women, the third in eleven months, it is intense pain that I feel. Pain so intense that I am numb. But the pain is reassuring. It is feeling. Therefore, I am. Pain then is the reaction and not the action. Perhaps, anger is the action? What I do know is that my experience of both pain and anger are integrally connected to my experiences of racism.

Racism is often defined in the academic literature as "White skin privilege plus power."[12] At the outset I want to express clearly that I do *not* disagree with this definition. It conveys a powerful and necessary message to White people[13] about their responsibility to unlearn racism. And it is a responsibility I am speaking about. It took me many years to understand that I could not fix racism. I can label it. I can point to it. I can explain why that particular behavior or action or attitude is racist. But I cannot stop it. I cannot stop you. I can report what I have said earlier:

> When are those of you who inflict racism, who appropriate pain, who speak with no knowledge or respect when you ought to know to listen and accept, going to take hard looks at yourself instead of at me. How can you continue to look to me to carry what is your responsibility? . . . I will not carry your responsibility any more. Your pain is unfortunate. But do not look to me to soften it. Look to yourself. (Chapter One, p. 21).

This is why a critical race analysis is so essential to academic study, and particularly legal study.

A clear and agreed upon definition of racism is not available. This should not be surprising. Experiences of racism are as different as the different racial and cultural communities that have those experiences. Racism is not a monolithic experience.

Within the academic literature racism is a much used and little defined concept. In Kallen's 1982 text on ethnicity and human rights in Canada, racism is defined as "the misunderstandings that have often influenced the kinds of prejudicial attitudes and discriminatory practices toward particular human populations" (2). From this we can understand that racism is a process. Later in the text:

> The tendency to evaluate, indeed, to judge, other races from an ethnocentric European-Christian perspective led many scientists to arrange these races in an hierarchical order of innate superiority and inferiority ranging from primitive to highly civilized. (4)

Not only is the failure to define racism in any succinct fashion interesting, but the failure of the law to embrace this word is also notable. In law, we do not discuss racism. We discuss discrimination. Discrimination is only the visible edge of racism. Perhaps then, combating racism through law can only be a partial solution, at least until the parameters of law are redefined in a way that is inclusive to all experience.

It must also be considered if a single definition of racism is sufficient or even possible. Racism operates at many levels, including the personal as well as the theoretical. The theoretical definition that I have provided ("White skin privilege plus power") assists me in understanding at an intellectual level. It helped me to understand that I was not the only individual that was responsible to erase racism and this was an essential understanding. But it does not help me live my everyday life. It does not help me on a personal level with the everyday experience of racism.

Here, I am assuming that an academic definition should relate to my everyday life. The way of my people is holistic. It does not separate my mind from my heart from my spirit. A student in my public law class complained to me that he did not understand what Aboriginal rights had to do with public law. Nor did the student think the topic was being portrayed objectively even though we were reading Canadian court decisions and not the writings of First Nations Peoples. I have heard that complaint many times. What it fails to acknowledge is the fact that Canadian court decisions do reflect a specific culture, even if that culture is not named. As I am willing to share my perspective and acknowledge that it is an Aboriginal perspective, I am criticized for my failure to be objective. I see my willingness to share my perspective and its biases as an effort that is honest. I was raised to be honest not objective. The criticism is a result of a failure to examine the contours of academic and legal bias.

It is easy to provide further examples of the system's failure to be self-reflective and the contradiction this creates for me. I have heard about several law professors who emphatically assert that they do not understand how the teaching of property law has anything to do with Aboriginal title. Some professors of criminal law refuse to examine the bias inherent in Canada's criminal justice system because they see it as separate from the application of the criminal law. I have reviewed outlines of children and the law courses where Aboriginal issues have never been mentioned. And then, another First Nations woman commits suicide at the Prison for Women. I grieve for each of them. But I am also angry. These emotions are not captured in the academic definition of racism. For me, therefore, the definition remains incomplete.

What I am attempting to do is to re-claim racism, as a word, and as a concept, and as an experience. I want it to speak to me, of me, for me. I am tired of it defining someone else's experience who has the luxury of not living racism. Racism, both as a concept and as an experience, creates a subject outside of me and leaves me being object. The fact is that racism creates an unnatural inversion. It is therefore a neat little trick which oppresses the individual or collective who is already struggling to overcome their oppression. This is the neat little trick. As soon as I point out to most people, "HEY, that's racist," it is distancing. You become defensive. Perhaps you blame me for calling you names or maybe you distance yourself by calling me angry. I feel guilty as I had never intended to hurt you. That is not my way. I have the responsibility to be kind. Kindness is one of my original responsibilities. The power to define my own experience is then taken away from me because racism is a bad word!

Racism is turned against the "victim"[14] in this kind of labelling process. This inversion of racism is partially the result of the well-established principle that academic training, and especially legal training, does not involve feelings. At the threshold this contradicts my experience and what I have been taught. My First Nations teachers have told me that I must double understand. It is not enough to get the knowledge into my head. Instead, I must also get the knowledge to my heart so that I will live what I have learned. This is why the learning from experiencing everyday life is so valued in First Nations cultures. It is also a further profound example why the study of language must become essential to the study of law. The power to define is essential.

In an effort to help clarify an understanding which I believe to be difficult, I offer a second example. Much of the discussion at a political level between First Nations and the levels of Canadian government over the last decade or so has focused on deliberations around "self-government." In the same manner that racism has become inverted and is often used against the collectivities that experience it, so has "self-government" been definitionally inverted and made devoid of meaning. *Osennontion* explains:

Naturally, our own people, as continues to happen time and time again, have wholeheartedly embraced the buzz-word [self-government]. Of course, the word itself is not the culprit; what it means to people, how it is interpreted, or misinterpreted, and how it comes about are causes for debate and dissension. When the Feds talk of recognizing "self-government" they mean delegated authority to "Indians," for example, to govern their affairs on the reserves wherein they were displaced, and this is accomplished through their legislation. When an aboriginal person, who knows what s/he is talking about, speaks of "self-government," s/he means the particular system of government that was given to the people when they were placed in their territory on Turtle Island. This government needs no sanction through legislation or otherwise; rather, the "others" need only honour the original agreements to co-exist, and through their actions, show respect for our ways. However, because so many of our people don't know our ways, they have become involved in processes whereby they have attempted to gain recognition of our "right to self-government," instead of working on finding ways to effectively assert and exercise our own governments. Before I knew better, I myself supported and took part in some of those processes—this was before I knew what things like "Nationhood" and Sovereignty" really meant. I came to realize my mistakes; I am praying for others to do the same before any more damage is done on behalf of "the people."

If we are going to use the English language, I prefer the term "self-determination," as it better describes, for me, the action that needs to be taken. The establishment, exercise and enforcement of government, is only one aspect of "self-determination." In our own language, we have a word that, of course, even better describes what we have been instructed to do. TEWATATHA:WI best translates into "we carry ourselves"—a rather simple concept, some might say, but I think it says it all. (Kane and Maracle 1989: 10)

In searching for meaning and for language that expresses our experience, we must be careful of the words which we chose to embrace our experience. What is also important to understand is that it is not the word that is the problem, but the process by which and by whom it is given meaning.

Academic understanding is more than mere thoughts and ideas. As it involves sanctioning of thoughts and ideas, it is fundamentally about sanctioning knowledge. Knowledge only involves those things that can be objectively proven. In the instance of law, knowledge, as it is understood in the dominant culture, reflects the preoccupation and continued assertion that law is objective. But what if my cultural experience teaches me that I cannot separate my feelings from my thoughts. This brings us back around to my criticism of the conventional understanding that jurisprudence involves only the study of form.

It is important to understand what is the result of the emphasis of objectivity to the study of law. We must study only what we can see and scientifically prove. Therefore, my only difference to you is the colour of my face. There is a person, a woman, beyond this brown skin that is different from you. In discussing the *Charter* and its underlying monopolistic value structure, Professor Mary Ellen Turpel articulates this position:

> I intentionally use the term "culture" and "cultural difference" instead of "race" or "racial difference" because I view this as more accurate and more expansive: race or racial differences are too readily equated with "colour" or visible biological differences among people; whereas cultural differences should be understood more as manifestations of differing human (collective) imaginations, different ways of knowing. The expression "cultural difference" conjures up more than differences of appearances (colour), it allows us to consider profound differences in understandings of social and political life. (1991a: 503)

Perhaps we value the same things, but the importance that First Nations attach to the values is different from that attached by the dominant society. Until we have examined the values upon which the legal system is structured, primarily to determine exclusivity, then we continue unwittingly to reinforce and support oppressive structures.

As we earlier noted, racism is not a word that is embraced within the legal discourse. For example, the laws we have prohibit only "discrimination." I believe that racism covers a broader range of behaviors than discrimination does. Discrimination involves actions or practices. It is the incident. Racism is about the way we think, the way we feel, what we believe, and how we structure our realities. Discrimination is only one aspect of racism. There is another parallel here too. In law, thinking (the mind) is superior to feeling (the heart and the spirit). As discrimination is the actionable, seeable, thinkable, portion of racism, law has again given priority to thinking as opposed to feeling. A brief examination of the law of discrimination should help to clarify what I am suggesting.

It is largely the field of human rights which has come to reflect the development of anti-discrimination laws in this country.[15] The history of human rights legislation in this country is rooted in legislation of the 1940s[16] which prohibited by quasi-criminal sanction actions expressing racial or religious discrimination (Tarnopolosky 1968: 567). From the outset, the nature of these early statutes as quasi-criminal sanctions introduced the necessity to prove the intent (what is in their mind) of the wrong-doer. This created an almost impossible situation for the individual seeking to bring forward a claim. It left the complainant a next-to-impossible burden of proof to discharge. Without proof of a mental process, the discrimination was not illegal. The result was that legislation was grossly inadequate in dealing with discrimination.[17] What we must also consider, therefore, is not only what we are including but what (and who) we have excluded.

In the United States and Great Britain, by the early 1970s intent as an essential element of discrimination was being disregarded by the courts (Vizkelety 1987: 24-25). It was not until 1985, that the Canadian judiciary accepted that intent is not relevant to a determination of discrimination. In the case of *O'Malley* v. *Simpsons-Sears*[18] the Supreme Court of Canada articulated this definition of discrimination:

> To take the narrower view and hold that intent is a required element of discrimination under the Code would seem to me to place a virtually insuperable barrier in the way of a complainant seeking a remedy. It would be extremely difficult in most circumstances to prove motive, and motive would be easy to cloak in the formation of rules which, though imposing equal standards, could create injustice and discrimination by the equal treatment of those who are unequal. Furthermore, as I have endeavored to show, we are dealing here with consequences of conduct rather than with punishment for misbehavior. (549)

Although this step is laudable and certainly essential to the development of effective human-rights sanctions (anti-discrimination legislation) in this country, it remains an insufficient advancement.

My real concern is with the insidious nature of racism and the ways in which racism is structured and sanctioned in this society. Merely going beyond intent is insufficient. Therefore, discrimination as a legal concept still remains an incomplete remedy. Two necessary considerations are fundamentally overlooked: by focusing our legal attention on intent, what did we exclude, and as a theory, is discrimination complete? This brings us back to legal theory, or the business of jurisprudence. Through the examples I have given, we can see how legal theory is incomplete. The essential question to ask is formed around an examination of: Whom are we excluding? and Whom are we silencing? Effectively, legal theory has so simplified the questions that I wonder if the answers that have been historically sanctioned are in fact answers. Marlee Kline expands on this notion with regard to feminist theory:

> Because of the simultaneity of their experiences of oppression, women of color must directly confront contradictions White middle-class women do not face when attempting to understand and theorize about their oppression. White middle-class women are "unusual in the extent of the choices [we] can exercise and in the lack of contradictions in [our] personal lives." However disadvantaged we may feel as women, we experience great privilege in terms of race and class. As a result, White middle-class feminist theorists have tended to discount "the complexity of the contradictions which most women are embroiled." As just one example, consider the family, which is a site of contradictory experiences for women of color of ways unknown to White women. Although both women of color and White women sometimes experience the family as an institution of violence and oppression, for women of color the family often functions as a source of support for its members against the immediate harassment of racism and provides a site of cultural and political resistance to White supremacy. The failure of many White middle-class feminists to account for the contradictory experiences of the family by women of color and thus to concentrate only on gender oppression is but one illustration of bell hooks' observation that "[c]ertainly it has been easier for women who do not experience race or class oppression to focus exclusively on gender." (1989: 122-23)

My experience of law is largely one of negotiating the contradictions.

As distinct nations who come to the study of law, I cannot tell you what it is that you need to do to make legal systems work for you. What I do know is that First Nations have a right to live without oppression and contradiction in the ways we were given. The most that I can do is maintain and nurture my voice. It is the voices for those who have been traditionally excluded who bring the tension to bear on all those systems that are oppressive to human life. It is that tension which is the site of true human development and knowledge.

Notes

1. When I wrote this article I believed that the term First Nations captured the experience of all original peoples resident in this territory now known as Canada. Since then, the term First Nations has become more narrowly defined and generally to refers only to the registered Indian population. Minimally, First Nations (as I intend it to be understood here) includes the peoples known as the Indian (status and non-status), Inuit and Metis.
2. In the First Nation's way there are four races. They are the red, yellow, White, and black. It is believed that each of these races had a traditional faith teaching such as the First Nation's teaching that I have begun to share with you.
3. This article was written after Richard Devlin (the editor of the text in which it first

42

appeared) telephoned seeking my permission to republish "Flint Woman." I was not comfortable with this idea. I did not want my ideas about the experience of racial oppression to be frozen in time in that one article. Racial oppression is a topic upon which I continually reflect. I had been thinking about issues of race/ culture and gender since the time when the first article was published. I sat down and wrote this piece (which was already floating around in my head) as a result.

4. I do not primarily consider that my work involves speaking to feminism or women's reality. This is not to deny that I am woman. My work primarily focuses on exposing racism. I do not mean to disappear gender. It must be realized that my race and culture shape my gender experiences as my women's identity flows through and from my experience of my culture and traditions.

5. For examples of how courts have treated collective rights, see *Boyer* v. *Canada* (1986), 65 N.R. 305 (FC); *Dumont* v. *Canada and Manitoba* (1988), 52 Man.R. (2d) 291 (CA).

6. This is an Ojibwe teaching shared with me by Shirley O'Connor.

7. Over the years, I have noticed that much confusion is caused by statements such as this one. Please do not understand these words through Euro-centric constructions of family and the role of women assigned in a different (and dominant) culture(s).

8. I am not a traditional language speaker. This story was first told to me by Tom Porter of the Mohawk Nation, Akwesasne Territory.

9. *A.G. Ontario* v. *Bear Island Foundation et al.* (1989), 30 O.A.C. 66, at 69.

10. In the summer of 1988, I had the opportunity to hear Lee Maracle speak at a conference in Toronto, Ontario. These are ideas that were very much inspired by Lee. I would recommend her book, *I Am Woman*, to everyone.

11. These are the Manitoba Justice Inquiry, the Inquiry in Alberta of the Blood Reserves, and the Nova Scotia Inquiry into the wrongful conviction of Donald Marshall, Jr. Also important is the Report on the Task Force of Federally Sentenced Women, which is the only inquiry focused on women, and a substantial amount of that document focuses on the over-representation of First Nation's women in the federal prison systems.

12. This theory was discussed by Esmeralda Thronhill at the Law and Society Conference, Learned Societies Conference, Windsor, 1988.

13. Please do not look at the colour of your skin and be immediately offended. Race is a particularly unsatisfactory label because it focuses our attention on skin colour. It is what is going on behind my skin, or yours, that is so fundamentally different. It is a difference of culture and not race or biology.

14. Victim is not a word that is empowered. Being a survivor of racism is a positive and inspiring label.

15. Walter S. Tarnopolosky (1968) traces the legal history of human rights legislation in Canada.

16. The two earliest enactments were the *Ontario Racial Discrimination Act* in 1944 and the *Saskatchewan Bill of Rights Act* in 1947. The Ontario legislation focused only on the publication or display of materials that were discriminatory on grounds of race or religion. The Saskatchewan enactment was much more broadly based.

17. For a discussion see Vizkelety 1987: 13-58.

18. [1985] 2 S.C.R. 536.

3

Self Portrait: Flint Woman

THIS ARTICLE IS THE THIRD IN THE "Flint Woman" series and was written in 1991, during my second year of law teaching at Dalhousie Law School in Halifax, Nova Scotia. Two important events have happened in my life since the writing of this article. In 1991, I married. My husband Denis is Cree. We currently live in his community, the Thunderchild First Nation. I am now bi-cultural in two ways as I am now significantly influenced by my Cree relations. The second event occurred in January of 1993 when my first daughter was born. Kate's birth and the vulnerability of bringing female life into the world forced me to confront my sexual abuse at a different level. In preparing this article for re-publication in this book, I have continuously noted that these two events have had a significant impact on how I see myself today. This article now feels incomplete.

This article was first published in Voices: Being Native in Canada, *edited by Linda Jaine and Drew Taylor, Saskatoon: University of Saskatchewan, Extension Division, 1992, pp. 126-134. This volume is currently in its second printing.*

My people are a storytelling people and my efforts here are a desire to capture the oral tradition within these square white boxes we call pages. As I have come to understand it from listening to the Elders and traditional teachers, the only person I can speak about is myself. That is how the Creator made all of us. When we speak badly of someone else, we are really only telling the world something about the kind of person we are, not the person we are gossiping about. All I have to share with you is myself, my experience and how I have come to understand that experience. This is true even when you ask me to speak on a topic that is supposedly objective, such as the law.

All that we can experience and share is ourselves. We can only experience the world through that prism of self. This is one of the basic differences between the two cultures, First Nations[1] and Canadians, that I have experienced. In academic writing, the rule is that authors do *not* identify their voices. They speak from a pedestal of knowledge. The individual speaking is not a central part of that knowledge nor is he or she actively involved in the knowledge he or she has produced. The knowledge is outside the self.

Once I wrote a piece on First Nations women and the violence many of us have experienced.[2] When it came back from the editor, he had removed all of the pieces of "my" story and all the "Is." He had created an academic piece for me and I think he felt very good because in his mind he had somehow elevated the status of my work. For me, I felt violated; the "me" had been stripped from my work. And I wonder what made that editor think I could not write in the academic style? Was it because I was a citizen of one of the First Nations? Was it because I was a woman? Was it because I was a newly appointed academic? Or perhaps, maybe some combination of the above? In my culture, not speaking from the "me" is a violation. The only true knowledge that I can have is that which is learned from what I have experienced. For First Nations, the rule is that all knowledge is what we have learned about the self.

If I have a further motivation for writing this piece, it is to empower the First Nations reader. By sharing my story and my pain, perhaps you too will remember how to dream. It is our dreams that make the future possible. I cannot ever become more that I am able to dream.

The first piece I wrote had a very long Mohawk title that roughly translates to "the way that Flint Women do things." Through circulation within academic and feminist communities, that has become shortened to simply "Flint Woman." Mohawk people are "People of the Flint." That is a very simple translation of the word in our language. And I have become "Flint Woman" through the process of writing these articles. This is the third in the series of articles bearing the "Flint Woman" title. They fit together.

The first piece is a story about one particular conference I attended, and it is about racism. More significantly that first piece is about my experiences at law school. The second article in the series is "Reflecting on Flint Woman." It is my professor speaking back to my student reflecting on what I have learned about racism. This third piece is what is behind the first two, the Mohawk woman. It is about the search for my identity and for my healing. It is meant to be personal. My choosing law as a profession is the culmination of my fascination with law, my word mongering and my preoccupation with searching for meaning.

When I was a young woman, I had read all the Perry Mason books on the library's shelves before I had finished public school. One day, reflecting back on my life, I realized I grew up fascinated by the law. I looked to the law to satisfy my craving for a total triumph of justice and fairness. I was clinging to a naive belief that somehow both justice and fairness existed in the world outside of myself. Reflecting on my life, the first thing I can remember really wanting to be "when I grew up" was a writer. I am a die hard "word-monger."[3] Words were the doorway to the world where meaning is questioned. Words are the realm of the intellect. They are the vehicle by which I can share my ideas and quest for meaning with you.

Words were also my solace, my comfort. I was lonely as a young woman. And as far back as I can remember, I always read by the hour. Reading provided me the first world I had to escape into. It is no wonder I grew up wanting to be a writer, since the written word brought me so much comfort in my youth. Escape was important as I learned at an early age just how unpredictable life was. My mother died of surgical complications the summer I was six. My father had his first heart attack shortly after my mother's death. His heart finally gave out on him in November of 1967 when I was nine. It was the world of words where I sought my escape and comfort from age nine to twelve. I can remember reading *The Diary of Anne Frank* and the quotation, "Paper is more patient than man." I then understood my own desire to write.

At twelve, I discovered drugs were a much more effective way to push down one's pain. Added to my confrontation with death at an early age was the experience of sexual abuse. It began shortly after my father's death. The sexual violations are still the most difficult for me to talk about or think about, and even to admit. I allowed my memories to surface a mere two years ago. I remembered the memory of being raped by two young men when I was just twelve. Many other memories came erupting to the surface once I had taken that first one out of storage.[4] I turned from books and the comfort of an imaginary written world to drugs as my spirit screamed louder.

There were two periods in my life when I spent a considerable amount of time cruising the streets of London, Ontario. These were between the ages of twelve and sixteen, and between eighteen and twenty-one. The brief interlude was spent in Chatham, Ontario, with a maternal uncle and aunt. That was a relatively peaceful period in my life in which time I was able to complete high school. It was, however, the street where a lot of my values were shaped. I still carry many of those values with me today. It is how I think because it is honest and makes sense. All of these pieces of my history are important not only to understanding who I am, but also to understanding how I think about the law. My study of law has been shaped on searches for "equality and justice."[5]

Particularly during my late teenage years, I felt more than lonely. I felt alone and different. I felt caught in the middle. I was half White and Whites clearly thought I was an "Indian." They tended to not want me around. But the "Indians" also felt I did not belong with them. Having been raised off reserve, I really could not be an "Indian." For many years I believed the middle was nothing but lonely. It was not until much later in life I learned that middle was the place to be. I can walk both ways. I have the benefit of traditional teachings as well as my university education. I can pick the best from both worlds. More importantly, the Creator chose to put me down in the middle. And it is in the middle, the place between two cultures, where any bridges of understanding will be constructed. This is my real work. Law is just the means by which I carry out my real work.

This "I'm on reserve, you're off reserve" is a split in our communities that troubles me greatly. It is directly, if only partially, responsible for our youth feeling lost, caught in the middle. It is a variation on the divide-and-conquer game that has been used by the settler populations to oppress our people. And it is time we stopped being so compliant with the rules to somebody else's game. The on/off reserve distinction is a construction of Canadian law. "Indians" did not dream up reserves, the Canadian government did in an effort to ensure controlled "settlement" of our lands. The *Indian Act* is not ours. It is not a reflection of how we are a nation, or how we govern ourselves. Reserves are not our creation, so the distinction between being raised "on or off" is one that should not be central in how we think about ourselves. It is a false distinction. It is a distinction that oppresses us. Having a territory is a different way of understanding where I come from. I am a Mohawk and my people have a territory. It spans the borders of New York State, Ontario and Quebec. It is that territory I come from and not the so-called province of Ontario.

Reserve-based thinking is thinking that remains colonized. This oppressive thinking, which so many of my people have picked up, predisposes us to leading a life of oppression. Oppression is a central concept that assists me in organizing the little bit of knowledge I have earned. No course of study in the university has ever helped me understand oppression. My understanding of oppression has grown in the margins of my university experience. It is what I have learned in spite of what others have tried to teach me.

There is a question that I am often asked when I speak about my personal history. How does one move from the streets and drugs to the university? It is necessary to unpack what is loaded behind that question before going further. The question presumes that there is intrinsically something "better" about the university compared to the street. And the same goes for the people that occupy both spaces. I have walked both roads and I do not find that presumption to be true. There are good-hearted people in both places. And fundamentally, I am still the same woman I was before I had the degrees to hang on the wall. I have learned important lessons both at university and on the street. What makes the lessons different is one type of knowledge is sanctioned and the other is disregarded. If what we truly value is knowledge, these presumptions ought to be questioned.

I have often been amazed that I landed at law school in Kingston, Ontario,

47

only eight blocks (or so) from the federal Prison for Women. I have always felt that I should have properly landed on the other side of that high limestone wall. It was both anger and amazement that took me on my journey to university. My quest to find meaning coupled with my preoccupation with words made university a logical choice.

The anger that motivated me grew out of what I saw on the streets—the pain, the anguish and the senseless suffering. It belonged to me and others I came into contact with. Especially, it was the suffering of women at the hands of men. This experience of abuse of women has not changed for me between the street and the university. Perhaps the shape of the experience has changed, but not that it is the experience of pain and abuse. I do not want you to think of me as a victim, because I have survived. And it has been good. I just have not been able to accept that pain and anger is what life is about.

The amazement can best be symbolized in the recounting of one experience. In 1979, I signed up for two introductory courses in economics and sociology at the University of Western Ontario. The first examination I wrote in sociology I received a grade of 78. In high school, I infrequently if ever earned such a grade. In fact, my guidance counselor in my last year of high school told me to forget university, I simply was not smart enough. Those are almost his exact words and they rang in my head for a very long time. The amazing part of receiving that first examination back was not the mark—that was just the initial shock. I was amazed by the professor's comment, "You can do better!"[6]

His words were simple but they certainly challenged my reality and inspired me. I have carried them with me for a long time. I immediately began wondering, "Better, eh? So just how much better?" And the challenge began. I kept pushing myself harder and harder to see just where the limit was, how high a grade I could attain. Maybe I was more than a "stupid Indian!" Every good grade I earned challenged the "inferiority complex" I had been dragging around with me. The secret desire I had harboured for some time to be a lawyer perhaps was maybe not so crazy after all. And I began to dream.

This one small incident is important to consider in another respect if you are still struggling with how people move from the street to the university. That little bit of encouragement given by one professor inspired me and gave me confidence.[7] It is important to recognize the possible impact of our actions on another person's life. Even small words of encouragement can be the basis for significant changes in our life circumstances and self-confidence.

When I reflect upon the transformation from street person to university student, I see that my behavior was still "addictive." I truly am a creature of habit! But at least this time I was living an addiction that was positive in result as opposed to dysfunctional all around. I see a definite relationship between my over-achieving woman qualities and the fact that I am a survivor of sexual abuse. It is very easy for me to live in thought, exerting all my energy in the realm of the mind. It is living in my own emotions that is such a struggle. It was in the month that followed my law graduation that my memories of sexual abuse in my childhood and teens popped up. That does not seem to me to be a coincidence either. University allowed me to easily escape into the world of the written word. I remained alive only in my mental energies, avoiding and pushing away the pain I carried in my emotional being. Being active and well in mind is not enough. We must also care for our bodies, our spirits and our emotions.

In March of 1984, I had my first baby, a son. I was taught by my aunties that children are our teachers, not the other way around. The children have just come from the spirit world and remember the lessons of innocence and purity that we adults have forgotten and set aside. And through the birthing experience, I first began to understand what it meant to be a woman. Having a son for me was very symbolic. Having been a survivor of child sexual abuse, my son was the first male spirit I willingly allowed to enter my woman's circle. And he has brought a great healing into my life. And this is something our men have forgotten, to ask before they enter a woman's circle of life (and here I am talking about more than just mere sexual relations). It is this simple abuse of our sacredness that is hurting my people, both the men and the women.

I wish equality seekers would come to understand that women are sacred because we bring life into this world. First Nations women are respected as the centre of the nation for his reason. Perhaps if in the talk of legal equality there was room for me to speak in this way, I would think more positively about current Canadian developments in law such as the *Charter*. But as long as equality law forces me to step outside both my culture and my gender in order to participate, I will remain a cynic.

My experience of Canadian law has very much been an experience of contradiction and confusion. Equality as a value and the rule of law as a legal principle, clearly expresses my experience of both contradiction and confusion. Most of us have a sense of what equality is. The phrase "rule of law" is not so well understood. It is the idea that law applies equally to all, that both kings (and I suppose queens) and commoners can sleep under bridges (not that kings or queens ever needed to). It seems to me that the rule of law is a notion which is based on the concept of sameness. In Canadian equality jurisprudence, this notion of equal means sameness (that we treat likes alike) has been rejected as simplistic.[8]

Not only is equality as sameness simplistic but such a notion of equality can create situations of grave injustice. Why is it that many Canadians accepted the Oka occupation based on the Minister of Justice's rationalization, which was built on the rule of law? The rule of law seems to me to be a shaky foundation upon which to build armed confrontation. It seems that the rule of law is a matter of perspective. Laws are applied equally in Canada only if you have the power to decide what laws we are talking about. Canadian politicians are emphatic about their equal enforcement of criminal laws but suffer from a historic forgetfulness should you ask them to apply the same principals to treaty provisions (which is exactly what the Mohawks at Oka were doing).

My words are about anger and frustration as they are the result of experiencing so many contradictions. My words are also about anger and frustration with myself. I have been busy chasing myself around. In my final year of law school, I received a letter in response to my application for graduate school saying I was on the waiting list and had not yet been accepted for the program because I was a "lesser qualified candidate." Two weeks later, I learned I had won one of five national scholarships to pursue graduate studies in law. It is funny now but I did not laugh much then. But I did learn something very important from the experience. All my years at university, I had been running from what I perceived to be the total brutality of the street. I had universities and law schools (and the people in them) way up on the pedestal. I was aiming to improve myself so I would be as good as those people. And what I learned was how I had fundamentally deceived myself.

On the street, life is honest. If you are going to hold a knife at my throat and threaten my life, I can see that knife. It is real. And I know why I am afraid. However, at law schools when they drive a knife through the core of your being and your hope, they are not even honest enough to admit that they are "packing."[9] You cannot see the knife and your fear seems irrational.

My ten-year effort to turn myself into a lawyer has been full of many struggles. It is a constant struggle. In the summer after I finished my law degree, I filed a law suit against the Attorney General of Ontario and the Law Society of Upper Canada. Before you can practise law you must have a law degree, have completed your articles and received a call to the bar. When you get called to the bar, you are required to take an oath. It is an oath where you swear your allegiance to the Queen. I will not take this oath. I am not a Canadian before I am a citizen of the Mohawk nation. This is what the Elders explained to me when they suggested that perhaps I should consider whether I should take that oath. I would like to pay my respects to Jacob Thomas, Cayuga Chief who laid this challenge at my feet and spent many hours supporting me in this struggle. Did I want to be a Mohawk first or a Canadian? I feel very strongly about the self-determination of my people. It is an inherent right. I cannot allow myself to do something that flows against what I believe myself to be. The oath case represents my refusal to continue to turn myself inside out to become a lawyer. Whether I am aligned with the Queen or the Mohawks does not influence my ability to be a truthful and honest person or to be a good lawyer.

It would not surprise me to learn that many First Nations people have taken this oath, but not taken it seriously. I never did before the Elders came to me and explained the significance of what I was doing, that I would be saying I was no longer a Mohawk first. I do not mean to imply that it is wrong for anyone, First Nations or otherwise, to take the oath. It is wrong for me as I do believe I should not be forced to denounce my Mohawk citizenship in order to be able to practise law. I can still be Mohawk and respect Canadian law. The oath case is not based on any disrespect for the monarchy. Canadians have had the right to choose how to govern themselves. Why is the opposite not true? Why can Canadians not only respect their laws but also respect laws of First Nations, not to mention the agreements our ancestors made. That is really the centre of the problem that caused the oath case.

The oath case is a very small stand to take, but it was so important to me. I did not think that doing the honest thing was such a big deal that it should have been splashed all over so many newspapers. I even spoke to a Japanese reporter and someone sent me an article that appeared in a British newspaper! That really surprised me.[10]

I have been chasing myself around for too many years, trying to fit into that system of law and legal education that First Nations or women had no hand (or heart) in shaping. Why would I think for a minute that these institutions would be accommodating, warm or receptive? Why would I go there looking for my identity or a reflection of my ancestors? The truth is not out there for us to find. It is in our hearts. And all those years of living in my mind just took me further away from developing a full understanding of myself.

I will keep teaching law or in the university as long as I can hold on to the belief that my mere presence in the law school makes a difference. That this brown face strolling the corridors and standing at the front of lecture halls in some small but fundamental way changes the institution. It ends the exclusion.

This fall I have been struggling a lot with questions of my identity and where happiness rests for me. I am frustrated with the image of myself I see the world reflecting back: "lawyer," "professor," "academic." All these images are rigid and they repel me. Do not put me in a box I had no hand at carving. The beauty I possess is as a woman and particularly as a mother. My children are my teachers. My woman's identity, in turn, flows through my culture. It does not surprise me that this latest transformation of self-identity corresponds to the birth of my second son.

The images—lawyer, professor, academic—that I am, but do not want to be, are all empty of any real meaning. I do not want to be known as an academic. I want to be a writer, an artisan. The creative side of me has been suffocated. And I only want to paint with words. And perhaps it is not my identity that needs to change. The creativity and the emotion have always been here inside me. What has been suffocated is the societal recognition of the existence of the creative, emotional me behind bricked and mortared images of the lawyer. "I am Flint Woman," I call to myself. Perhaps what needs to change are the social stereotypes that separate me from me.

My words are a colourful tapestry. They are my art. My struggle is to recover the identity that allows me to walk in the way of beauty. And how do you remake the image of a lawyer into a beautiful red likeness?

Notes

1. In this article I intended the term First Nations to be inclusive and refer to all original people including those now known as the Indian, Inuit and Metis.
2. No citation is provided in order to attempt to provide the editor with anonymity.
3. I have borrowed this phrase from another Aboriginal author, Lee Maracle.
4. There are a number of people who supported me in these first steps of my healing process. If not for them, I would not have the strength or patience to write this book. They are Penny, Pat, Fran, Darrell, Blaine and a psychologist who's name I cannot remember.
5. My interest in law is an interest in public law (primarily criminal and correctional, child welfare and constitutional issues including Aboriginal rights) and *not* private law. In law school I intentionally never attempted any corporate or business law courses.
6. Here I pay my respects to Dr. James J. Teevan for helping me open an important doorway.
7. In January 1994, I participated in organizing a small meeting, a talking circle, on justice for the Royal Commission on Aboriginal People and the Native Law Centre at the University of Saskatchewan. During this meeting, a young man who has served more than ten years of his life behind the bars of Canada's federal prison system, was asked what would have made a difference in his struggle to re-adjust to life in the so-called free world. His response underlines the importance of my lesson. He said "It's the simple things that would make a difference. A letter from home, letting me know what's happening in my family. Letting me know I belong and I am cared about." I pay my respects to Darrel Tait.
8. For example, please see *Andrews* v. *Law Society of British Columbia*, [1989] 1 S.C.R. 141 at 164.
9. Street slang for someone when they are carrying a weapon.
10. The oath case struggle (and it was not an easy decision to make to file the suit) had a happy outcome. The Law Society agreed to change its rules and make the oath optional. The case never went to court. In January of 1994, I was called to the Ontario bar.

4

Flint Woman: Surviving the Contradictions in Academia

An earlier version of this paper was prepared as an introduction to the book Breaking Anonymity: The Chilly Climate for Faculty Women, *The Chilly Collective, Kitchener-Waterloo: Wilfred Laurier Press, forthcoming. Many of my colleagues over the years have helped me process these ideas and encouraged me to write about them. I am most grateful to Professors Constance Backhouse, Darlene Johnston, Irene Linklater, Sanda Rodgers and Mary Ellen Turpel.*

The overwhelming sense I had of my first few years of university education was of having found a place where I belonged. I can always remember being a "thinker." My friends tell me I am very logical. I was well suited to the requirements of a university life. It was years before I understood that this sense of belonging was a false one. My sense of belonging grew out of my status as a survivor of various forms of abuse. In university, I did not have to feel, just think. Feelings were what I was trying to avoid. Years later I came to understand that the sense of belonging I felt was really the comfort I took in finding an environment where feelings were not an essential requirement for success.

I have a number of stories to tell about what I have learned about surviving the contradictions of my life as both a university student and a university professor. The contradictions arise because Aboriginal culture is not the dominant culture of the university and my gender places me in another minority in the university teacher population. Being able to name and describe the contradictions I experience on a daily basis is very much a part of the process I have adopted in order to continue to survive within the university.

The experience of women in universities is not unlike the experience of women in other institutions and professions. This is only one of the reasons

53

I believe it is important to document my experiences of survival. It should be easy to recognize that women are under-represented in the academic fold. There are still fewer people of colour and Aboriginal people who hold faculty positions within Canadian universities. Aboriginal women and women of colour are dramatically under-represented in institutions of "higher learning." Universities remain a bastion of White male privilege. My experience of the university, and in particular the demands of an academic career, are complicated by the fact I am both Mohawk and woman.

Many times during the last six years of my teaching career, I have felt either confused about or uncomfortable with certain aspects of my job. This feeling is rooted in my difference either as a woman or as an "Indian" or some combination of the above.[1] I have named these uncomfortable and confusing experiences contradictions. The experience of contradiction is my expression for a state of being that I often slam into head first and the experience leaves me overwhelmed and motionless. I now understand my relationship with the university as a process of negotiating those contradictions. The negotiation part of this process implies there is no good solution to my experience of contradiction. Often naming the experience is the best solution I can hope to secure.

In an effort to minimize the numbness and pain that results from experiencing contradiction on a daily basis, I made a conscious decision a year ago to leave the law school. After making this decision, I was fortunate to secure a position at the University of Saskatchewan in the Native Studies Department. For less than a year now, I have been experiencing the university from a different and welcomed perspective. I am both healthier and happier now that I have found an environment where my ways of being as a Mohawk woman are not as alien as they were in the law school.

The majority of the experiences I am about to share, occurred within one of four Canadian law schools in the past decade.[2] I began my legal studies in September of 1984. The basic nature of my experiences of legal education has not changed even though my position within the law school has changed. As a professor, however, negotiating solutions to the contradictions has become more complicated. It is complicated because I now have access to a certain amount of power by virtue of my position as a professor. As a student, the lines around my oppression were clear. As a teacher my race/culture and/or gender oppression is complicated by the fact that I can choose to and do exercise power over others. At the same time, my professorial privilege is complicated by experiences of discrimination and oppression.

When this article was first written, there were only three Aboriginal people (and I must also point out all three of us are women) who held tenure track positions in law faculties.[3] We were all appointed on July 1, 1989.[4] Only one, Mary Ellen Turpel, continues to teach at a Canadian law school.[5] I can be angry and feel that the extraordinary demands on my time are unfair, but that does not change the sad reality that there are only limited choices available to cover issues of race and/or culture (Aboriginality) and gender. I must continually balance my sense of responsibility against feeling like I am perpetuating the silence around certain exclusions by deciding not to participate. Eventually, I decided to write about my personal experiences because I have spent a lot of time thinking about my position within the university over the last few years. I have made some important realizations that I need to share, perhaps only to purge my soul.

In purging my soul, I have decided not to name names although I will provide dates and locations, and identify institutions. Although writing is one of the thin strands of sanity that allows me to continue to maintain a grasp on my professional life, it does not come without inner turmoil. I often worry about the pain my writing may inflict upon others when they recognize themselves in the stories I tell. I often wonder how this has become my responsibility—your pain—as though I was somehow the author of it. I am getting very tired of "talking out" or as I think of it now "talking back."[6] I am very tired of always being in the position of responding to someone else's agenda rather than participating in the re-creation of our own Aboriginal space.

Things happen and I write them all down, sometimes quite compulsively. Writing—talking back—is the process through which I come to terms with my pain, anger and emotion. It is the process through which I often am able to come to terms with my oppression, the oppression of my people, and the corresponding feelings of helplessness and hopelessness that sometimes ride over me like a tidal wave. In itself my writing is not often within accepted academic traditions and another contradiction is named. Often only through the process of writing does the feeling of contradiction become actuated. It is real because I can make it appear in bold black letters against stark white paper. Writing is a place where I have found both strength and empowerment.

The process I went through before making a personal commitment to write this article is obviously important to me. This is only in part a result of my concurrence with the body of knowledge known as feminist analysis. This body of knowledge often focuses on process and process is the first thing that is important to me here. Choosing when to participate and when not to is one of the least frequently discussed ways that power is exercised in academic circles. Equally important is an examination, both personal and systemic, of what the consequences of my involvement are.

I frequently find myself struggling when my colleagues would like to ask me to do something but feel their asking puts an extraordinary burden on me. This is an experience which is most commonly experienced in my relationship with my feminist colleagues. Not being involved in issues affecting Aboriginal women can leave me feeling isolated or inadequate even though I know this is not the intent of my colleagues. Not being involved often means that there are no Aboriginal women involved and that also has particular consequences for me. This is only one of the contradictions where I can be caught. I know that this dilemma is not the creation of my colleagues but that it is the result of the systemic exclusion of Aboriginal women (and other women of colour) from universities. The under-representation of members of equality-seeking communities within Canadian universities has particular consequences for the first few members of these groups to claim a previously forbidden position. This is even more disturbing in institutions that have a commitment to equity. The demand on these few professors sends our quality of life into an irreversible tailspin.

I know that the naming of this contradiction will be unsettling for a number of my colleagues. I do not carry this responsibility well. Recognition of this contradiction results in their understanding that whenever they ask me to participate the delicate balance in my life may collapse. Yet, not asking results in my exclusion and more importantly not asking likely results in the exclusion of all Aboriginal voices.[7] Only through naming and sharing my experiences and my reflections on those experiences, do I believe that we can collectively reach a satisfactory solution.

Reading has always been a comfort to me. Because I am a mother of several small children, I often read in the wee hours of the morning. I have turned to women's literature on a number of occasions to help me understand my struggles with oppression. Taking comfort in the quiet hours of the night—children sleeping—I began to understand that I was neither alone nor was I crazy. I have sat with these women's words of their own pain and exclusion and I felt empowered by our common experiences. All too often missing from the gendered analysis was an integrated and detailed analysis of the way race and culture impacts on our gendered lives. I have often seen my experiences as woman during my ten years of schooling and my five years of university teaching reflected on the pages, in neat black type on bold White background. At the same time, I also began to feel invisible. Invisible because race and culture have such a significant impact on my experiences of university and this layer was almost totally absent from the women's storytelling.[8]

My experiences of culture are complicated by my gender and the fact that the dominant culture in this country also oppresses women. Sharing my Aboriginal experience with other Aboriginal people helps me uncomplicate my own experiences. One of my male relatives, a cousin, is a graduate of a professional school at the University of Western Ontario.[9] We attended the university at the same time and often got together to support each other and share our experiences. Once he told me about the student reception he went to in the first few days of his enrollment at the medical school. The reception was held in a large "L" shaped room. He was greeted by the appropriate student dignitaries. They encouraged him to meet some of his colleagues. He was taken to the back corner of the "L" shaped room, which was not visible from the entrance, and introduced only to other people of colour. He interpreted this as a profound message about his place within the institution and whom he was expected to associate with. Perhaps, those responsible bore him no ill-will (perhaps they even thought they were being kind) and acted only in their own ignorance, but what they did was clearly wrong. More than ten years later when I talked to my cousin about writing this article, my feelings of ambiguity and contradiction, he re-called the event I just described to you.[10] There is no doubt in my mind that these events may not be remembered by those who perpetuate them, but they are the events that taint our experiences of those institutions.

I remember my second year of law school at Queen's University. It was the first year of the overt "gender wars" at that law school.[11] I still marvel at the imagery that the label "gender wars" instills. Men in trenches, combat clothes, weapons, fighting for their cause. I am also reminded of the Mohawk men, the Mohawk women and their supporters who a few summers ago stood toe to toe with the Canadian military defending a small plot of land. The image of war is a contradictory one for me, as a Mohawk and as a woman. I, as woman, did not feel at war during my tenure as a student at Queen's law school. I felt excluded and battered. My reality and my people's proud history in the country were continually denied over and over again. Not only did I feel excluded but that feeling was reality. I was excluded. To describe this experience as "gender wars" takes the naming of the experience away from me and other women. This recognition is a reflection of just how powerless women sometimes are—even the popular name for our struggle is not ours. War also implies a battle between equal forces with equal resources. This is not the truth about women's struggles.

Naming is clearly an issue of great importance. Language reflects gender relationships as the naming of a particular woman's struggle as a "gender war" reflects. Women's worth is disenfranchised by the English language. English also makes difficult the expression of my race and culture experiences. It is not just a question of the "right" words not existing. It is more complicated than that. Even when I can find English words to convey my meaning, the meaning that the listener attaches to those words is often different.

I have told before a naming story to make this point. When I am talking to other Aboriginal people, I can describe myself as a Mohawk woman and they all understand what that is and means. When talking to non-Aboriginal people, I cannot be so sure they will know that word for my people. I am forced to find another word. I can choose Indian, or Native, or Aboriginal. It does not matter that none of those words fit me right. It matters that I use a word that others can understand; I am forced from my comfort zone through no choice of my own. It is so symbolic to me, that uncomfortable choice of what to call myself. It tells of the totality of disenfranchisement that Aboriginal people have faced in this country; when you cannot even find a name for yourself!

While a student at Queen's, in February of 1986, I attended a conference in Winnipeg, Manitoba, sponsored by the National Association of Women and the Law. Five students from my law school were able to secure funds to attend this conference. We all went seeking solace with professional women involved in the law who we, at least initially, believed shared our common experiences of oppression on the grounds of our gender. At the registration event the first night, I experienced more conversations than I could count where other women (both lawyers and other students) expressed their concern about our ill fate of having chosen to attend Queen's law school. Many of the women suggested to us that their schools were not bastions of White male privilege and that they were treated with respect within their faculties. At the time, I was more than stunned. I was in no way prepared for this response and found it beyond credibility. It spoke to me volumes about the extent of the denial that many women experience in order to accomplish their goals.

I felt fortunate to be attending Queen's. Even if the institution did little about the gender oppression and the multiple exclusions that women faced, our experience at least was on the table, written in large neon pink letters. This naming of our oppression allowed me to begin to understand that the problem was not within me (some form of personal inadequacy), but within the environment I was actively surviving. For me, that was progress beyond living the denial that seemed to proliferate in the other Canadian law schools. This Winnipeg conference was one of the first times that I felt overpowered by the experience of contradiction. It is an experience that has stayed with me for many years.

At the end of my first year of law school, I was very disillusioned. I knew that I would not be able to grow into the role of practising lawyer and all the assumptions of what a good lawyer is, especially a criminal defence counsel. I felt that there was no sense in continuing on the path I had chosen, because the outcome I had first envisioned was no longer possible. During the eight months while I was absent from the law school, I learned that perhaps I was confused about what my path was. I wanted very much to be an advocate for my people. I did not like the idea of quitting anything. I knew the study of law was still important to me. In the back of my mind I began to formulate a new idea. I wanted to teach law. At the time, I could not say these words out loud. No other Aboriginal person, especially no other Aboriginal woman, had ever secured a career as a law professor. If no one else could, what made me think I could? I quietly returned to law school, head down, not daring to mention my dream. Partially, this dream reflected my desire to change the experience of law school for others as well as a recognition that change can be accomplished by being on the inside of a powerful institution.

It was a very difficult lesson for me, to learn to bring law down from the justice and fairness pedestal on which I had placed it. It was (and remains) difficult to accept that it was not me who was the problem but the very structure of law. It is still difficult and the lesson is continually placed before me. It is one I can never seem to fully grasp. However, I am not going to take full responsibility for this ongoing struggle. It is one of the continuing contradictions that I negotiate. I went to law school not only to escape the abuse and oppression that came my way solely because I was an Aboriginal woman who was orphaned at an early age. But I also went to school to do something to change that reality for others as well. The hardest lesson that I have had to grapple with in the last two years is that my objectives were fatally flawed.

During the almost-last edit of this paper, I realized that one of the repetitive responses I have had to the law over the last decade is a desire to quit or run away. I used to see that as a negative behavior trait. I am starting to understand it differently. Law has been a painful experience for me. To know that one does not deserve to be in pain is not negative. For an individual struggling against both colonization and abuse, the desire to move away from what pains us so greatly is a logical response. Acting on that desire has negative consequences. Acting on the desire fully denies the possibility of securing a (legal) education. I know that Aboriginal students who are presently enrolled in law school continue to struggle with the amount of pain they experience. I know this because of the constant ringing of my telephones. I know because of the tears I have shared with these students. There are specific reasons for the pain that Aboriginal students are struggling to survive and I want to share what I have come to understand about the source of my own pain.

When I enrolled in law school, I honestly believed that Canadian law would assist Aboriginal people in securing just and fair treatment. This is why I agreed to study law. Since then, I have learned that the Aboriginal experience of Canadian law can never be about justness and fairness for Aboriginal people. Every oppression that Aboriginal people have survived has been delivered up to us through Canadian law. This is true of the taking of our land and our children. Residential schools were established through law. The same is true for the outlawing of our sacred ceremonies and what is currently done to our people in the criminal courts of this land. What I learned long after my law school graduation was that Canadian law is about the oppression of Aboriginal people. My years in law school were so painful because oppression, even if only in study, is a painful experience.

It is important to document some of the ways in which my experiences and my reality were excluded from my educational experiences, as this is one of the major sources of my feelings of alienation and pain. It is only through examinations such as this that any of us will come to understand the current difficulties Aboriginal people face in Canada's education institutions. Law school curricula (or curricula in other disciplines) were not developed with the Aboriginal student in mind. Granted, I could always enroll in a single course in Aboriginal Rights. Law touches the Aboriginal person's experience in multiple ways. There are tax problems, child welfare problems, criminal law problems, questions of prisoners' rights, religious issues, personal property issues such as the repatriation of cultural objects, land claim issues, and issues of copyright to songs and stories. There are corporate law problems, environmental questions, questions of matrimonial property, and the issue of who is granted status under the *Indian Act*[12] regime. There are issues of government powers and responsibilities. And the list of Aboriginal issues in Canadian law continues.[13] It is as broad, if not broader, than the problems faced by every other individual or collective domiciled in Canada. Yet all of this is covered in a three-hour-per-week seminar course for approximately thirteen weeks (and some schools do not even offer this course with any regularity from year to year). In the same way, because I have some level of recognized expertise in Aboriginal law, I am expected to understand every Aboriginal legal problem from tax to criminal law, from child welfare to incorporations, from the *Indian Act* to the constitution. No non-Aboriginal person is expected to develop an expertise in all aspects and fields of Canadian law. Yet, very few people recognize the imbalance they create when the expect Aboriginal people to be all knowing. This is a factor which greatly contributes to our marginalization.

The great majority of Aboriginal law courses are offered by non-Aboriginal scholars who have developed an expertise in the area of Aboriginal rights as they are understood in Canadian law. I have often wondered how women professors would respond to the suggestion that men can, could, and should teach courses about law and feminism. It is so apparent that this would create quite a controversy. But when non-Aboriginal people teach courses on Aboriginal people and how Canadian law is applied to our lives, this is somehow an unrecognizable controversy. This speaks volumes to the power that women have secured within law faculties or more importantly the degree that Aboriginal people have not.

The courses that are currently offered in Canadian law schools are just a small component of what Aboriginal law students need to learn about Aboriginal rights. Curriculum construction reflects the complete ignorance of most law schools to understanding the needs of Aboriginal would-be lawyers and the legal problems that our communities face.[14] The way in which legal education is structured may prepare you for the large corporate firms that occupy plush offices in Canada's large cities. It does not fully prepare us for the practice of Aboriginal law. I suspect that this observation is true for other collectives of "outsiders" across all university disciplines.

Curriculum problems do not reside solely in the construction of the course offerings. Within each course a variety of difficulties arise. When I was at Western, I enrolled in an anthropology course which was a general survey course on the Aboriginal Peoples of Canada. Until the handful of Aboriginal students in the class revolted, all of the materials utilized in the course were written by non-Aboriginal people. All of the guest speakers were non-Aboriginal people. When we confronted the teacher, we were told that she had no access to materials other than the ones presented. This thin excuse (which seems to be closely related to arguments about academic freedom) completely missed the point being made. The offering of only non-Aboriginal authorities delegitimized Aboriginal ways of knowing and being. Even after expressing our concerns we were excluded, denied and marginalized.

Over the last few weeks, I have been troubled by my most recent experience of the law school. Upon arriving in Saskatoon this summer, I was almost immediately approached by the Dean of the law school to teach a course in Aboriginal title. After several rounds of discussion and negotiation, it was agreed that I would teach Aboriginal title as a five week segment of the personal property course. The course would be offered during November and December to the entire first year class. This was a first for the College of Law at the University of Saskatchewan. It was the first time that Aboriginal title was a significant component of the required first year property course. It was also the first time Aboriginal title was offered by an Aboriginal professor.

The way the course was structured meant a class of close to ninety students, more than double the size of most law school courses I had ever taught. Professors tend to avoid large classes as they are not pleasant experiences for either the students or the teacher. Yet, if I did not teach all the students, there was no guarantee that the other section would receive as thorough a view of Aboriginal title. I had reason to be suspicious about how the other section would be taught as there was no other Aboriginal professor available to teach the other section. I knew if the other half of the first year class was taught by a non-Aboriginal person my ability to teach this course from an Aboriginal perspective would be totally compromised. I knew from experience that when I am teaching one section of a course and a non-Aboriginal person teaches another section, the non-Aboriginal teacher and class becomes the accepted norm. I am expected to conform to that norm. If I do not, then the way I am teaching is seen as inferior. This is true (amazing as it seems) even when the substance of the course is Aboriginal people.

The class size was intimidating and I did experience some anxiety before the day I arrived to begin teaching. My discomfort was more deeply rooted than in just the class size. I did not want to be near the law school or law students. My reception by my Native Studies students had astounded me! It was the first time in my teaching career where I had the opportunity to teach a regular university class where I was respected and not resented by the class. I did not want to return to the law school environment, an environment I had experienced as openly hostile, after experiencing this.

My Aboriginal title course went fairly well, at least until it was time to mark the examinations. There were times when I felt that familiar law student hostility, but it only came from a few students who huddled together in their resistance in one corner of the lecture theater. The examination papers were unlike any I have every seen before. Some were openly hostile. The hostility did not manifest itself so much in overt racist comments (such that I could show them to the Dean and be certain he would understand the problem). They were subtly hostile in the way in which the students used the law. The air of European superiority found in the early cases seeped off the pages of some of the examinations. The examinations were very difficult for me to mark. I had a physical reaction, a constant nausea, to the marking of those papers. I am still angry about the racism I was forced to inflict upon myself. I am still angry because there are no current mechanisms or structures within the university that would protect me from such hostility. As the course instructor, it was unquestionable in my mind that I had the responsibility to mark those examinations.

At the same time that I was feeling intense anger at the university's ignorance of the poisoned environment I was working in, I was still busily trying to understand the hostility and racism that seeped off the pages of some of the examinations. Had I done something wrong in how I taught or structured the class? How do you teach a class of ninety in a very large lecture room in the physics building, about a different way of being and knowing? I have taught this course four years running now and never had an experience like this one. Those classes were so much smaller, only twenty students. In those classes, there was space to address attitudes. At the same time, I understood the irony of the situation I found myself in. I was taking responsibility for the racism displayed by some of those students. In the classroom, I am powerful, the professor. There is no room in this equation for the discrimination that exists. My race, culture and gender are pushed behind that title, professor, into obscurity.

I was already feeling bad enough about the class and the examinations, when the class evaluations arrived one Monday morning in the mail. I want to share the tone of some of the anonymous comments I received. These comments were the deciding factor in my choice to write about my most recent experience as a law teacher. Although teaching from the case law, I was told that I was not objective and that the course was about political opinions and propaganda, not law. I found these comments to be interesting. In almost every other course in the law school, only Euro-Canadian perspective is taught. It is never discussed as a perspective but as rational and reasoned truth. The uni-cultural (White/Canadian) truth is never described as cultural or racially biased. When another view of the world is introduced it is written off as emotional and not objective (irrational) rather than having to confront and understand that the White/Canadian world view (legal view) is not universal (or objective). I (or my ancestors) had no hand in creating the great deception propagated in Canadian law. I often wonder when and how it became my responsibility?

The comments also focused on the students disgust because I had made them feel guilty. I cannot accept that it is my responsibility to carry the guilt of the oppressor (or silence myself for the sole purpose that the oppressor will not feel badly). No one has ever offered to carry the pain and anger of being oppressed for me! Trying to force me to be responsible (at fault) is a powerful tool intended to silence. The contradiction between the expression I found in some of the examinations and the standard I was held accountable to has me half-stunned still.

It is not just my experience of some students that is disturbing or discouraging. Racism and sexism transcends all social and economic boundaries. As a professor I have often tried to encourage my colleagues to include Aboriginal ideas, materials, issues and perspectives in their courses. I am frequently met with the same kind of distancing as the anthropology professor provided us years ago. My colleagues tell me that they have no expertise in that area and therefore cannot teach these kinds of materials or present these kinds of issues. Or there is my favourite excuse, that being academic freedom. I wonder if I decided to teach only Aboriginal constitutional law problems in the general survey course required of all second year law students, and justified this decision on my lack of knowledge about White law problems or academic freedom if anyone would take me very seriously! Obviously, both of these arguments are thinly disguised attempts to continue to adhere to the status quo and must be seen as such. Furthermore, they are attempts to refuse steadfastly to examine the way race and culture impacts on the power relationships which exist within the university environment.

Problems with curriculum (or the lack thereof) have not disappeared now that I am the teacher and not the student.[15] When I do try to make the materials inclusive of the Aboriginal perspective, it is not necessarily an advantage to the Aboriginal students. Rather than attacking me for forcing them to study materials that they feel are irrelevant, non-Aboriginal students place their immediate anger at the feet of the Aboriginal students in my class. The Aboriginal students are not only more accessible but they also have little power within the institutional hierarchy. There are a number of interesting conclusions that can be drawn from this recognition. It is as though the Aboriginal population of the school is seen as one conglomerate; we are not individuals, but that single Aboriginal "thing" over there. The anger (many would call it backlash) at what I have included in my courses is placed on the backs of those most vulnerable within the institution. It is difficult for me to decide whether it is better to include or exclude Aboriginal perspective (presuming I could exclude my own perspective if I tried!).

There is an interesting double edge in my experience of my teaching position. I am required to carry out the same duties as any other of my colleagues and perhaps it is to their credit that the other professors do not treat me as different (that is, lesser). However, the reality is that my experience is different. The study of law for me is the study of that which is outside of myself and my community. It requires that I be expert at both the ways in which "White" people do things, as well as continuing to learn as an Aboriginal woman. In fact, my survival of the law school depends on my intimate knowledge of who and what White people are. The same does not hold true in the reverse. White people have the opportunity to fully discard my reality and this is at least one of the significant sources of my marginalization. The result is that my workload, at the intellectual level, is at least double. On top of this recognition, it must be accepted that professors with experiences of "other" are in great demand within the student body, on the conference circuit and on committees within the school.

In 1993, at Ottawa law school I was asked to sit on the admissions committee, the Aboriginal advisory committee, the equity committee, the hiring committee, one special committee struck to resolve a dispute involving two students (one Aboriginal and one not), and my colleagues elected me to the executive committee. This far exceeds the committee responsibilities that the collective agreement required or that was required of my colleagues. This is not a specific complaint about the institution in which I taught. I firmly believe that I taught in the "least worst"[16] law school in the country. When I brought my concerns to the attention of the administration, my suggestions for making my workload bearable were heard and accommodated. My problem is that it was me who had to seek out that accommodation. This is an important theme which will be returned to in a moment.

The law school in which I last taught is committed to education equity. Because I belong to and identify with an under-represented and historically excluded group my particular experiences and expertise are valuable to the work that the committees conduct. All this is very well as long as the only consideration is the quality of experience of the law school and the students. When the quality of my life is added to the equation, obviously, the commitment to equity is a burden that I disproportionately carry. Equity stops somewhere before my office door. I am excluded from where I most want to be included.

Marginalization is just one layer of the problem. Fragmentation is equally important. It has already been identified that Aboriginal people are under-represented among university professors. If we have managed to break into the university, we are spread out across various departments and faculties across campus. Even when our numbers in a particular university may reach the point of critical mass we do not have the opportunity to share with our Aboriginal colleagues on a daily basis. I am busy with my law school or my Native studies duties, and my friends are in English, Classics or Education. The university is not structured to allow us an Aboriginal place.[17]

In my lifetime, I have learned more from reflecting on my personal experiences and from my Aboriginal teachers than I have from any educational institution. I spend a good deal of time contemplating my role as professor. This is the process by which I am able to first name and then examine the contradictions in my life which constantly require mediation. Obviously, any discussion of my personal experiences of law still focus on the law school in which I work (or last worked). I have already said that I firmly believe that I taught in the least worst law school in the country.[18] I am fond of this least worst idea because I do not feel that any law school yet offers a legal education which is meaningful to Aboriginal individuals (or a teaching position that fully allows us to be who we are). Best is a high standard and we have yet to reach this peak.

My next story is told with the hope of examining the work that still needs to be done. In December of 1991, the dean of my faculty agreed to hire an outside consultant[19] to interview as many Aboriginal students at the University of Ottawa as could be located, and document their experiences. Several of us had urged the dean to undertake this study because we felt a lot of inroads had been made since we attended law school and wanted to be certain that as we mapped out our future we were in touch with the current needs of the students. In the few years that had passed since I was a student there were several Aboriginal law professors who could serve as role models, the curriculum offerings had increased, the school had an education equity program, and most importantly a critical mass of Aboriginal students existed in the student body. This was more change that I could have believed possible ten years ago as I sat silently in a first year law class. The results of the study were daunting. The Aboriginal students still felt extreme alienation during the course of their law studies. This alienation was often expressed in exactly the same words I had used years earlier. All of the inroads we had made amounted to nothing if the standard of success adopted was the experience of the students.[20] It is also worth noting that one of the biggest complaints brought forward was the near total irrelevance of the courses they were assigned or offered.

Curriculum content and offerings is an important topic and a central concern of a good number of the students whom I have spoken to over the last few years. This is where the story takes another odd twist. I am a law professor. With that comes a certain responsibility. I am a member of the institution, and often the Aboriginal students waste few words in pointing this out to me. When the institution harms the Aboriginal students, I am responsible for that harm as I am a member of that institution. Yet within the structure of the institution, I have little if any immediate power to change the curriculum offerings beyond what I do in my own courses.[21] This is true even in the face of a very supportive and understanding administration.

The problem that all of these examples describe is one of structure. This is where we return to a theme ("who is carrying the majority of the workload associated with equity commitments") introduced earlier. It includes the assumptions upon which educational institutions are based. It might be helpful to provide a clear example. As a professor, I wield a certain amount of power. It is true, I decide whether a student passes or fails; if an "A" or a "C" is earned.[22] However, when I stand in front of a class, many of the individuals have more privilege and power than I can ever imagine having. This power is carried as a result of their skin privilege, or their gender, or their social status, or family income. The law school, however, functions shaped solely on the view that I am the powerful one. Students are protected against my "alleged" bias by grade-appeal processes. However, I am not any professor. I am not male, White and my family is not economically advantaged. I am heterosexual, able-bodied and a mother of five. I am Mohawk and follow my ways. There is no protection available to me in any policy if the situation arises where I experience a student who discriminates against me based on my gender, culture or race. Within the law school, the only construct of professor is the individual who holds the power.

In every class I have taught over the last five years, there are at least half a dozen students who challenge my authority. The easiest way to alleviate the conflict my presence creates (that is, as a Mohawk woman) is to de-legitimize me. This, coupled with the failure of university structures and procedures to recognize that I am not (as others are not) "any" professor, complicates my experience. This is not a problem I encounter only in my exchanges with students. The complexity of my involvement in the institution as professor is not recognized in the tenure and promotion processes. Although universities are attempting to diversify their faculties, few attempts are made to alter the policies and practices of the institution to reflect that diversity. There is only one outcome: I am forced to find ways to accommodate my own difference and to protect myself.

I came to this realization through the actual experience of a number of student complaints directed at both myself and other faculty who are members of other specific collectivities. The details of these complaints are not important for my present purposes. What is important is that I have tried to find ways to insulate myself from complaints. My teaching has become more conventional. I try to dress to look like a professor more than I did in my first year of teaching. This decision was my response to receiving a teaching evaluation that suggested I wore "too many beads and feathers to class." Try as I may, I can never remember wearing feathers to class. I am overly hesitant to cancel classes. I make every effort to return assignments immediately. I avoid doing anything that I know the students do not like. I continue to try to find individual ways to protect (some might say hide) my difference. I am also aware that many of my colleagues have never had to consider many or any of these things. At the same time, I know that my individual efforts only operate to partially insulate me from the true problem. My individualized efforts do not remove the structural barriers which give rise to the majority of contradictions and conundrums I encounter. Real change requires a full and systemic institutional response. Such a response will never be found unless the institutional commitment to eradicate all barriers is sincere.

In an effort to find a more hospitable environment in which to teach last year, I very excitedly accepted the invitation to teach an Aboriginal women's course in the women's studies department. I naively thought that getting away from the conservative faction at the law school would bring me further insulation and an experience that was more rewarding. Over the first month that this course has been offered, I was inundated with "White students" (who make up at least two thirds of a class of close to forty) who feel threatened in the classroom. They are responding to several women of colour who are logically angry and fed up with an education system that has offered them little. The anger of the women of colour is, in my opinion, an expression of a collection of experiences of alienation and exclusion both within the university and in their other life experiences. I understand and identify with the anger of the women of colour even though I recognize that our experiences are not the same. One of the students who came to see me in my office complained to me that the "class unit" was disrupted. I was overwhelmed by this comment. In my more than ten years as a student and my five years as a professor, I have never experienced the classroom as a safe place. The gulf between our experience seems to be wider when the criteria is race/culture as opposed to gender. After thinking about my conversation with this student for a long time, it seemed very ironic to me that my efforts to insulate myself by claiming a women's space only highlighted for me the differences of my race/culture experience again.[23]

At the end of the course, many of my women's studies students expressed how much they had learned in the class. For many of them, it had been a good class. For me, it was frequently a lesson in surviving trauma. The solidarity I felt with the anger of the women of colour contradicted the responsibility I felt I carried as a professor. In particular, I felt an obligation to provide a safe learning place for all the women in the class. No matter how I taught, someone's sensibilities were outraged (or perhaps only potentially so). This contradiction also manifested itself in my own awareness that I could not fully support a feminist agenda, an agenda which some students felt all professors in a women's studies program would be required to support. Ironically, in the standoff that developed between some of the White women and some of the women of colour, the Aboriginal women withdrew. In a class on Aboriginal women, it seemed as though there was no space left for them. I am not sure I understand how to keep this tragic outcome from repeating itself.[24]

Through my years as a university teacher, I have frequently been forced to examine the concept of anger. It is a consistent theme in all of the "Flint Woman" pieces. I hesitate to use that imagery of anger because it is so full of someone else's negative assumptions about my own personal culpability for my anger. Trying to name what I was truly feeling helped lead me to the conclusion that English is a fully inadequate language for the expression of my experiences. English is the language of my colonization. Language is implicitly loaded with a series of cultural presumptions which I do not necessarily share and perhaps may not even be aware of. This, in part, is a result of not sharing the same culture with other speakers of the English language. What I am naming as anger feels more like thunder, thunder in my soul. Sometimes, it is a quiet distant rumbling. Other times it rolls over me with such force that I am immobilized.

None of what I have written so far is meant to suggest that I regret any of the choices I have made in my life. I do not regret my legal education although sometimes I contemplate denouncing it. My education and subsequent employment has changed the pattern of individualized oppression I face. But changing my position within Canadian society has done little to change the overall oppression that most Aboriginal people face in this country. I still get the phone calls from people whose children have just been arrested, apprehended by child welfare authorities or committed suicide. I still hear of the experiences of forty men in a community abused by one Jesuit priest and the devastation that has been brought to bear on that community. I know that the women and children are still being abused. I see so much pain. Others believe that I have the power to change things, and only sometimes can I. Law is often the mop used to clean up the mess. It offers rare opportunity to change things before the blood is let. I exist in a contradiction of being expected to be grateful for my success and recognizing that success reflects a pitiful amount of real change for other Aboriginal people.

Last year one of my colleagues was doing some work on a problem concerning an Aboriginal community. During this time period, he had the occasion to introduce me as one of the least tactful members of the faculty. This was not done in an offensive way and I was not offended by an introduction that rang the truth. A few days later, this same colleague and I were discussing his work on an Aboriginal issue. He expressed frustration that he was getting little cooperation from the Department of Indian Affairs. In fact, he insisted that the only thing he felt he had accomplished was to speak to every department and person within the Indian Affairs bureaucracy! I was not very sympathetic at his one encounter with such evasiveness on the part of a bureaucracy charged with the welfare of registered Indians in this country. I jokingly turned to my colleague and asked if perhaps he now understand how I got to be so tactless having been weaned on the Department of Indian Affairs.

This story is a poignant example of another shape in which the contradiction appears before me. I do not share with my colleagues a common view of the world. Nor do I share with them a common personal history. Often, my colleagues do not recognize that we share little in the way of a common background because they can choose to see me as a (law) professor. We have been thrown together as a coincidence of our chosen profession. The two conversations that occurred between the male colleague and myself would never have taken place among my Aboriginal friends, family or acquaintances. We have all experienced the Indian Affairs "baffle-gab."

Despite all of our differences, I still believe in educational systems as a site of future change. I do not cling to the same hope for law as a vehicle for change toward Aboriginally inclusive systems. What I have come to understand through my last ten years of involvement with the law is that it is not the answer I am looking for. Every oppression that has been foisted on Aboriginal people in the history of Canada has been implemented through laws. This includes child welfare apprehensions, residential schools, the outlawing of our sacred ceremonies, the prohibitions against both voting and hiring lawyers, the impact of the criminal justice system, and the list goes on. Law is not the answer. It is the problem. My experience of law has been about coming face to face with oppression, both my own (individual) and that of other Aboriginal people (systemic and individual). This is why the study of law is so profoundly painful for so many Aboriginal people.

I do not intend to discourage any Aboriginal person from pursuing a legal career. We are in desperate need of more front-line lawyers, the lawyers who spend every day in the trenches of criminal court and child welfare court (for example). We also need good Aboriginal legal philosophers and theorists who will continue to provide the intellectual insight in the re-claiming of our own relationships with one another. I am just concerned that would-be Aboriginal lawyers know exactly what the job is before us. My study of law is the study of my own de-colonization. I am reminded of Audre Lorde's warning. You cannot take apart the master's house with the master's tools (1983: 98).

The conclusion that I am able to reach is not a particularly cheerful one. I am where I am today because I decided to make a difference both in my own life and its somewhat tragic beginnings but in the lives of my Aboriginal relations. Naively, I believed that once I could write enough letters behind my name that White people would accept me as equal. I no longer proscribe to the theory of equality because it does not significantly embrace my difference or that I choose to continue to remain different. As I climbed that ladder of success I never understood that I could not climb to a safer place. I now understand that the ladder I was climbing was not my ladder and it cannot ever take me to a safe place. The ladder, the higher I climbed, led to the source of my oppression. Being so close to the fire explains for me why I now feel the contradictions and conundrums at a new and heightened level. Although the lessons that led me to this realization were difficult, I do not regret them.

I may no longer live in a situation of overt violence but I still live with the knowledge that overt violence surrounds me. I have found success in my effort to change my personal circumstances even though structural and systemic change can still feel elusive. As a result, I have begun to understand that I am still battered—intellectually and spiritually battered. But like the women, I am not yet beaten.

This text tells stories of courage. It also exposes experiences that should inspire great shame in the hearts of the perpetrators. It is my hope that by breaking the silence, meaningful and systematic change will occur within my lifetime. This change will occur when we all begin to accept our responsibilities and begin to examine more fully the contours of all oppression.

Notes

1. I am certain that there are also class issues involved in the way I experience the university. Based on present income, my family and I are privileged (especially in comparsion to the Aboriginal population). However, this is not the backgound I come from. I have just begun to unpack the impact of "class" on my life. These issues are present in the text, but still are largely submerged.

2. I studied law at Queen's University and at Osgoode Hall Law School. I taught law at Dalhousie University and the University of Ottawa's Common Law School.

3. There are several others, at least three men and two women, who have since secured positions within Canadian law faculties. These positions either involve an obligation to a special Aboriginal program or are term appointments only. By pointing out that these positions are not "regular" (tenure track), I do not mean to insult my Aboriginal colleagues. This point is made to illuminate the unacceptable nature of their appointments within those faculties. The lack of permanency in some of these positions seems to suggest that at some point in time in legal education, Aboriginal people and perspectives will no longer need to be included. This suggests that access initiatives are complete and will someday "fix" the problem. This is false and quite frankly, racist.

    In fairness, I also want to point out that several Canadian law schools (Osgoode Hall, Queen's and the University of Toronto) have all made concerted efforts during the 1993-94 academic year to hire Aboriginal legal scholars. However, all of the law school hirings to date have been on terms the law schools define. No school has made an effort to involve traditional Aboriginal legal scholars on terms that are acceptable to Aboriginal people or Aboriginal communities. Hiring Elders or traditional teachers to teach courses is not within the current vision of any Canadian legal institution (and perhaps it should not be).

4. I agonized over the decision to leave the law school for a long time. My decision rests on the simple principle that remaining full-time in the law school takes me too far away from my people—in geographic, spiritual, emotional and intellectual terms. I remain committed to the de-colonization of Canadian law; however, I no

longer believe that my efforts within the law school bring sufficient results. I am not running away from a painful experience, but adopting what I hope are more effective strategies for change.

5. Professor Darlene Johnston who taught at the University of Ottawa is on leave and has returned to her community to do legal work.

6. This was a phrase that was used to discuss the experience of compiling the racism volume recently published by *Canadian Journal of Women and the Law*. Please refer to volume 6, number 1 (1993). I recalled our involvement in that work:

> I can start by talking about the name of this Volume. If I remember rightly, the name—"Racism . . . Talking Out"—was my idea and is therefore my responsibility. The idea came out of our discussion that this Issue should not be the end of the road for the *Journal's* coverage of racism, but should be just a first step. We were talking about "audience" and our priorities. We were concerned that this Issue might be mostly about giving a message to non-Aboriginal people and White people about our experiences and what our lives are about. But what we really wanted to do was to start having conversations amongst ourselves, so that we can start comparing our experiences and begin to figure out where we have shared understandings and where our experiences are different. The idea of having one *Journal* issue called "Racism . . . Talking Out," and a later issue called "Racism . . . Talking In," was supposed to capture something of the different needs and aspirations of our audiences and ourselves . . . (at page 224).

7. One of the strategies that I have begun to use to combat the exclusion versus exhaustion conundrum is to suggest that people contact other Aboriginal women who can also speak to the issues. It is a personalized access program. One of the problems of under-representation is that the mainstream does not know how to access the talent and wisdom in Aboriginal communities. My connection to the community is a small doorway. This personalized access commitment has two effects. It relieves the stress created in my life that is the result of being over-extended, and it also opens the door of opportunity for other Aboriginal women. It is a way of re-distributing the nominal personal power I have acquired and turning it into something more powerful.

8. I know that within the dominant culture and especially within the academic tradition the concept of "story" has a negative connotation. Stories are not truth. Experience does not necessarily meet academic standards. I find myself hesitant to use this concept as it will in some circles, in all likelihood, be misinterpreted and read down. However, storytelling in the Aboriginal tradition occupies a central place within the culture. Perhaps stories are even the central vehicle for sharing knowledge. I use this word "story" in the respectful way of my people.

9. He is Dr. Michael C. Monture a graduate of Western's medical school. My family is very proud of his accomplishments.

10. Michael's story is repeated here with permission. His support and trail blazing have had a profound impact on my ability to chase my own dreams.

11. For a detailed accounting of these times please refer to McIntyre 1987-88: 362.
    During the fall semester of 1985, I was not enrolled at the law school. I had

taken a leave at the end of my first year of law because I was so disillusioned by my experiences. It was during this semester that Professor McIntyre wrote her memorandum and circulated it to her colleagues. It was eventually released to the national press (and to this day Professor McIntyre does not know the identity of the individual that catapulted her to national attention). I returned to school in the winter term of 1986, to confront the fall-out from the memorandum.

12. R.S.C., 1985, c.I-6.

13. This is something very different from traditional systems of Aboriginal law.

14. I have discussed the difficulties of Aboriginal students at law school, including the exclusionary construction of law school curriculums, and that article is reprinted as Chapter 9 in this volume.

15. As I worked on this paper, this sentence continued to feel awkward to me. I puzzled for awhile over this feeling. I eventually settled on the words "teacher and student." In the way of my people, I am too young to be anything other than a student. There is a constant conflict between my image of myself in a cultural sense and in my professional life. It was not the sentence that was awkward but another contradiction that is nestled between my cultural beliefs and my professional life.

16. It was Professor Sanda Rodgers (now Dean of the University of Ottawa's Common Law Faculty) who first acquainted me with this term.

17. At the suggestion of Sakej Henderson and under the authority of the President of the University of Saskatchewan, a committee called the Aboriginal Caucus has been established this winter. This caucus is meant to be the first step to address the marginalization and fragmentation of around twenty Aboriginal academics and staff at the university. We meet once monthly in the President's Board Room. I know of no other Presedential initiative that as fundamentally challenges the way in which the university structure is oppressive to Aboriginal scholars. Changing the shape of the university landscape to be inclusive of Aboriginal people does not have to be a difficult task.

18. As I examined my experiences of law over the last decade, I realized that many of the stories I wished to tell focused on the University of Ottawa. This caused me some concern. I want to say clearly that these reflections are based on the coincidence of my employment and not any kind of ranking of where I believe the most work in legal education needs to be done. In fact, I am not sure that any such ranking would serve a useful purpose. If least worst is the best that we can do, then our energies seem to be better spent improving the situation for those of us who have been outsiders for too long rather than engaging in a competitive game of who is least worst.

19. I can imagine the university administrator sitting back in his/her chair wistfully thinking of the good old days where he or she would have the money to do such hiring. I am not very persuaded by fiscal restraint arguments. They are racist. Just when Aboriginal people have some access to previously denied spaces, the country goes bankrupt. This is still my land being shared, and an obligation is still owed. Fiscal restraint is not my problem!

More realistically, fiscal restraint requires that we become more creative. Instead of having the luxury of hiring an outside consultant a graduate student could be provided the opportunity (preferably an Aboriginal graduate) to complete some work that had immediate relevance for course credit.

20. I have not even factored into this discussion the great amount of energy it takes just to maintain the few small successes that we have had against attack from conservative factions within both the law school and the larger legal community. Unfortunately, much of the energy I spend in the law school is spent dealing with "backlash." Backlash is another of those words that I really do not like. *Backlash is nothing more than racism, pure and simple.*

21. Over the years I have also found myself augmenting course offerings by making myself available to do at least three independent research courses with students. Generally, the students who seek out this opportunity are Aboriginal students. They tend to have interests that are not explored in the courses that are presently being offered. When a student asks me to supervise such a paper course, I am acutely aware that if I say no they have few, if any, options. It is important to me to emphasize that I really enjoy this work with students and plan to continue to encourage them to avail themselves of this opportunity. On the other hand, I am also aware that this obligation is not one that is equally shared across faculty members in the institution where I teach. Another conundrum is located.

22. Interestingly enough, when I do assign a low grade to a paper or examination, I frequently find myself challenged by students. I do not think this is an odd or unfortunate phenomenon. If the challenge is a substantive one, I have no complaint. It keeps the professoriate honest. However, all (in fact most) of the challenges I face are not about substance. Many students challenge my marking in such a way that it is obvious that they do not believe I have the authority to grade their work as anything other than excellent. I believe that some of these challenges, at least, are based on either my gender or race/culture, if not all of these qualities.

   Until a friend told me of the work of Patricia Williams (1991), a Black legal scholar in the United States, I was beginning to feel a little inadequate. Professor Williams' article on student evaluations brought me untold comfort.

23. This student later disclosed that she was a student of Aboriginal ancestry. This complicated greatly my ability to analyse what had happened. It is a reminder of the diversity of our experiences as Aboriginal people. It is also a reminder of the importance of perception.

24. I have not ruled out that the fact that I was committed to teaching the course cooperatively, which in my mind includes a responsibility to be non-hierarchical and let everyone pick up their individual responsibility to learn, complicated the pattern that developed. By this I mean to indicate that I think the fact that I do not assume the role of learned professor, the sole source of wisdom and authority in the classroom, challenged the students in a way that I found very surprising in an institution of higher learning. If I had assumed the classic professor stance, I think that some of the controversy and tension would have only percolated in the undertones of the classroom. As the course was a course on Aboriginal women, a topic of great diversity, I did not believe that I had the right to assume sole authority for the experiences of all Aboriginal women.

Politics of Oppression

1. Education

5

Alienation and Isolation: Patterns of Colonialism in Canada's Education System

THIS PAPER WAS ORIGINALLY PRESENTED as the keynote address at the third symposium of the National Indian Education Forum, Kamloops Indian Residential School, Kamloops, British Columbia on August 15, 1990. This paper has been prepared from the audio tapes of that oral presentation.

As I look around the audience, I feel very young—I am just 31 years old. There are many of you out there who are obviously my Elders. I am just a baby learning how to walk and yet I have been put up here. It confuses me. I do not know why you put me up here as opposed to some of the old wise ones who have taught me and who I am still learning from. In the way of the First Nations, I am too young to be the teacher. I am still struggling to learn. Most of the wise people I know do not have university degrees. Wisdom comes from what we do with our life experiences. Wisdom is about how we make our life experiences work for us, after we have worked to understand what the experiences mean. True wisdom requires much self-reflection. It is in this way that First Nations recognize and credential people.

To get a degree, you jump over a certain set number of hurdles and presto, credentials. Those hurdles though cannot guarantee you have truly learned something except how to jump over that particular set of hurdles. First Nations have had a difficult time understanding and respecting such a process. I, therefore, want to say that it is not the degrees that are important—the fact that I have a law degree—the fact that I almost have a Masters in Law—those are not the important things about me. They are just pieces of paper. The fact that I teach law is not the important thing. My job as a law teacher just makes it a little bit easier to do what my real work is and that work is with my people.

I do not want you to think for a minute by my saying, it is not the degrees that are important, that I am saying, "Oh, formal education including university education is not important." That is *not* what I am saying. Education is very, very important. It is a tool. It is a skill. Education is a way of looking at things. First Nations have had little opportunity to affect the shape of formal educational institutions. Where the problem lies, as far as I see it, is in how and who has been able to define what education is. Education does not mean something in and of itself. Education is a "means" not an "end." It is in how we put education to work for us that education is most important.

There is a gap between formal education programs and First Nation aspirations. I understand this gap to be a problem in education. I think there are others who have a much better understanding of what education is. My understanding has been developed as a university student. I studied at university for ten years. I have only been a teacher for two years now. It is also important to understand that I have no formal training as a teacher. My understanding of teaching, studying and educating has been developed as a process of struggle. It is understanding built on my desire to survive.

The way I understand things, each of us has at least one gift from the Creator which is meant to be shared with the people. It is important that each of us is able to identify and understand what our gifts are. My gift is the ability to tell stories about life (usually my life). Perhaps the most important thing I learned through all my years of non-Indian post-secondary education was to have some confidence and respect for myself. This was not an easy lesson and it is one I still struggle with. Confidence was not learned because of my formal education but in spite of it. It is a gift I try to instill in my son. I also recognize that this is one of the greatest failures of the current education system. First Nation children do not leave that system with a positive First Nation identity.

Many of us worry about the children and what they are learning. Bernice Hammersmith says in an article I read while editing this paper:

> We lose a lot of our children from the educational system in grade eight or nine or even earlier. They're always pointed at as the problem; they never think of themselves *as the solution*. And that is how they grow up. (1992)

Encouraging positive self-images must be a fundamental building block on which Aboriginal aspirations are built into the education system.

In thinking about my own life, I recognized something else that is important for me to share. The path of formal education I have chosen to follow both as a student and a professor sets me down in the middle. I am committed to maintaining and following a good "Indian" path. At the same time, I can function in the White world. Because of the choices I have made in my life, I can chose to act as a bridge between my people and non-Indian people. I have a friend who describes this place as the home of the boundary warriors.[1] It is my connection with First Nations communities that keeps me strong enough to continue to press the university to provide educational spaces that are meaningful to First Nations.

First Nations must take the time to consider exactly what we mean when we talk about providing education for our children. When we have figured out what education means to First Nations there is the need to talk about how we are going to put First Nations dreams in place. We must remember what education means to us before we consider what exists in systems of formal education. Meaningful educational opportunities as First Nations define them is the standard to which we must compare existing patterns and beliefs in current educational institutions. To begin with the formal (non-First Nations) educational system means we embrace certain assumptions that we may not really agree with. What presently exists in formal educational institutions may in fact be the problem and not the solution. What we must remember is how we traditionally educated our people in a good way. It is probably presumptuous that I speak in terms of "we." Not all First Nations (or even Mohawk) people will agree with what I have said or what I think. I use "we" because I believe no single individual has the complete vision for the future. What must be built requires the collective vision and action of First Nations.

I think that the starting place for traditional First Nations education is an understanding of who we are as individuals. Therefore, I also want to talk about who I am in the sense of what is important to me, about me—that is, how I define myself as a First Nations woman. I am a Mohawk. And that is very, very important to me and to how I understand myself. First Nations are not all the same. It is important that each of us is able to carry our distinct nation identities, be that Cree or Mohawk, Ojibwe or Maliseet, Dene or Lakota. I am also a mother. I have a six-year-old son named Brandon and another one on the way. It is difficult for me to talk today because I am really rooted in that baby I am carrying and the work that my woman's body is doing. My baby is coming soon. It is becoming very hard to jump from that space into talking to a group of people. The two most important things about me are that I am a Mohawk woman and a mother. The core of my identity is not located in the fact that I have survived formal education.

Re-claiming our place in formal educational institutions is going to be a very difficult task and it is going to require a lot of patience. We must remember that schools in Canada were once part of the government's plan to assimilate us. We must question if education institutions that were founded on a belief in our Aboriginal inferiority are really part of the answer or has education been part of the problem? It is not schools as institutions we must depend on but the creativity of all First Nations people. We must learn to rely on ourselves and not on institutions of colonial governments. We must always have in our sights the process and nature of our oppression and colonization. Education is important if and when we are able to educate our young in a decolonized way. Colonialism and its consequences are the obstacles.

One of the other concerns that I often hear from people is a fear about making mistakes. This fear sadly keeps people from taking action toward their dreams. I also understand this fear as one of the consequences of our oppression. One of the things that I was taught about a mistake is the first time that you make a certain mistake, it is not a mistake at all—it is a teaching. It is once you have had that teaching and when you do not pay attention to the teaching, that you have made a mistake. That is when you become accountable. The first time it is always a teaching. I am thankful for that. I am respectful of that. What all my fears and worries are rooted in is my real fear that we are just going to wrap education up in a pretty red wrapper and call it "Indian" education and say we are done.

The best example of what I am talking about that I can provide for you is my experiences as a student of law. My concerns about law are similar to my concerns about education. Both the systems of law and education that we now live have been forced on us. Law and education are two of the central institutions or processes through which First Nations have been colonized and oppressed. There are similar patterns in both systems of order. A body of Canadian law has developed over the past hundred years, and especially since 1982, that is called "Aboriginal Rights." Even First Nations people are talking about our "Aboriginal Rights." What we have to remember is that the legally recognized source of this kind of right is in fact the Canadian legal and political systems. "Aboriginal Rights" are not the traditional First Nations way of doing things or understanding law. Canadian law has *not* yet successfully embraced our ideas of tradition—what is often called natural law. This is in spite of the fact that the 1982 constitutional provisions clearly provide room for such an opportunity. Canadian law has only come a very little way toward embracing Aboriginal understanding; they occasionally speak of "Aboriginal customary law."[2] This recognition of Aboriginal customary law has unfortunately *not* been developed from within a legal perspective which respects the underlying values on which First Nations laws and societies are based.

Canadian legal systems are based on the principle of adversarial relations, that is to say conflict. First Nations law is not based on a presumption of conflict. Instead it is based on the principles of relations and consensus.

Therefore, "Aboriginal Rights" is merely Canadian law wrapped up in pretty red paper. Only on the surface does it appear to be "Indian." Once you carefully examine it, it is obvious that it is *not* about First Nations ways of "doing law." This is the biggest lesson that I learned at law school even though it was not one of the lessons any law teacher was trying to bring me to understand. I learned this because I examined my own pain and my own life experiences. My experience of formal education as painful is not an exception. In all the conversations that I have had with "Indian" people about their post-secondary education, isolation and alienation are always mentioned. It is very difficult for any individual to learn when what they are feeling is isolated and alienated. I want to continue to talk to you about my experiences at law school to explain this.

Sitting in first year Property Law for eight months there was never any mention made about the relationship between First Nations and the territory that has become Canada. It was no more than six or seven years ago at the most that I took this course and we talked about property for nearly a full year and never once mentioned "Indians"! I was so shocked I could not say and did not say a word about the total disappearance of First Nations, First Nations history and belief, or the colonial relations Canada was built upon. The entire system of property law in this country is built on a great lie—that colonial myth. "Columbus discovered America and claimed it for the Europeans!" None of my colleagues in law school saw we were surrounded by that colonial myth or that the property law system they all supported was built on a great lie which disappeared all of my people. None of my colleagues knew the impact that Canada's colonial past was having on me as an Aboriginal person. I was the only Aboriginal person in my class at law school and this compounded the experience of alienation and isolation. Nobody in that law school was conscious about the fact that they were lying and I was overwhelmed at being expected to quietly participate in the disappearance of my people. This is one example of how I experienced isolation and alienation during my legal education.

This realization about education as an experience of alienation and isolation put me on to something else. I had to start thinking about who I was as a Mohawk woman and what did it mean to be a Mohawk woman. This self-examination was initiated because I felt so alienated during my first year of law studies. What did it mean to be a Mohawk woman and a student of Canadian law? I saw very clearly that I had two sets of responsibilities, especially since I was a mother. I had the responsibility to learn about those Mohawk ways so I could teach my son but I had also voluntarily, even if unknowingly, made another commitment to learn about the Canadian legal system. So I had these two really big jobs to do for the three years that I was at law school. I think this realization helped me combat the isolation and alienation I was feeling because I understood that these feelings were not sourced in my own inadequacies. The feelings of alienation and isolation were much larger than just me.

When I looked around me at the other students at law school, they did not see that they had two really big jobs to do. I did not see those non-Indian students and even some of the other "Indian" students who were there with me recognize that they had two responsibilities. They did not see that if communication across cultural differences would ever occur in a good way and in an honest way, we had to work at being able to understand both of these ways of being, including the two legal systems that are here. And when I figured that out, I was pretty mad. I probably wanted to whine around a little bit and feel sorry for myself. It felt very unfair that I had twice as much responsibility as the other students around me. This was especially true as I knew I was being held accountable to the same standard as other students, notwithstanding the fact I knew I was doing twice as much work. After awhile I understood my need to whine and feel sorry for myself was a condition of "learned helplessness" that grows out of my status as an oppressed person who is a citizen of an oppressed nation.

The next thing that I figured out when I was busy whining around and being mad about having figured out that I have these two responsibilities and my colleagues at law school had only one, is that I was *not* the disadvantaged one. I was mad at first because I thought, I have this awkward and heavy burden, and the rest of the students were responsible for one job. Slowly I began to understand that I was the lucky one and I felt sad for those other people. Those people had nowhere else to turn when they discovered that they were dissatisfied with the condition of Canadian law, while I was lucky to have those Mohawk teachings to turn to—lucky because that was where I was able to go to find things that talked to me about my emotions, that talked to the fact that I was a survivor of child sexual abuse. I found teachings that talked to my spirit and teachers that taught me about body, mind and spirit and how they are braided like sweetgrass.[3] That is how we have to keep ourselves if we are going to be healthy people. And my mind works even better today because I learned to value my body, my spirit and my emotions.

When I think about being a law teacher now and when I think about teaching law, I need to think about both these sets of responsibilities. People are always saying that I am some kind of an "expert." Well, I am still trying to figure that one out. The experts that I know are back home. They are all the old aunties, uncles, grandmas and grandpas back in my territory.[4] I try and think about bringing their wisdom into the law school. How would we start using Elders within the law school framework? How would you start to incorporate their knowledge, because they are our experts, those old

"Indian" people. They are our PhDs. If we are going to educate our children and young people in meaningful ways, then we will begin involving the Elders in all levels of education from primary to post-secondary.[5] This is a decision that must occur on a community to community basis. It must be remembered that Aboriginal communities are diverse. I do not use the word community to mean solely the idea of an Indian reserve or Métis settlement. Aboriginal communities exist in cities as well as on reserves. I have an Aboriginal law family and that is no less community than the kinship relationships based on the fragmented territories (commonly called Indian reserves) that we have left.

As I discussed earlier, First Nations legal structures are not recognized because of the ways our systems are so differently structured compared to the Canadian education system. If you do not have that little piece of paper that signifies the end of your education to wave around, it means you do not know anything. That is not true. We have to start uncovering all of the myths, not just the ones that are so obvious to us now. Education is not just about formal learning. Formal education is just the very tip of the iceberg. Education is also about understanding our real life experiences in both our hearts and minds.

In an attempt to fulfill my obligation to double understanding, that is, thinking and feeling, I have tried to learn by examining the process of my own education. My education has been a contradictory experience of learning while struggling to survive the system that I saw as a pathway to personal freedom. I want to share with you some of the things that I have learned about why the process of my own education was such a struggle. The most obvious barrier I have identified is the inhospitable environment that the university presents. I think this is not just true of universities but of the majority of Canada's educational institutions. I do not think of environment as just the physical setting. This is just one of the important aspects of environment. Classrooms tend to have a rigid form. I am not sure that the physical structure of most classrooms facilitates Indian learning. For example, do we want to put people up front so they feel really uncomfortable looking out at all the youths who want to make circles? There are many physical constraints that form barriers to providing a learning environment that is comfortable to First Nation students. These barriers are often easily identifiable. Desks in rigid rows with fixed seating, pedestals and podiums for professors, and windowless rooms are some of the obvious examples. In fact many of these things are recognized as constraining for all students, independent of their racial and cultural heritage. It is into this inhospitable environment that we place Aboriginal individuals and ask them to develop their minds. The fact that the physical environment is not supportive of the opportunity for learning creates a barrier that is an additional responsibility for Aboriginal students.

Universities in particular are places where people develop intellectual capabilities. This involves exercising and developing one's mind. But to a First Nations person this exercise is an incomplete way to develop knowledge. True knowledge involves not only mind but also body, spirit and emotion. As a result of my years of university education, I have got a real good brain. My brain usually works great. What about my spirit? What about my body? What about my emotions? None of those things were dealt with through the course of my experience in that so-called higher form of education. Body, spirit and emotion are systematically disappeared from so-called higher education. I cannot be a healthy individual without a good mind, a healthy body, as well as balance in both spirit and emotions. These observations also involve a recognition that concerns about learning environment include physical, mental, emotional and spiritual aspects.

I want to give you an example of why teaching the mind is not enough. I went back to my reserve and I had the honour of sitting with several Confederacy Chiefs for a whole day. We talked about many things that day. Towards the end of the day, one of the men started talking about all the different treaties that my people had made with the Canadian and British governments and all the other settler nations that had come here. Of course, I did what every good little law student would do. I grabbed a pen and paper and started writing quite furiously, as he talked to me. He probably talked for two hours. At the end of it, he said to me, "I want you to tell me what you learned." Then, he took those papers away from me. Well, I could *not* think of one thing to say! I had not learned a thing. I had put it all down on the paper and trusted that little piece of white paper to remember everything for me. The minute he took my papers away from me, I did not have any understanding left. I learned a really big lesson that day about learning. And I realized that one reason we must be able to "double understand" is because if we have got it twice, if we are listening with both our heart and our mind, only then have we really learned. This is the way we are supposed to be learning when we are sitting and talking to those Elders. Once we have it in both our heart and mind, there is less chance that we are going to forget it. So I am really hesitant now to trust that piece of paper with what is my traditional responsibility. I have to take that knowledge when it is given and I have to keep it. And I know that I learned to trust that piece of paper before I trusted myself through the process of formal education. Our definition of formal education must therefore respect the oral traditions of our nations.

The other thing that really worries me is what is happening in this country today. I look at Mohawk territory and I look at young men picking up weapons, picking up drugs, arguing that gambling and cigarette smuggling is economic development. Mohawk people and all First Nations people have what is called natural law. Mohawks have what is called the Great Law of

Peace. It is not called just the Great Law. It is called the Great Law of Peace. The button I am wearing says, "The bravest warriors are those who stand for peace." I do not want my son ever to have to make the decision about whether he is going to pick up some automatic weapon and stand on a bridge or at a roadblock. I do not want his mind and heart to be forced to think only of violence and resistance. That is not a good way for a spirit to be forced to live. As I understand it, picking up a weapon is a fundamental violation of that Great Law of Peace. So I do not condone what is going on at those barricades. I worry when I see people getting so excited about weapons and violence; especially when they are thinking that it is all right to do. At the same time, I do not condemn it either because I understand it. I understand about our young men who have grown up being lost, and someone puts out their hand to them and in their hand is this beautiful golden warrior image—an image that says a warrior is someone who protects the land, protects the people, so the young men hungrily pick it up. Just like I learned through the process of education to trust that piece of paper more than I trusted myself, our young men through the process of their informal education, perhaps from what they learned on television or in criminal justice institutions or in residential schools, learned that force and violence *are* answers. And the beauty of our men and the true meaning of warrior becomes "Rambo-ized." I understand that and I pray for those young men that they might understand what they are doing.

My view of the activities in some of the Mohawk territories are not going to make me very popular with some people. I can accept that as long as what I have said is respected as my own view of the situation. I want to say clearly that I am not judging what others have done. I have never been in the immediate situation where I was forced to make those choices of armed resistance. My education has privileged me in a particular way and I know it is unlikely that I will ever have to make such a choice. I live in a way that is very insulated from individual acts of oppression directed specifically at me. I am concerned with the effect of the situation that exists in Mohawk territory and that we see blasted all over national television. I am concerned with acts of resistance because mere resistance as the measure of a human life is wanting.

I have heard some people suggest that the only people who can talk about the armed confrontation at Oka are the people who were there. I do not think I have the right to judge those individuals, only the Creator can do that. At the same time, Oka has also profoundly affected many people. One day during the summer of 1990, my son raced into the house after playing outside. He found me reading in the living room. I looked at him, kerchief pulled up over his face, as he proudly announced, "I'm playing Mohawk, Mom." This is not the way I raised him. I raised him to *be* Mohawk.

I pray for the young men and my prayers sound very much like what the Elder was saying this morning, "You have to walk what you talk." I do not know of a more peaceful people than First Nations people. That we have been pushed so far that our men believe the only choice they have is to pick up a weapon terrifies me. How did we get this far? And by we, I do not mean only Mohawks or First Nations, but also Canadians of all races and ethnic origins. This is a challenge that we all collectively face and a responsibility we all must meet. What we have not done is when the little boys are six years old—we have not taught them right. As a mother, if my son ever goes and stands on a barricade, I am really going to wonder about where I went wrong with him—because I know his spirit cannot be healthy when it is surrounded by force and violence. And this is a burden that First Nations mothers ought not to have to bear. It is a luxury for Canadian mothers to not have to face this burden. Because that is not what being a warrior is about—not about picking up guns—not about fighting. I see a direct relationship between a failure among our people and a failure of the education system to educate our children properly. And it is time that we stopped it. And it's long past time that we ask, "What is education?"

There is a teaching that explains that you must know where you have been in order to know where you are going. This explains why it is so important for us to understand the history of our nations. This is also the reason why I try to identify myself as Mohawk and not as Indian. In this regard, there is a further reason why we must carefully pay attention to how we are defining First Nations education. It was the Creator who put First Nations here on Turtle Island (North America) "in charge" of the natural law. It was we who were made responsible to care for Mother Earth, for the water, to respect all other life beings. Therefore, I think the answer, today, rests with us. I think it is time the Canadian government took a full stop in order to take a fresh look at First Nations. Canadians need to start looking at that natural law and learn from us. I think that is why, with Elijah Harper, First Nations were able to stop the Meech Lake Accord. This is the big message in the stand of Mr. Harper. We, First Nations, have that answer that is so necessary now. We know that answer. The answer is about living in respect. I know the settler people came to us and asked us for help a very long time ago. I know it was my Aboriginal ancestors who taught the settlers about surviving in this land. They are going to have to come back to us and ask again for help. Will we have educated ourselves enough that we are ready and willing when they come looking to us for the answers, for help? Or will we still be trapped in colonized minds?

Let me give you just one more example about what I am talking about. Even this morning when we are talking about education, we spoke about "fighting" for our "rights" to education. I have a really hard time understanding if something is really good, why do we have to fight for it. It does not make any sense to me. It is contradictory. We have to *protect* good things, not fight for them. Responsibilities are taught not fought for. We have to learn how to live our rights because that is our responsibility. Fighting for good things is like mixing fire and water, and that does not work. If something is really good, you just have to do it. You just have to live it. You do not have to fight for it. I think this is another example of how careful we must be when we rely on the English language to express "Indian" ideas.

When I went to the law school, I learned all about rights. It was rights, rights, rights, all the time. Do you know what kind of rights you have? My Elders taught me that I have only one. Do you know what that one right is? It is the right to live as a Mohawk woman because that is the way the Creator made me. That is the only right I have. After that, I have a series of responsibilities, as a Mohawk woman, because that is how I was made. Did I speak to you about male responsibilities? No. I cannot understand male roles and responsibilities because I have not lived that particular experience. As a woman, I can only say to you, "Look, I have trouble with this warrior image. The image of violence located within that warrior image is not how I want our men to be. But I cannot tell you how it is those men are supposed to be in a traditional way. I do not know." I know how a woman is supposed to be but I cannot teach men about how a man is supposed to be.

I know that the legal system that we have in Canada is a very big part of our problems today. Pick up and read any introductory book on Canadian law. You know what assumption they start with—conflict. "We have laws because we are born to be in conflict. Law is a way of resolving that "natural" conflict. Their law starts on the premise that there is going to be fighting. My people have the Great Law of Peace. Identified here is a fundamental contradiction. Mohawks assume with our law that we can and will live together peacefully. Law is not a battleground. Mohawk law is about living in a good way together. For me there is something fundamentally the matter with a legal system that presumes only conflict. If you base laws on conflict then conflict must exist. If you think conflict is going to exist—yes, it is going to exist. It is self-perpetuating. As I understand it, the conflict presupposed in Canadian legal relations goes a very long way to explaining why and how the conflict in Mohawk territory began. It is difficult for me to believe that the kind of change we need now can be planted within a system based on the ideology of conflict. I no longer believe law is the solution; it is the heart of the problem.

How does this realization about Canadian law relate to education? Looking back through recent history, it seems appropriate to me that we are sitting in a residential school to have the conversation we are having today. The goal of these schools was to make us more like "people" so that Indians could live in a "civilized" way. Today this is seen as offensive. Part of our alleged civilization through residential schooling, of course, included learning about and accepting that system of law which presumes that there is going to be conflict. This form of education is built on a colonial philosophy. In the educational system today, when I send my son to school, I still see him surrounded by the remnants of Canada's colonial history. I still see in his experiences traces of the belief that Indian people need to learn civilization. There are many examples of this system treating our children as inferior. This must remind us that the system of education that we are working within was and remains a tool of colonialism.

Even though the government and their officials apparently embraced the idea of "Indian control of Indian education" in the seventies, I do not think their mode of education is yet the same kind of education that First Nations dream about. I aspire to education that is holistic, which is the basic way that I understand belongs to First Nations people. We still have this education system that is subtly perpetrating the colonial philosophy of Indian inferiority. We have not fully erased it from our view. When I teach law to law students, I have to teach all the colonial ideas about conflict, conquest and discovery. You cannot understand step two in Canadian law if you do not buy step one. Step one is the great lie that Columbus discovered America. With the privilege of being professor, I can challenge the usual terms of reference, values and beliefs in my classroom. This is not enough as long as some people hold onto the belief that there is one way, one truth and one knowledge. Even as professor, I am outside of that one knowledge, and my work and teaching is attacked and devalued. This has left me with the understanding that there is still a lot of work to be done. We are not finished challenging education just because a number of us have become educators. Rather, as First Nations numbers have increased within the academy, we are able to more readily identify the problems and barriers that exist within the structure of education.

I have thought a lot about what education is. For me, what education must be about is inclusion and not exclusion. It must be about giving each and everyone of us our own good voice. Some of us are going to be the speakers, some of us are going to be the artists, some of us the teachers and spiritual people. We each have a beautiful gift given to us by the Creator. What our education system should be doing is helping us to live those beautiful gifts rather than asking us to set them down and be like everybody else. This is the challenge that faces us all in the 1990s, whether we are First Nations or members of other racial, ethnic or national groups. I pray that through striving to reach First Nations educational aspirations, we can begin to remember how it was meant for us all to walk in a good way.

Notes

1. Again I am indebted to James Youngblood "Sakej" Henderson for his insight.
2. Customary laws have been recognized in adoptions and marriages. See for, example on customary marriages *Connolly* v. *Woolrich,* (1867) 1 Canadian Native Law Cases, 70 and on appeal *Johnstone* v. *Connolly*, (1869) 1 Canadian Native Law Cases, 151. In the case of customary adoption, see *Reference Re: Katie's Adoption Petition* (1961), 38 W.W.R. 100, 32 D.L.R. (2d) 686 (NWT Terr. Ct.).
3. Sweetgrass is one of four traditional medicines that the Creator gave to Aboriginal people. It is a medicine that is used in prayer.
4. Reserve is a word that I think we should not be using. Nations have territories and not reservations. It is important to consider the English words we have been conditioned to use and what their subtle meanings are. Colonial languages must also be seen as one of the structures that oppresses Indian thought.
5. Not all of the experiences I have had bringing Elders into the university have been positive. Non-Indian students do not always understand how to be with an Elder. I worry that this lack of knowledge leaves the Elder feeling disrespected. This is one aspect of renovating education to be inclusive of First Nations that cannot be forgotten in the discussions we are going to have.

6

Now that the Door is Open: Aboriginal Peoples and the Law School Experience

CHAPTER 9 WAS ORIGINALLY PUBLISHED in Queen's Law Journal *15, 1 (1990): 179-191.*

> When our grandmothers sent their children to school it was with self-sufficiency and mastery over the production of new things in mind. They did not realize that we would never be taught to create the iron cooking pots from the ore of the earth. This is the third generation of our education and our children know less about the production of the stuff of life than our grandmothers. Schools have showed themselves to be ideological processing plants, turning out young people that cannot produce the means to sustain themselves, but who are full from cover-to-cover with the ideological non-sense of European culture.
>
> We have learned something in the last two decades. We have learned that to change things will require tremendous power and that we lack power. We are going to acquire it in the same fashion that we lost it, tenaciously and doggedly. We are going to pursue empowerment. (Maracle 1988: 113)

Our grandmothers expected that education would provide opportunities based on the skills their children would gain while away at school. We now understand that the dreams of our grandmothers were never realized and could not have been realized. Both the academic literature[1] and Aboriginal experience[2] document the many dismal failures of the attempts to educate Aboriginal Peoples within the institutions of the dominant society.

A review of statistical data completes this picture. The 1986 Census data details that only 8.1 percent of the Aboriginal population[3] have a high school certificate (3.5 percent of males and 4.6 percent of females). This is demonstrably lower than the general Canadian high school achievement figure of 12.8 percent (5.5 percent of males and 7.3 percent of females). When turning our attention solely to university education the figures are even more disparate. Of the Aboriginal population, 3.5 percent have university degrees (1.7 percent of males and 1.8 percent of females). Nine and a half percent of Canadians have university degrees (5.5 percent of males and 4.0 percent of females).[4] Aboriginal people are less than half as likely to hold a university degree (Statistics Canada 1989, IV).

Although gains have been made in both access to mainstream, post-secondary education and control of Aboriginal education in the last two decades, inroads must still be made if we are to achieve at least numerical equality. I would argue that numerical equality *may* only be one of the relevant goals. Equality of numbers alone will not be enough. Numbers cannot act as an indicator of the meaningfulness of the educational experience. It is against this single criterion, meaningfulness, that the greatest inequality has been perpetuated against Aboriginal Peoples.

Education is of primary importance in our modern world. It is a pre-condition to most forms of employment and thereby access to income. To state the obvious, educational success significantly impacts on one's enjoyment of life. Education is a significant gatekeeper to the opportunities we are able to access. This is the first way in which education can be defined as meaningful.

The stark reality, however, for Aboriginal Peoples is that our education has not been about access to opportunities but rather forced assimilation to a different and foreign cultural worldview. This is appropriately labelled the "missionary" approach (Deloria 1974: 24) to education for reasons which shall be made clear in the body of this paper. It is in this second way of defining meaningful education, as a tool of cultural survival and as a means of reaffirming the validity of Aboriginal culture, that the worst injustices have been committed against Aboriginal Peoples and our distinct cultures. This can be demonstrated in several ways—first legally:

> In the 1880s the Federal Government enacted amendments to the *Indian Act* in which Indian children were legally required to attend schools as established or directed by the Minister of Indian Affairs. This was some time before compulsory education existed for the rest of Canada. The only schools established by the Minister at that time were residential schools patterned on the Industrial school model then popular in the United States for Indian children and juvenile delinquents. Indian children were taken from their parents

(and from their influence), the Minister was appointed their legal guardian and they were educated in schools run sometimes by the Department, but generally by missionary societies. . . . (Sinclair 1990: 9)

That the education of *all* the Aboriginal children sent to residential schools was based on the punitive model of an Industrial school where delinquent behavior was corrected is telling as well as most appalling. To be born an "Indian"[5] child therefore equated to being born criminal, or perhaps "wild" or "animal-like."[6] It seems unnecessary to emphasize that education administered on these terms is unlikely to be meaningful to the students.

This image of the "Indian" as criminal (or wild, or animal-like, or savage) exists not only in the philosophy of the residential school but can also be traced through the philosophy of child welfare legislation (see Chapter 10) and is obvious in specific provisions of the *Indian Act*. The *Indian Act* education amendments of the 1880s went hand-in-hand with the *Indian Act* provisions which criminalized our ceremonies such as the Potlatch and the Sundance and forbade the wearing of ceremonial dress.[7] There are direct links between Christianity's desire to protect us from our "pagan" ways thereby ensuring our civilization, and the removal of our children by means of education in their so-called best interests. Education of Aboriginal children has been one of the central tools of forced assimilation and the destruction of family relations and social relations, as well as the traditional forms of education.

In the House of Commons in 1920, when the compulsory education amendments were being discussed, it is unquestionable that the goal of these provisions was to eliminate Aboriginal cultures. At the time Deputy Superintendent General Duncan Campbell Scott declared:

> Our object is to continue until there is not a single Indian in Canada that has not been absorbed into the body politic and there is no Indian question, and no Indian department, that is the whole object of this Bill. (cited in Haig-Brown 1988: 27)

It is clear that this was an intentional and deliberate invasion of Aboriginal culture based in the belief that European culture was far more advanced. This philosophy is one that should be easily recognized today as racist.[8] Cultural invasion by education is today unlikely to be so intentional and deliberate, but the result of well-intentioned professionals who bring to teaching their own worldview based on their own upbringing. It is equally devastating (Freire 1970: 154).

Turning to the political sphere in more recent times, on June 25, 1969, Jean Chretian, then federal Minister of Indian Affairs and Northern Development, introduced what became a controversial White Paper on Indian Affairs (Canada 1969).[9] This document was the last official policy document which expressly provided that education would be advanced as a primary tool of the cultural assimilation of Aboriginal Peoples. In 1972, The National Indian Brotherhood (now the Assembly of First Nations) responded to the White Paper's education provisions in a document entitled "Indian Control of Indian Education." The response was the Indian control of our children's education through parental responsibility and local control as "only Indian peoples can develop a suitable philosophy of education based on Indian values adopted to modern living" (as cited in Barman et al. 1987: 2).[10] It was not until 1973 that the federal government adopted the National Indian Brotherhood position, but adopted it only in principle. Amazing as it may seem, it has only been twenty-two years since the Canadian government *formally* abandoned the principle of assimilation through education. There remains a reasonable doubt that this policy has yet to be abandoned in practice.

The last twenty-two years of political negotiation surrounding our children's education[11] has resulted in an impasse quagmired in the concepts of jurisdiction and authority. This is a familiar pattern in Aboriginal/Canadian political relations. We have experienced this very same theoretical roadblock in the constitutional discussions, the child welfare negotiations[12] and the criminal justice initiatives,[13] to give only several examples. What is unfortunate is that all of our energies are devoured by the political debates. Our time is spent on talk not action. Action is required to change the desperate life circumstances of Aboriginal Peoples in this country. I would assert that jurisdictional disputes are a very effective way of oppressing a people.

The nature and scope of the injustices perpetrated by both the state and the church against Aboriginal Peoples through education can also be understood through the personal accounts[14] of students who survived that experience. Describing the first day of residential school, one student comments:

> And then, all of a sudden, we seen somebody coming down the hallway all in black and just this White face and that's when I started just shaking and we all started crying and backing up. . . . We were doing that of sheer fright. This sister is coming towards us and what has been going in her mind is, "Here's these little wild animals." You know when you go to touch a little wild animal, it cringes and we say right away, "Oh, it's a wild animal. We've got to tame it." I could just imagine what was going on in her mind,

"These little wild Indians: I've got to tame them." ... And here me, I'm saying, "I'm so scared. What is she going to do to me?" And after hearing about them killing our own people, "Are they here to butcher us or what are they going to do to us?" (Haig-Brown 1988: 46)

And another woman remembers daily life at the same school:

In the morning, we had to get up at six o'clock, perfect silence. We all took turns going into the bathroom: we'd fill our basin full of water and we'd take it to our bedside. We'd wash, take that basin, empty it, clean it out, put it back, fix our bed, get dressed and as soon as you're finished—you only had half an hour to do all this—brush your teeth, get in a line and stand in line in perfect silence. If you're caught ever speaking one word, boy, you got cuffed around. (54)

For anyone who has studied criminology and the development of the prison system, the parallels between residential school and the early penitentiary are obvious. Absolute silence that governed the prisoner's day, long hours of prayer and physical labour were also requirements of repentance. The same woman continues with her description of life at the residential school, as follows:

And then we marched from there down to the chapel and we spent over an hour in the chapel every morning, every blessed morning. And there they interrogated us on what it was all about being an Indian. ... He would just get so carried away; he was punching away at that old altar rail . . . to hammer it into our heads that we were not to think or act or speak like an Indian. And that we would go to hell and burn for eternity if we did not listen to their way of teaching.(54)

The themes that I have identified—such as the children being perceived as wild and in need of taming and the relationship to the same punitive model which shaped prison justice at the time—are witnessed through these accounts of the residential school experience. Such accounts must lead us to the conclusion that we completely reject the "missionary" philosophy, in all its forms, as appropriate for the education of Aboriginal people.

One more reflection on education and its potential harm, completes this picture:

In the beginning when the English needed the Indians they were very friendly and got along very fine. And in fact our traditional Thanksgiving is a commemoration of that friendship. Indeed the sense I had in high school and before that when we were to celebrate in an Anglo kind of environment, what Thanksgiving meant in the United States, the sense I always got out of it was that the European colonists had invited the Indians to dinner and had fed the Indians and that was sort of the way it was kind of promoted. I think history shows that the person who showed up at the doorstep with the turkey was not the colonist, it was the Indian, and it was the Indian that had to teach people how to catch those birds. Not only that but the Indians were the ones who knew where the cranberries were, the Indians brought corn and the Indians brought potatoes, actually it wasn't potatoes, it was artichokes. The Indians brought the squash, all the stuff that are the trimmings and whatever of the Thanksgiving dinner were provided by the Indians. There isn't a bowl of barley soup in the whole meal. (Mohawk 1987: 5-6)

This analogy points to the failure to accurately reflect and portray the truth about American history and the same is true for the Canadian historic memory. However, the relationship between history and education is significant. Education is one of the mainstays of creating and spreading historical (mis)understandings. Relationships such as these should not be allowed to slip our attention when considering educational reforms.

The point is clear, Aboriginal Peoples now understand education for what it has been—a tool of our oppression. Education is merely a reflection of Canadian society—its version of history and its values. If our[16] society is racist, and this is a fact that Canadians are now coming to understand, then our education systems can only reflect and further entrench that racism.

What is it then that we are to do? We must use what we now understand to continue to question our existing institutions and their philosophical bases. We must use that new understanding to craft a future direction for our society and our institutions:

To whine around about the destruction of our language and customs, without trying to come to grips with the why of the destruction is pure mental laziness. The appropriation of knowledge, its distortion, and in some cases, its destruction, was vital to the colonial process. The conqueror relies on his victims for obeisance. The culture of the conqueror is justified by the notion that some sort of 'godly' or inherent right to conquer belongs solely to him. The process of colonialism has as its ideological rationale, racism. It is the relations of the colonial system that we must alter fundamentally, not dress our enslavement in Native garb. (Maracle 1988: 114)

Our challenge, and it must be a collective challenge, is to transform educational systems as we know them today. One reason that the challenge must be a collective one between Aboriginal Peoples and Canadians, is that it is only in this way that we can break the patronizing, parochial and colonial nature of our educational relations. We must expose and denounce the racism. Aboriginal Peoples do *not* need to be "helped" to attain some higher status or a greater degree of civilization. We need to be respected for who and what we are, as well as for how we have helped to shape this nation. We are not founding people. We are original people. And that is not found in our textbooks, or in Canadian history, or in our classrooms, or in our laws. Only through accepting the truth about Canadian history can education for Aboriginal people become a path to our freedom rather than a tool of our oppression.

The emphasis I have placed on the history of educational relations between Aboriginal Peoples and Canadians may lead to the criticism that this discussion is backward looking. However, I am not complaining about what has been lost. Many Aboriginal nations have a teaching that you must know who you are (and that would be your nation, clan, language, song, and spiritual name) and where you have been before you can know where you are going. In this way history is not of the past, but history is walking in strength and pride with your ancestors today. From this perspective, culture cannot be lost. It is also most important, as I have tried to document, to recognize that the "missionary" philosophy in educating First Nations in Canada has not been eradicated. It is insidious in our educational institutions of today. Perhaps, legal education is one of the clearest examples of the festering of current education policy in days past.

I do not consider the legal context to be a complete, totally appropriate or the only beneficial forum to finally resolve the educational dilemma challenging us. The adversarial system[17] produces a "winner" and a "loser." No one, especially based on racial and cultural criteria, should "lose" when it comes to accessing the benefits, that is, the meaningfulness, of education. It is contradictory to define educational equality in terms of balancing interests. However, this does not mean that we should ignore the legal framework. We must recognize that it is only a partial forum in which we can seek solutions.

My thinking on education focuses on what is a just way to treat people. However it must be remembered that there exists a sound legal basis for characterizing access to Aboriginally relevant education as an Aboriginal right or a Treaty right.[18] Let us hope it is unnecessary to take this battle to the courtrooms of this land. In addition to this first basis for a legal claim or a right to education, human rights documents such as the *Universal Declaration of Human Rights*, (United Nations 1948) the *Declaration of the Rights of the Child*, (United Nations 1959) the Canadian *Charter of Rights and Freedoms*, and the *Canadian Human Rights Act*, all support the legal belief that education is a basic human right (MacKay et al. 1989: IX).

The central challenge to education institutions is how to encompass this respect for a basic human right within their goals and curricula. The challenge is much too large to be shaped by one individual. My purpose in writing this piece is to start, perhaps provoke, discussion. My concern is centred in legal education because it is what I have experienced and continue to live. But I would hope that not only is cross-cultural discussion fostered but cross-discipline discussion as well. There are many valuable teachings that we can all share with each other.

The Challenge of Legal Education

Just as the expectations of my grandmothers were never met, I felt during my law student days that I was always waiting for my legal education to begin. I always felt that "something" was missing or perhaps that I was missing something. Nor am I certain that I am now able to clearly define what exactly this "something missing" concept is. I know it is very important though. And I know it is a concept shared among many other Aboriginal students who have studied law. In my first year at law school, I felt it was *my* problem—similar to the way in which Duncan Campbell Scott and many others in the 1920s and later were able to characterize the "Indian problem" as the sole fault of Aboriginal people. Then the solution rested on changing the "Indian" into a civilized and assimilated being. In first year, I internalized this characteristic of colonialism and oppression, believing if I could only change, perhaps fit in a little better, my law school experience would be rewarding. Both the institution and some of my teachers reinforced this belief. Since then I have understood that the greatest obstacle was not myself, but the very structure of the institution and the legal studies program.

In speaking to other Aboriginal law students, it is easy to recognize this "something missing" feeling in their own personal stories. The feeling that "something" is missing is knowing that you *are* an outsider. Often, this feeling is internalized. Frequently the Aboriginal student is left feeling, "There is something the matter with me because I do not fit in here." Many of us want to leave after first year, if indeed we were fortunate enough to be one of the ones who did not fail.[19] It is, therefore, easy for me to conclude that something specific is "wrong" in legal education.

At some point in time in my first year of law school, I bumped into the

Dean of the school in the corridors. We discussed how we were and how school was going for me. He asked how I had enjoyed the Saskatoon program and if it was helping me adjust to law school. I had not accessed law school through the Saskatoon program. (The Dean's assumption or stereotype of Aboriginal experience can be interpreted in a number of ways.) We made small talk for awhile. Eventually, I asked him, "Since law schools have now thrown open the doors to their hallowed halls and warmly welcomed Aboriginal students, what are you going to do with us next?" The Dean indicated to me his agreement with this concern. Access programs alone are not enough. Access programs do not address the situation of being an outsider. Access programs speak primarily to equality of numbers.

Failing to address the "what now" question will likely only result in further unintentional perpetuation of the "missionary" approach to education within law schools. "We are doing a good job because we are helping these people!" The result will then be that Aboriginal people are required to assimilate to current models of what it is to be a law student or lawyer. There is no reason to believe that assimilation through legal education would be any more than the dismal failure it was at elementary and secondary levels. Quite the contrary, it is more reasonable to expect that the "missionary" philosophy as it is currently subtly embraced at law schools will continue to act as a major obstacle to the education of Aboriginal legal professionals. That question, "what now?" still haunts me.

Knowing oneself to be an outsider is intensified by attempting to maintain ourselves within competitive, hierarchical structures and relationships. Further, curricula at all levels of education are grounded within a White, patriarchal, middle-class system of values. This reflects the understanding that educational philosophy was and still remains grounded in the idealism of the "missionary" approach. This value system bears little or no relation to local Aboriginal concerns. This is not only true for Aboriginal people wishing to pursue legal education but is merely a reflection of our experience of the dominant society in general. Professor Rennard Strickland relates:

> In a sense, the challenges and the questions which face young Indians who are considering becoming lawyers are related to the one which has long troubled all Indian people—the dilemma of living in two worlds, one traditional and one modern. To the lawyer the question is: How can I be both an Indian and an attorney? How can I be true to myself and true to my people? How can I be both prosperous and proud? How can I be loyal to my tribal heritage as an Indian and faithful to my oath as an attorney? This is quite a challenge. (1974: 47)

At this point in time, it should not surprise anyone that Aboriginal students experience extreme alienation within educational systems which I believe is proportionately related to the degree to which they are connected to Aboriginal communities and/or traditional beliefs and values. There is no reason why this struggle is not addressed as part of the preparation for a legal career. If we are able to train "better" lawyers, then we should be doing just that.[20] It is more realistic to expect that this can be achieved within the law school environment than during the articling period or during bar admission courses. This is not to say that this concern cannot and should not also be addressed at those later junctures.

Where I do not clearly agree with the perspective of Professor Strickland (and granted he was writing during the 1970s when we were just beginning to confront these challenges) is in his inference that somehow Aboriginal people must chose between their "Indian-ness" and being "successful." It is not impossible to do both! When we ground our ideas in a conflicting dichotomy of either "Indian" or "White"; traditional or modern, "Indian" or successful (and one will ultimately triumph), we ground our thinking in racist stereotypes of Aboriginal people. There is a relationship between this kind of thinking and the assimilationist philosophy of the "missionary" approach to education. This assimilationist philosophy sounds like this: through education we will naturally better the lesser status of these individuals to a greater degree than the general benefits of education to people who do not belong in this lesser category. It is unacceptable that we continue to support, even subtly or unconsciously, this perspective.[21]

Consider a different perspective on the issue of being an outsider. Viewing life, even momentarily, from a perspective other than your own is necessary if members of the mainstream are ever going to understand the complexities of racism. Alex Christmas, President of the Union of Nova Scotia Indians, in his address to the Racism Forum held at Dalhousie Law School in February 1990, challenges:

> We are now entering a new era of race relations in Canada, an era where Aboriginal people cannot and should not be treated any longer as second class citizens. We have now crashed through the racial barrier that has kept our people from participating *meaningfully* in our own traditions. Canadians can no longer ignore or treat lightly our aspirations because of their beliefs of superiority and dominance over Aboriginal Peoples. We are not inferior as some believe. We are different—different in our views, in our hopes and in our ways—but, by no means, do we accept the notion that we are any "less" of a people! Those who still cling to those ideas are still practicing, consciously or unconsciously, racism in its most deceitful

form. They have deceived themselves about their own attitudes.

Have you ever stopped and thought about how the Mi'kmaq think about you? You have lived in our territories for years. We have watched your society take our lands, ignore our treaties, destroy our livelihood, deplete and pollute our resources and try to convince us that we should be grateful for all the government welfare programs? Do you honestly believe that we think everything is all right when we suffer unemployment in the 60 to 90 percent bracket, where our people die at a higher rate than yours and where our young face only despair and prejudice? Is it possible that we, as a people, know what the problems are and how to approach them? Maybe we have been underestimated in our wisdom, endurance and strength. In one way, underestimation is our big advantage because we can easily surprise others when they try to deal with us with less than honourable motives. We understand far more than many believe.

Our advice then is—look at yourself first. The one major hindrance in the development of our people is the racial barrier. Many believe: "They're only Indians. They can't manage the wildlife and the fishery. How could they ever run a justice system anyway?" Are these your attitudes as well? I sincerely hope not.[22]

As Mr. Christmas so eloquently points out, it is only when the mainstream is able to acknowledge the existence of outsider experience that fundamental changes will begin that will eventually transform society and institutions such as law schools. It is important to note the difference between acknowledging and understanding. Understanding can only be gained through experience. I am not suggesting that members of the mainstream will ever fully understand Aboriginal culture as they can never live the life of a Aboriginal person (and logically then, mainstream membership clearly precludes "expertise" in "Aboriginal rights").[23] What I strive for is the day when we can live in respect with each other, walking side by side.[24]

The basic tension buried out of sight in Aboriginal/Canadian legal relations is based on our differing worldviews. I want to provide several examples of how this tension manifests itself within legal institutions. S.M. Waddams has written a book which is often referred to students preparing for legal studies. It is a worthwhile text but it is also a problematic text. Teachers referring Aboriginal students to this text could perhaps provide an initial caution which embraces the following concern. Professor Waddams firstly defines the human person as a political animal in the Aristotelian sense (that is human beings naturally live in communities). Building on this *natural* development of civilization, he then defines law as:

A universal feature of human society has been conflict. Individuals have individual interests. On occasion, they conflict with each other. If a society is to survive it must develop a system of resolving conflicts between individuals, and conflicts between individuals on the one hand and the community on the other. The law is the system of resolving those conflicts. (1987: 2)

Not only is conflict natural but it is universal! And law, then, is the solution in civilized societies. To Aboriginal people, this ideology is nothing short of ridiculous. Harmony is the center of our relations with the universe and all other beings, be they human, animal or plant. Not only is this the basis of Aboriginal legal relations, but it is a total and integrated philosophy around which all social relations are constructed. The separations of law, government, family, education, religion, etc. simply do not exist within the Aboriginal worldview. Therefore there is tension and disagreement at the fundamental level of construction of legal relations. The Aboriginal worldview is disappeared within the legal systems of Canada, in much the same way as Professor Waddams fails to recognize that he (and many other profound scholars) disappear other worldviews in their unquestioned belief of "universality." Uncovering these myths on which the legal system is built is one of the fundamental challenges facing the legal system. In my view, it is the philosophical source of centuries of oppression of non-European based philosophies.

The work of Canadian legal scholars, the judiciary, politicians and in fact all those involved with the shaping of Canada as a nation state have actively, by omission or commission, participated in the direct oppression of Aboriginal Peoples. It is the mythology which underlies the development of Canada as a nation state which we must expose and denounce. This mythology is in fact a great lie, which unravels like this:

The new European nations have worked diligently to wipe out the indigenous history and intellectual thought and replace these with European history and intellectual thought. The great lie is simply this: *If indigenous peoples will only reject their own history, intellectual development, language, and culture and replace these things with European values and ideals, then indigenous people will survive.* It is from this twisted thinking that European nations have convinced millions of indigenous people all over the world to surrender their freedom and accept subjugation as a way of life. (Ryser 1984: 28-29)

There should be no mistaking and no misunderstanding exactly what the consequences are in failing to deconstruct the mythology surrounding the great lie and those who continue to chose to perpetuate it. It must be understood that the relationship between participation in education, including legal education, and participation in social relations, including the political realm, are inter-related. Access to meaningful education is one road to self-determination and it must be understood that this is what I am talking about.

The personal consequences of participating in the processes which continue the perpetuation of the great lie must also be examined—for these personal consequences are one of the greatest barriers to establishing meaningful educational experiences. I would assert that the meaningfulness of education is jeopardized for both the mainstream as well as members of the outsider population. Education that does not foster respect is not meaningful but oppressive. The reality of "minority" participation in law school is that we are continually defined as exceptional because we are Aboriginal or that we are successful only because we are tokens.

Remembering back to my first day at law school, I was confronted in the lounge by another student who, in a quite hostile manner, explained that perhaps one of his friends was not present because of me. And this made him angry because the only reason I could have reached the hallowed halls of the law school was by virtue of a special access program. And of course, by implication, this friend was more qualified to be there. The reality of my admission to law school was that I was accepted as part of "regular" admissions with an entrance scholarship as well. I had attended no so-called special program. But, my colleagues, be they students or now professors and practitioners, readily and repeatedly assume every Aboriginal student has attended the Saskatchewan Program. Of the 150 First Nations lawyers and the 125 First Nations law students in Canada, approximately one third have *not* attended Saskatchewan (Brown 1989: 2). I never bothered to explain this to the angry young man because I knew it would not change anything. His attitude would remain the same, only his perception of me would change. I would become not really "Indian-like" but the exception. It feels rather like a vicious circle. I am either negatively labelled as either lesser by virtue of my attendance at a so-called special program (and I do not think for one minute that this is an appropriate characterization of access programs) or exceptional and somehow fundamentally different from all the rest of my people. What I have been describing is the racism inherent in legal institutions. And what must surely now be clear is that the task—transforming the law school—before us is overwhelming.

The "wrongness" of legal education (which is better described as the inability of legal education to address Aboriginal experience and other sources of diversity) must be discussed by law teachers, administrators, students (particularly Aboriginal students) and Aboriginal communities.

This assumes that pursuing relevant legal education for Aboriginal Peoples is a relevant goal of Euro-Canadian[25] legal systems. Quintessential to that discussion is a discussion of what we collectively and individually are doing right. These types of discussions are glaringly absent from within the institutions that house legal programs. Providing a forum for these conversations will call on the creativity of law schools because the administration of these schools as well as the teachers are largely non-Aboriginal. Furthermore, within the structure of law school there is no mechanism for involving Aboriginal communities.

The literature currently available on Aboriginal people and legal education is disappointing. The bulk of the literature is of a descriptive, program review or a program evaluation nature.[26] It is largely congratulatory, as opposed to providing critical assessments. The articles are generally written by those directly involved in providing these special programs and services and therefore have a stake in advancing the unquestioned success of the program. The authors are almost all non-Aboriginal. The articles embrace the "missionary" approach to education and legal relations (which allows for the perpetuation of the great lie—become like us and everything will be fine). This is not to suggest the efforts of these individuals were not well-intentioned or of great benefit to the development of Aboriginal access to legal education in Canada. The fact that the literature available on Aboriginal legal education has not yet begun to examine the underlying difficulties with the philosophical principles of legal and educational systems is disturbing but not surprising.

The Canadian literature in particular is only written by those outside the culture. Once it is understood that there are at least two seemingly contradictory worldviews, the importance of who controls the means and mechanisms of discussion should be readily apparent. This is not criticism directed at any one non-Aboriginal author of articles and/or theories on Aboriginal rights under Canadian law. It is a criticism of the collective memory loss of a particular set of individuals. What has been lost is half of the duo-vision of what we know now to be Canada. What must be addressed is the reality that current Canadian legal scholars speak only from within their *own* tradition of "two founding nations."[27] The myth of these traditions is not questioned. And the great lie lives on and on. A doctrinal framework which holds these two valid theoretical perspectives, the Aboriginal view and the established Canadian view, on Aboriginal rights must be constructed. This new legal doctrine, which will enhance the validity of both perspectives, is essential to establishing fair, just and peaceable relations in this country. Both of the equally valid legal traditions of this country must be willing to participate to each other's mutual satisfaction and agreement.[28] This agreement cannot be reached by negotiation but can only be developed through processes of mutual respect. The current state of affairs is that one view trumps the other by default—that is the collective memory loss. Nothing is gained by or for Aboriginal Peoples, or Canadians for that matter, in this adversarial "my way wins" dichotomy where our legal rights have descended. The only result of the "my way wins" process will be a stand-off.

Even more disturbing is the type of literature typified by an article which recently appeared in the *Canadian Lawyer* magazine, "Lost in a Sea of White" (Coates 1989).[29] This article begins in a deceivingly radical tone, documenting the racism confronted by a "prominent Toronto lawyer" who is Black, incidents such as "the time he was detained outside a provincial court by a security guard who insisted on checking him for weapons while other lawyers—all White—breeze through the door" (27). The article however, quickly degenerates into an opinionated discussion of the new law school programs at schools such as Dalhousie and Osgoode Hall which admit students on "relaxed academic standards."[30] In 1980, Roger Carter, former Director of the Native Law Center and former Dean at the Faculty of Law, University of Saskatchewan, had this to say about such assertions:

> A further comment should be made dealing with the assessment of the program. In a few isolated cases objections to the course have been voiced on the footing that it provides some kind of easy access to law studies and thus places the native student in a peculiarly advantaged situation. *It should be clear from the foregoing that such comments are wrong.* For one thing there is nothing novel or remarkable about "discretionary or mature" admission policies in Canadian Law Schools. They are long standing and are open to any person of whatever ancestry he or she may be. Secondly, no "ordinary" applicant is required to undertake, and succeed in, an intensive and demanding eight week summer program before finally being considered for admission to his or her law school. In summary it can fairly be said that these students are faced with, and have to satisfy, added requirements—rather than the contrary. (32, emphasis added)

When the debate becomes divided on lines of choosing if one supports affirmative action standards or not, then the debate is one that has been successfully narrowed in a very unfortunate way.[31] The areas of discussion where we could productively be channeling our energies are not even mentioned.

Two examples should illuminate the difficulties in this process of exclusion. The truth about law school admissions is that race has historically been a factor. Criteria for admissions such as the LSAT and undergraduate records have been demonstrated to advantage White applicants. Historically race criteria have existed *silently* that advantaged White applicants over non-White applicants. The expression of the eradication of this historic bias, often expressed in a way that seems to advantage non-Whites, often brings vocal criticism. This is both illogical and backward thinking. Consider whether or not race and/or ethnicity should be viewed as a positive factor in the law school admissions process. Legal systems must serve all sectors of society if the goals (such as the rule of law, justice and fairness) of the legal system are to be served. It is beneficial to strive to ensure that all sectors of society participate in the delivery of legal services to the community (Ramsey 1980: 385). Given the under-representation of certain groups in law schools, the existence of affirmative admission standards furthers the goals we all profess to respect within Euro-Canadian or Euro-American legal systems. The failure to consider race or ethnicity as a positive factor in the admission process and clinging to the old-fashioned beliefs that neutral, colour-blind standards are objective and fair forcibly impedes the ability of the legal system to respect its own core values. There exists a relationship between the desire to cling to old standards of discourse and evaluation and the nature of literature that is available. Defensive posturing around the belief in old ways versus the challenge brought forward by "minority" participation does not facilitate discussion or development.

Defensive posturing also excludes from the discussion an analysis of the important benefits of an affirmative action law school program. It is not merely a question of to admit or not. Affirmative action programs send a strong message to the "minority" applicant as well as their community.

> . . . an affirmative action admissions program at a law school may reasonably be view by minority applicants as an indication that the school has a commitment to the education of minority students, that there is a fair chance of their being admitted, and that the overall environment at the law school is more likely to be supportive than hostile or indifferent. (Ramsey 1980: 391)

The apparent clustering of Aboriginal students at Canadian law schools with programs in Aboriginal rights law, such as those at the University of British Columbia and the University of Saskatchewan, documents the collateral effect of the "special" admissions program. Unfortunately, the debate about admissions standards tends to become narrowly focused by critics of the programs on the misinformed discussion of so-called lower standards in such a way that the overall beneficial effects of these programs are either impossible to consider or entirely forgotten. The "Lost in a Sea of White" article is a perfect example of how the process of exclusion operates.

The article in *Canadian Lawyer* discusses a concern about the lowering of academic standards at law schools. This discussion is really a thinly disguised perpetuation of racism. First, an undisclosed quantum leap precedes the conclusion that different standards are somehow lower standards. This is qualitatively not different from the assumptions made by Europeans at the time of initial contact some centuries ago. It is the modern-day equivalent of the desire to "civilize the Indians" to a European standard of so-believed advancement. It is known that the history of law school enrollment has been White and male. The standards that have effectively evolved are therefore grounded in Whiteness and maleness. Failing to recognize the exclusionary way in which the standards of admissions have evolved is the first quantum leap. A second quantum leap occurs when you take these historically developed standards and allow them to define the norm, when in reality White or male is not the norm.

The way in which the author of "Lost in a Sea of White" integrates "minority" viewpoints is also most reprehensible. All of the quoted comments of the minorities are critical of the new access programs for "racial minorities." The task of defending the new access programs is left to the White directors or facilitators of these new programs. This technique subtly adopts the stereotypical image of the "great White father/mother" who will save the poor (also read that as "criminal," "animal-like," "wild" or "savage") "Indian." This is a perspective which has dominated journalistic portrayals of Aboriginal Peoples for a very long time[32] and is a perspective that one would expect, perhaps naively, to have been eradicated or at least no longer tolerated by 1990.

And if you are not firmly convinced of the racism which seeps from this issue, then the "Back Page" editorial should send a flood of clear white light through our minds regarding the motivation of the magazine's editorial staff. George Jonas writes a simplistic defence of liberalism and law schools' new admission standards. It is simplistic because he never expounds on why liberalism must be the prevailing theoretical paradigm, while he levels an attack on the critics of liberalism (and supposedly the supporters of access programs), which merely amounts to child-like name calling.[33] His characterization of affirmative action in law schools to a "Nazi-like quota system" is reprehensible. After all, law schools are not lining up White legal professionals and gassing them on the front steps of Canadian law schools. The parallel is highly inappropriate and trivializes the injustices inflicted on the Jewish people in Hilter's Germany.[34] Perhaps Mr. Jonas needs to focus his attention on this side of the ocean and the history of this "great" country—small pox blankets, the hanging of Riel, the annihilation of an entire nation of people in Newfoundland, and so on. I recognize that this editorial piece is an opinion. I do not believe that no limitation exists regarding moral responsibility for the publication of such pieces. The right of free speech is not absolute but must be mitigated against the right of "minorities" to lead meaningful lives. I value the right to a meaningful life free from racism more than the freedom to speak racistly.

The debate about lower standards is really a thinly disguised smoke-screen for an unimaginative suggestion that perhaps the status quo should remain entrenched within law schools. Unfortunately, the author of "Lost in a Sea of White" does not have the courage to make express his motivation or his opinion, whatever those may be. The result is a dangerous and harmful article which masquerades itself behind the respectability of a magazine published by those involved in the legal profession. This is, I believe, an issue of professional responsibility.

In considering this issue of professional responsibility, both within the law school context as well as the field of journalism, the treatment of four of my Dalhousie Law school colleagues' joint letter to the editor of the *Canadian Lawyer* is insightful. The title appearing before their sincere letter criticizing the two pieces on "minority" programs at law schools in the previous issue is, "Now, From the Peanut Gallery." I think the position that they put forward was due at least honest concern and a sincere response.[35] The "Editors Note" following the printing of this letter, is so repugnant that I will let it speak for itself.

> Intrigued by the erudite and level-headed arguments raised by these academics, we called the Dalhousie Law School admissions office on the morning their letter arrived to again inquire about the standards applied in the program for disadvantaged blacks and native people.[36]
>
> A representative of the admissions office told us in no uncertain terms that candidates for this program do not have to meet the standards set for the average candidate. In particular, she said that whereas the typical applicant would have to have an LSAT score in the "mid-30s," a native or black applicant would only have to score in the "mid-20s." She added that while a "B-" was the threshold academic average for most applicants, blacks and natives wouldn't be held to that since most don't come with any sort of scholastic track record.
>
> Further she comment that school marks play a very minor role in cases involving minorities.
>
> Perhaps we're missing something in all this, but those do seem like "relaxed" academic standards for admissions which is what our story said. . . . (Canadian Lawyer 15, 1: 5)

The editorial goes on, but I hope that my point regarding the sincerity of the tone of the magazine's response is well taken by this time. The attitude of the editorial is more reprehensible than the original article. Perhaps, I come to this conclusion because the article may be excused as a well-intentioned effort to understand new initiatives at law schools while failing to understand the complexities of racism. The editorial however conveys a different message. To me it says, I have a right to maintain the status quo and any racially misinformed attitudes I may have.

What the editor fails to mention while busy "noting," is that whoever called the admissions office at Dalhousie failed to identify who they were. In essence, to me that sounds like securing information under false pretences. Not that this should matter, the nature of the admissions policy should not change based on the nature of type of caller.[37] However, this failure to identify themselves, given the article previously published, seems improper and a breach of professional standards of the journalism "fraternity." Being a legal professional, I know just how easy it is to ask leading questions. The individual speaking on the phone should have had the opportunity to speak candidly or off the record. This choice was never given as the caller never identified their professional identity. This is particularly troubling as the journalist chose to speak to a person who holds a support position and *not* to the chair of the admissions committee. What the editorial response still fails to notice is that there are fundamental differences between different standards and lower standards. Regular admittees are not required to demonstrate such values as outstanding community involvement or work records.

Although articles of the *genre* of the piece in the *Canadian Lawyer* can only promote racism or profound disgust and, notwithstanding the current state of the literature and the constant battle against racism and racist attitudes, some progress is slowly being made within Canadian law schools. In the five years since this article was first written, I can again note that some small steps have been taken at some Canadian law schools. Some gains have also been lost such as the loss of the Department of Justice scholarships for Métis and "non-status" students. Change has been insufficient to affect the experience of alienation and isolation most Aboriginal law students face. Racism, both overt and subtle, is one of the significant reasons why legal institutions have failed to meet the needs of *all* their students. The shape of this failure, consistent over the years since this article was first published, will be examined next.

The Common Law Schools

The first formal Canadian development in legal education for Aboriginal Peoples was the "Program of Legal Studies for Native People" at the University of Saskatchewan's law school. Planning for the program began in 1969 (Carter 1980: 28) with the first course being offered to students in the summer of 1972. The creation of this program rested primarily on the initiative and insight of the then Dean of Saskatchewan's law school, Roger Carter. A planning committee was struck in 1972 comprised largely of university representatives (MacKinnon and Rhodes 1974: 40-41). The program was developed with the cooperation and approval of most Canadian common law schools. "The *general response* of these law schools was one of enthusiasm and a genuine desire to share in the overall scheme of legal education for native people" (MacKinnon and Rhodes 1974: 41, italics added). The program was structured to accomplish these goals; "to acquaint native students with the rigors of legal education, to provide them with a 'head start' in their study of law, and to assess their capacities to perform successfully in Canadian law schools" (41). In 1975, the administration of the program was taken over by the newly created Native Law Centre (Thompson 1988: 713).

The Native Law Centre, which hosts the summer program, has been since 1984 a department of the College of Law at the University of Saskatchewan. The summer program is one of the Centre's primary goals and its major teaching initiative. Other principal activities include research, publication and maintenance of a resource centre. A lecture series has also been hosted since 1986 (Thompson 1988: 715-717). The research function is comprised of several activities which focus on issues of Aboriginal rights law within the Euro-Canadian context.[38] The majority of the authors published are not members of any Aboriginal Peoples.[39] This has been cause for concern within some Aboriginal circles. Research initiatives are not focused on further advancing and understanding traditional Aboriginal systems of justice. Further to the bulletin service, the Centre publishes the *Canadian Native Law Reporter*. This is the only single source of Canadian case law on First Nations issues and is a very important contribution to the study of Euro-Canadian law. Of its two principle functions, teaching and resourcing, only the resource function is seen as a permanent need (Thompson 1988: 719).

Partially as a result of the completion of a program review, the Native Law Centre was able to hire its first Aboriginal director. James Youngblood "Sakej" Henderson began his tenure at the University of Saskatchewan in 1993. Under his guidance, the Aboriginal legal community is hopeful that the Native Law Centre will become more respectful and responsive to the legal needs of Aboriginal people *as we define them*. The administration of the law school (and indirectly the Native Law Centre) has yet to make a firm commitment to respecting this Aboriginal vision. In particular, the summer program's direction has not significantly changed in the last decade. This is disappointing. It would be easy to revolutionize an eight week program toward a vision of what Aboriginal people dream legal education could be. Such a program could then serve as a model for law schools to aspire to. The summer program in its current form serves law schools first and Aboriginal Peoples second. In my mind this is an unacceptable exercise of status quo power and privileges.

In cooperation with the establishment of the summer program in 1972 and, as a direct result of that initiative, the first step in transforming legal education for Aboriginal people was taken. This step was to question the failure to provide access routes to Aboriginal Peoples—the numbers game. Statistics compiled by the Native Law Centre in 1989 showed that the following law schools had been significantly involved in the effort to educate Aboriginal legal professionals: the University of British Columbia (61 graduates and students enrolled in classes), University of Saskatchewan (25), Queen's University (24), and Osgoode Hall (23).[40] No other common law school had enrolled or graduated more than fifteen students. The Native Law Centre compiled statistics again in October 1994. As of that date, 266 program alumni have obtained law degrees. The University of British Columbia has graduated the most students (78), the University of Saskatchewan has graduated 28 students, followed by Queen's University and the University of Saskatchewan with 27 graduates each. The University of Ottawa has 24 graduates. No other law school has graduated more than 20 students.

In January of 1990, I sent a general letter of inquiry[41] to all Canadian law schools. The response rate from the common law schools was excellent, with only two of sixteen *not* responding.[42] The response from the five Quebec law schools—Laval, Montreal, Quebec, Sherbrooke, and McGill— was poor. Only two Deans replied, Laval and Sherbrooke.[43] This fact coupled with my inability to communicate in French has directed my choice to discuss only common law schools here. This choice does *not* reflect any belief that Aboriginal legal education programs within civil law schools are *not* also essential.

Access to the civil law schools for Aboriginal people has lagged behind that of the common law schools. The Saskatchewan program first accepted students in the summer of 1973. It is a program based on the common law. However, I do not believe students wishing to study at civil law and/or francophone schools have been expressly excluded from the opportunity the Saskatchewan program offers (although the second language spoken by Aboriginal students—English or French—could be an excluding factor). In fact, three Saskatchewan alumni have graduated with law degrees from McGill as of September 1989, and two were currently enrolled there.[44] No Saskatchewan alumni have enrolled at any of the other Quebec law schools. In the summer of 1989, for the first time (seventeen years after the access program was offered in English for common law students and in the face of the promise of Canadian delivery of bilingual services), the University of Ottawa offered a civil law program in the French language.

I purposely attempted to collect only general information from Canadian law faculties. I know of no current source which makes available this basic information. Lack of both time and resources were also factors in this decision not to draft a specific and detailed questionnaire or other form of research instrument. It is my opinion that further formal and structured research is most necessary regarding the issue of Aboriginal Peoples and legal education.

The data I have collected is self-report data. It must be interpreted with caution. My letter to the Law Deans reads as follows:

> As a First Nation's (Mohawk) woman and a new law teacher, I have been critically considering future directions for First Nations peoples developing in my profession.
>
> I am interested in receiving information on affirmative action, access, or equity programs in operation or within contemplation at your law school. In particular, I am interested in programs for racial and cultural minorities with special emphasis on First Nation's peoples.
>
> At the moment, I am interested in determining what efforts are occurring on a national basis within law faculties. It is likely that I will soon be producing a paper for publication on this topic. I would be glad to share with you the formal results of my efforts should you request a copy.
>
> I look forward to your response.

It was the deans themselves who set the parameters for the information they provided to me. I can therefore not be certain at what stage of development the deans decided to report on initiatives being taken at their schools.[45] If deans did not expressly state that new policies were *not* being developed, it cannot be concluded that discussions or initial planning is not taking place. Therefore, the survey reflects only what *is* happening at law schools and only in some cases what may be planned. This is a serious caution that must be placed on these results. It further substantiates the dire need for further formalized and detailed research in this area.

It is encouraging that all of the fourteen responding law schools indicated that they have admission policies geared to the unique situation of Aboriginal Peoples in Canadian society. This reality is likely a direct result of the early 1970s initiative of Roger Carter and the pre-law program at the University of Saskatchewan. Looking to the future, the Canadian Council of Law Deans "are hoping to sponsor a symposium on the issue of admissions policy and racial and cultural minorities some time next year" (Mercer 1990).

Unfortunately, the picture does not remain as bright when seeking evidence of further advancements after the 1970 period of growth and awareness. Five law schools indicate that they have recruitment programs in place. Two other schools are planning or discussing such initiatives. One of these schools indicated that their difficulty operating the special admissions program comes not in the selection process itself "but in obtaining sufficient numbers to apply to begin with." Four law schools indicate that they are reviewing their policy on Aboriginal and/or "minority" involvement through the establishment of committees and/or reviews of the existing policy. A further two schools indicate that they have begun discussing Aboriginal and or "racial minority" access.

There are four law schools which bear special mention. Dalhousie University in 1989, University of Alberta in 1990, the University of British Columbia in 1984, and the University of Ottawa in 1989 established directorships of special programs for Aboriginal Peoples and/or other minorities.[46] The broadest based and most progressive of these programs philosophically is the Education Equity Program at the University of Ottawa. The program involves "the development and implementation of an outreach and academic support program for a broadly defined group of students which include Aboriginal Peoples, cultural and racial minorities, disabled persons, mature students and persons for whom economic hardship is a significant barrier to their pursuing studies at our faculty" (St. Lewis 1990). The program at Ottawa should serve as a challenge to the rest of us.

Also of interest is the realization that there is no absolute relationship between schools with directorships and the graduation and enrollment of Aboriginal students. There seems to be several things happening. Universities which have graduated significant numbers of Aboriginal students are British Columbia, Saskatchewan, Queen's and Osgoode Hall. As both University of British Columbia and Saskatchewan have had programs in existence for a number of years, a correlation between their success with numbers and the existence of the programs seems logical. However, the programs at Dalhousie, Ottawa and Alberta seem to be responses to a different set of variables. The inability to attract Aboriginal students, coupled with a recognition that it is not desirable to see this trend continue, has likely fostered the establishment of those three programs. In the years when the first two programs at Saskatchewan and British Columbia were established, the same factors seem to have governed the actions of those faculties.

It is only at the four law schools with directors that formalized tutorial programs for "special admission" students such as Aboriginal students were established prior to 1990. They are also the only four law schools that have further special supports in place, with one nominal exception. One other law school indicated that the university in which they are housed has just appointed two Race Relations Officers to serve the entire university community. Of the four schools with programs only two indicate that Aboriginal and/or Community Advisory Committees have been established. This fact is most unfortunate as twelve law schools are forgoing the unique opportunity (such as in the area of recruitment as previously discussed) that is offered by involving the Aboriginal community in the direction that the law school is headed.

It is at least disappointing that none of the other ten law schools indicated that they are even considering committing resources to directorships and programs of a similar nature to the four already established. In fact, *only* two other schools indicate that they are considering establishing tutorial programs.[47] These two plus one other school indicate that they have contemplated any further form of support to Aboriginal students. Interestingly enough, two of the three indicated that their actions are responses to demands from existing Aboriginal students and their associations. It seems that the leadership within the schools is coming from the community and the student body rather than from the law school itself. This is disturbing as it places on the Aboriginal student a unique burden not carried by mainstream students (a burden for which the existence of a tutorial program does not compensate). The very students who are perhaps least likely to be able to afford extensive extra curricular activities (because they are also negotiating colonialism and oppression at law school) are forced to assume this burden in order to maintain their survival within the legal institution. This is yet another reason why the formalized recognition of community involvement through advisory committees is so disappointing.

One further study completes the picture available from current research on the state of Aboriginal education in common law schools. The Canadian Bar Association (CBA) reviewed Aboriginal rights in Canada and published a report of their findings and recommendations in 1988. One small component in this report analyzes the status of legal studies in Canada. The Association wrote to all law schools inquiring about their curriculum. The first seminar on Aboriginal Rights was offered at the University of Toronto in 1967, followed by Osgoode Hall in 1970. As of the 1987/88 year only the University of British Columbia indicated that they offered more than one seminar in the area of Aboriginal rights.[48] The University of British Columbia has four seminars offered. Of the thirteen common law schools that responded to the CBA inquiry, seven offered no courses or seminars in Aboriginal Rights. Again, this data was reported during the 1987/88 academic year.[49] The CBA committee also inquired about the course content in such courses as Real Property or Constitutional Law to determine if the topic of

Aboriginal rights is covered. Although the authors indicate that the results they collected are not precise, they conclude:

> It does appear that quite a few law professors in Canada are making a conscious effort to ensure that their students have at least some limited awareness that there is a distinct body of Canadian law which affects aboriginal people. (87)

Only in individual cases, am I able to share the Canadian Bar Association's optimism and enthusiasm. When more than 50 percent (7 of 13) of the common law schools are *not* even offering seminars in Aboriginal rights, it is impossible for me to agree that the future for Aboriginal legal studies is yet to the point where it can be called optimistic. First, it is disappointing to note that change within law faculties appears to rely on the initiative of individual professors and not on the commitment of the institution *as an institution*. This marginalizes issues affecting Aboriginal people. Second, proportionately, one would expect there to be between 1,026 and 1,710 Aboriginal lawyers in Canada—there are only approximately 150, about one-tenth of what proportional expectations would be.[50] Although some positive steps have been taken it is much too early for optimism.

This simple survey indicates clearly the lethargy that has enveloped law schools. Once the door was opened in the 1970s, few schools have made further inroads which embrace Aboriginal participation. From the survey, only one school indicates the setting aside of special scholarship funds for graduate study, one mentions the establishment of discussions surrounding the establishment of an Aboriginal Justice Institute, and one is actively pursuing curriculum review. The picture created is indeed far from encouraging within 10 of the 14 common law schools.[51]

My conclusions should not be read to suggest that all law schools should move ahead in a similar manner as the schools which have already established directorships. There are already two models available—the directorship and the Native Law Centre. There are many ideas and options that law schools could pursue. The challenge we collectively face requires creativity, and a single solution, or merely one step, in the 1990s is no more satisfactory that the single initial step taken in the 1970s in Saskatchewan. The question that still haunts me, "what now?" still remains.

Moving Forward: Breaking Barriers

What is education? This is the question that we must begin to embrace. It is necessary to define education as inclusive, as opposed to exclusive. The historical structures (that is the "missionary" approach) and definitions of education which can only create and perpetuate otherness must be completely eradicated. This question encompasses a number of other questions, all equally challenging. What is the function of education? What is legal education? What is good law teaching? How do you appropriately embrace otherness (i.e., minority)[52] issues in law schools? How do you empower a silenced student? How do you reconcile the contradictions between First Nations law and the dominant Canadian legal system?

What we need to discuss is not merely access and equality but also quality. Are we providing meaningful legal educational experiences? This is not to deny that numbers are not an important game. I was the only Aboriginal student in my year at law school (there were several students ahead of me and some came along behind me).[53] As already indicated, recent statistics indicate that the Aboriginal citizen is still drastically under-represented in the legal profession. Largely, the numbers game (or the sheer lack of numbers) intensified the experience of alienation and isolation I felt at law school. The lack of Aboriginal peers while at school was not the only problem. Our under-representation in the legal profession results in a real lack of role models for Aboriginal people. At my law school, or others in Ontario, there were no Aboriginal educators or faculty.[54] Although the large Bay Street firms were frequently requested to come to careers day, few invitations went out to respected First Nations lawyers to visit at the law school. It was an unheard-of idea.

My law school experience was largely an experience of White culture and it remains so even though I am now in a position of authority/power as a law teacher. There exists very little reciprocal experience of my culture, by the institution or other non-Aboriginal students. It was and remains a one-way street. Those times when it was not a one-way street came largely at my (or another *student's*) initiation and insistence. This is not to say that support is not forthcoming from individual faculty members, but largely that the institutions as a total experience were not capable of providing a legal education equal to that of the education provided for individuals who came from the mainstream.[55] My concern is not only for what I lost but for what my colleagues lose as a result of a uni-cultural legal experience. Diversity is a source of inspiration, or should be, for all of us.

Law schools collectively must begin to firmly respond to articles such as the one recently in *Canadian Lawyer* and to the everyday experience of minorities at law school. Law schools must begin to affirm the message that racism will *not* be tolerated in any circumstances or under any conditions. There are a number of ways in which this message can be sent: institutional financial support for "minority" initiatives, including scholarships (rather than continuously using this type of program as a source of outside funding),[56] immediate academic sanctions against students who engage in racist activity and clear policies which set out these sanctions,[57] careful attention to ensure that so-called special programs do not become ghettoized but are seen as central to the law school program (that is, the formal rejection of the "missionary" approach to legal education), administrative action (as opposed to the usual inaction including the apology for racist incidents) which supports the perceptions of "minority" students and professors, the hiring of more "minority" professors and support staff, an ombudsperson, sympathetic faculty which means a faculty educated on issues of racism, inclusive curriculum development, the reassessment of the admission criteria such as the LSAT for *all* students, and the inclusion in the law schools of symbols to which we identify. (No matter how many pictures you hang around the school of White men, it is unlikely I will ever become one or feel comforted by their presence.) This is rather a long (though not complete) list of ideas and suggestions only. Each is worthy of further thought, description and discussion.

Initiatives that address participation and not racism directly are also essential if we are to fully address the challenge before us. Ideas in this category include the establishment of clinical programs. Existing law clinics should embrace the concerns and desires of local Aboriginal communities. This should be happening in a systematic and formalized way. Further clinical programs could be developed to address the over-representation of Aboriginal people in the criminal justice system. The Correctional Law Project at Queens University might be a logical place to begin such an initiative.[58] Issues of self-government from a traditional Aboriginal perspective demand research now and could be incorporated in existing clinical and community programs.[59] Programs in poverty law would also seem to bear a significant relationship to Aboriginal Peoples and the specifics of our experience should be incorporated into these programs.

Graduate studies programs in law need desperately to be developed, and Aboriginal involvement in graduate studies needs to be encouraged. It is only through graduate studies that our under-representation in the literature and within law faculties as professors will be addressed. As funding is now limited by the new Indian and Northern Affairs Canada education guidelines, funding for students is an essential requirement for Aboriginal completion of graduate studies.[60]

These ideas should not been seen as a conclusive list of accomplishments we should strive for. They are the reflections of only one woman. This brings me to another important point. I am only one woman and a Mohawk woman. I do not speak for all Aboriginal Peoples. I do not speak for the men of my nation. As Aboriginal populations are *not* homogeneous (that is, we are not all the same) we cannot address a multiplicity of community challenges with a single answer.

I want to focus on only one of these issues in my several lists of ideas to give an example of how detailed and lengthy such a discussion can become. Some of the problems with curricula demonstrate how the "missionary" approach subtly manifests itself in the law school environment. Property law is the most obvious example and most First Nations law students identify a struggle with this course.[61] The problem is simple. It is the idea that the "Crown owns all the land." This concept is taught as fact. It is not questioned. It is the basic founding principle of European-based property law systems. Yet, it is completely contrary to Aboriginal concepts of land ownership.[62]

Upon describing to me her first year experience at law school, an Aboriginal student described running into this property concept as "running full force into a brick wall." Her response to this experience was to question her suitability at law school. It was not until some time later, a subsequent year at law school, that this student came to understand that the manner in which property law was conceived was a structural obstacle to her attendance at law school. The "missionary" approach to education has been defined as one in which education professionals assume that all students gravitate to the same value base as they do. It assumes there is one history and that one history is the truth. This assumption is not usually conscious. It is the result of experiencing your own education as an "insider." Elsewhere in the literature, this phenomenon is described as the experience of "White privilege."[63]

There are other examples of subject matters, courses and concepts which create impediments to Aboriginal full participation at law school. The concept of *mens rea* in criminal law is one. Intention and guilt are not central concepts in Aboriginal culture. In fact, many Aboriginal languages cannot offer a literal translation of "guilt." The closest one can say, is; "Are you being blamed?" Aboriginal cultures are not built around concepts of punishment and coercion. The maxim, "to punish only the guilty," has little cultural relevance for First Nations.[64] Criminal law courses are *not* currently being taught in such a way that they give expression to this particular form of cultural diversity. Our cultural difference directly affects our drastic over-representation in the criminal justice system. Criminal law can be taught in a way that recognizes and affirms our cultural difference very simply. As there is a relationship or parallel between conceptions of intent in both criminal law and tort law, tort law should also be examined for the same type of cultural bias.

Through my experiences of law schools, both as an Aboriginal student and professor, I have learned that the nature of legal education is exclusionary. Exclusions are found in the composition of classes and the professorate, the subject matter of courses and the courses offered. Exclusions exist in the very structure of the institution. Examining exclusions is a responsibility of all law teachers.

I do not mean to suggest that the responsibility lies only with law teachers and that we should all do something *for* Aboriginal students. Aboriginal students and their non-Aboriginal peers must also closely examine their responsibilities. What I wish to see accomplished is a legal educational environment that facilitates the learning experience of *all* students regardless of our multiple differences and their multiple sources. The learning environment is largely the teacher's, and not the student's, responsibility.

When we work collectively to transform the law school environment, it is not just Aboriginal students who will benefit. We are all enriched by experiencing diversity. We must shed the attitude that we are somehow helping someone who is disadvantaged before we can fully share in this experience. In writing about their experience in the early years of the Saskatchewan program, one law teacher comments:

> I always feel proud at being associated with the program. In the first place the endeavor of introducing native people to the legal profession is clearly worth doing, and in the second place I think the program performs very successfully . . . we succeed in having the students work hard without their becoming resentful; they learn a great amount of first year law without suppressing their values and sense of rectitude; we are able to conduct tough and rigorous classes without the students becoming fearful, anxious or inhibited; we are able to promote solid law school standards without producing destructive competition; we are able to convey the uncertainties and anxieties found in first year law without causing the students to become withdrawn, resigned or defeated; we try to teach law in light of basic concepts in the legal process and subject to wide social criticism without our students demanding certainty and a purging of ambiguity; and, best of all, I believe that the teachers have been able to impose solid intellectual standards without being immobilized by feelings of guilt about the plight of Indians in general, or of our students in particular. The explanation for this type of success is found in large part in the character of our students. They are amazingly perceptive (much more perceptive than the usual first year students) and they seem to recognize the good things the program is doing and in what ways the program might go wrong. They have the degree of self-respect which enables them to accept the ways of the program without becoming changed by the process. All of us who teach law worry from time to time about the seeming personality transformation we cause in our students: the change from intellectual curiosity to intellectual conceit; from gentleness to bravado; from sensitivity to certainty. I don't get the same sense

of affecting the Indian students—they seem to be stronger people. (Carter 1980: 31)

It is this kind of experience that takes me to the conclusion that all our lives are enriched when we are able to embrace and welcome diversity. It is evidence of the incorrectness of the suggestion that existing initiatives in law schools have been "for" Aboriginal Peoples or in some way "helping" us.

The challenge of transforming the law school is not as simple as I have thus far led you to believe. It is not enough to embrace only race and culture. My experience of law school of course was shaped by the fact that I am not just a citizen of an Aboriginal nation. I am also a woman. As previously indicated in the 1986 census data, Aboriginal women are slightly more likely to hold a university degree than are Aboriginal men. This trend is opposite to that of the Canadian population where men are more likely to hold a university degree. However, the data available from the Native Law Center indicate that up until 1985 men were nearly twice as likely to be admitted to the pre-law program.[65] Attracting Aboriginal women to law schools must become an issue of affirmative action which to date has been largely overlooked. Attracting Aboriginal women to law schools brings with it certain unique challenges beyond issues of culture, such as, child care, economic support, role models and part-time education. These are concerns for women students generally and are already documented in the feminist literature.[66] Issues such as child care and economic support are of special importance considering both the recent funding cuts to education made by Indian and Northern Affairs Canada and the knowledge that Aboriginal women are more likely to be single mothers.[67]

The issues of gender and race are complex. I cannot separate one from the other as I experience them both at the same time. This experience of "women of colour consciousness" is a layered experience and the best written description I have found is in Mari Matsudi's work. First you must imagine the experience of a student with women of colour consciousness in a first year law school class. Now, try to imagine this experience:

> The professor sees his job—and I use the male pronoun deliberately— as training the students out of the muddle headed world where everything is relevant and into the lawyer's world where the few critical facts prevail.
>
> The discussion in class today is of a *Miranda*-type case. Our student wonders whether the defendant was a person of color and whether the police officer was White. The student knows the city in which the case arose, and knows that the level of police violence

119

is so high in that place that church groups hold candlelight vigils outside the main police station every Sunday.[68] The crime charged is rape. The student wonders about the race of the victim, and wonders whether the zealous questioning by the police in the case was tied to the victim's race. The student thinks about rape—the rape of her roommate last year, and her own fears. She knows, given the prevalence of violence against women, that some of her classmates in this class of 100 students have been raped. She wonders how they are reacting to the case, what pain it resurrects for them.

In the consciousness of this student, many facts and emotions are relevant to the case that are extraneous to standard legal discourse. The student has decided to adopt standard legal discourse for the classroom, and to keep her women-of-color consciousness for herself. . . . (1989: 7-8)

This student's women of colour experience dictates that she must peel away at the layers of her consciousness like that of an onion. In other circumstances (the example Professor Matsudi puts forward is a class with a White woman professor) she will rest in other layers of her consciousness (that is her gender and not her race or culture). We must recognize and affirm the extra work this student is doing as it is from within her efforts to survive that her outsider consciousness is developing. Many of us have previously described this thinking as crazy or schizophrenic. It is not. It is survival.

This is also similar to the skill that lawyers use to isolate the important facts and issues in case preparation. But the ease with which these students already bifurcate their thinking is not utilized in the teaching of law as an example of how to process legal thought. Professor Waddams in his *Introduction to the Study of Law*, recognizes the importance of this technique:

> The process of picking out the significant facts from the mass of those that are insignificant is one of the lawyers most important skills and the best way to learn to do it is by practice. (1987: 28)

Professor Waddams is speaking of the value easily attached to the case brief method. As Professor Matsudi suggests, women, and especially women of colour, already have significant experiences in isolating issues in our need to create safe places for ourselves. If we were to utilize this experience as a further example of the value of the case brief method to isolate facts and issues, we would accomplish at least three things. We would be teaching in a way that speaks to women's experience. Second, we validate women's experience. And third, the men in the class are exposed to the unique experience of women, thus challenging them to embrace diversity also.[69]

The discussion of women and legal education is much too brief to build conclusions on. Just as further research and discussion must be devoted to the serious concern of Aboriginal Peoples and legal education, research and discussion must also be devoted to the experience of women and legal education. The point I desire to make is simple. These two important and necessary discussions must not occur in total isolation from each other. Not only can valuable lessons be shared across these experiences of "outsider," it must be remembered that my experience as a woman flows through my race and culture. Do not force women of colour to stand on their heads for you. I am not woman first and Mohawk second. If indeed a linear relationship exists it operates in the opposite way. The experience however does not feel like a linear one, but layered like an onion (or perhaps more complexly). To achieve true equality we must resist the desire to simplify matters by creating artificial hierarchies of our "isms" and hierarchies within those experiences.

There is a quotation popular in the Canadian literature on Aboriginal education. It appears frequently and bears repeating in this conclusion. It is the words of Chief Dan George:

> There is a longing among the young of my nation to secure for themselves and their people the skills that will provide them with a sense of purpose and worth. They will be our new warriors, their training will be much longer and more demanding than it was in the olden days. Long years of study will demand determination. Separation from home and family will demand endurance.
>
> But they will emerge with their hand held forward not to receive welfare but to grasp a place in society that is rightly ours. (cited in Carter 1980: 28)

The time that Chief George dreamed of is now here. Do not let his dreams and vision go the way of the dreams of my grandmothers several generations ago.

Notes

1. See for example Barman et al. 1986 and 1987.
2. See for example Adams 1975: 151-162 and Haig-Brown 1988.
3. The census data relies on self-reported "Aboriginal origins" which would include the ability to trace ancestry to either Indian, Inuit or Métis populations. The usual caution on the reliability of self-report data must apply here. Census Canada provides two cautions for the interpretation on the data involving "Aboriginal origins." First, 136 Indian reserves (approximately 45,000 people) were improperly enumerated and were excluded from the data base. Second, the 1986 Census encouraged respondents to mark as many origins as applicable.

Thus, more people identified "Aboriginal origins" in the 1986 data. This should be born in mind when comparisons are made with the 1981 or previous Census data.

4. It is interesting to note that at both high school and university levels Aboriginal women are slightly more likely to be educated than are Aboriginal men. The opposite is true for the Canadian population holding a university degree. Canadian men are more likely to have degrees, even though Canadian women are more likely to complete high school.

5. The definition of Indian is a legal one based on the necessity of identifying the population against which bureaucrats will administer the *Indian Act* regime. This definition is based on blood lines and residency on a reserve. See *Attorney General of Canada* v *Lavell et al.* (1973), 38 D.L.R. (3d) 481 (S.C.C.).

6. Haig-Brown (1988: 46-47) documents the perception of residential school personnel in British Columbia as being based on the belief that the children were "wild" and their efforts were to instill European values into the minds of the children by whatever means possible, including physical violence and emotional deprivation.

7. See, for example, *Indian Act*, R.S.C. 1927, c.98, s.140; *Indian Act*, R.S.C. 1906, c.81, s.149 as amended by S.C. 1941, c.35, s.8.

8. Racism and racist are words which inspire defensive posturing on the part of those who believe they are being accused of this form of immoral behavior. It is clearly not my intention to insult or offend anyone. What must be understood is that racism is not a question of intention but it is an issue of understanding. Judgments are made about people, cultures or traditions which are based on ethnocentric determining criteria. Racism will not be eradicated from legal studies or society in general unless we can talk about it.

   For a further detailed discussion on my definition of racism and feelings surrounding it, see Chapter 2 in this volume.

9. For a discussion of the Aboriginal reaction to this document see Cardinal 1969: 1-17, Waubageshig 1970: 5-40, and Wuttunee 1971: 1-76.

10. The White Paper and education is discussed in Longboat 1987: 24-26.

11. It should be noted that these discussions of control were centralized on issues of children's education and *not* post-secondary education. The nature of the Canadian education system necessitates the consideration of jurisdiction as two separate processes—one for elementary and secondary programs, the other for post-secondary. There are a number of reasons for this. If you cannot successfully educate at the initial level, then it becomes very difficult to access the second stage, specialized university and college programs, although some inroads have been made through specialized access programs. Second, the cost of running a college or university is beyond the imagination of most reserve or settlement communities. The size and isolation of many Aboriginal communities also prohibits the establishment of local colleges and universities. Jurisdictional discussions of a local nature must therefore take on different dimensions for elementary and secondary programs, on the one hand, and, on the other hand, post-secondary programs. As it stands, Aboriginal Peoples must continue to access these specialized or advanced programs away from their home communities.

12. For discussions see Carasco 1986 and Johnson 1983.

13. See for example Sugar and Fox 1989: 465 and Canada 1990.

14. I am fondest of this approach to establishing a principle or fact as it reflects my peoples tradition of oratory and storytelling. That I have placed it last reflects only my tendency to save the best for last.

15. Similar but more extensive comments along the same lines as Mr. Mohawk's talk can be found in Weatherford 1988.

16. I do not find it useful to construct a conflict dichotomy of "White" versus Aboriginal societies and values. By virtue of the fact that we all share the same land mass, we are all thrown into this dilemma together. This is not however to suggest that power and powerlessness are not important variables in the consideration of providing meaningful education. This theme of powerlessness or otherness will emerge again later in this paper.

17. For a discussion of the difficulty with the rights paradigm, see Turpel 1989-90.

18. For a discussion of these concepts as the basis of a right to education see, Nahwegahbow and Johnson 1989.

19. For example, at the University of Saskatchewan, less than 30 percent of Aboriginal students who start a law degree finish that degree. Considering this is the home of the Native Law Centre and the summer program, this is a disturbing statistic. The law school has recently (at the time of editing), struck a committee to investigate this issue.

20. Unfortunately, there have *not* been significant changes within the structure of Canadian law schools since this paper was first published. Some minor changes have occurred with the offering of tutorial programs and increased course offerings in the area of Aboriginal and Treaty law. These changes still require the student to fit into a pre-existing mold rather than transforming the law school to reflect the needs of a diversified student body.

21. The difference in perspective is the difference between being colonized and attempting to become a person who is de-colonized.

22. A copy of this speech is on file with the author.

23. I use this phrase in a very specific way. Aboriginal rights is the study of law, culture, languages, practices and so on, of my people from a tradition that has been developed outside of our culture and ways. This is the case with Aboriginal rights law which has been and continues to be developed solely within the Canadian legal tradition based on the laws that were brought across the ocean by the colonizers and their descendants.

24. This is the teaching of the Two Row Wampum. This wampum is a treaty which was signed with the ancestor nations of the people who now call themselves Canadians and by my people. It is the 44th Wampum in the Great Law of Peace. This wampum can be simplistically described as such: "One Row represented the Whiteman's canoe or government and the other Row represented the Red Man's Canoe or government. These two Canoes or laws must never intermingle or interfere." Further discussions can be found in Yvonne and Jacob Thomas, *The Constitution of the Confederacy by the Peacemaker*, mimeographed volume compiled December 18, 1986 (copy on file with author). This is a valuable source of information concerning the Great Law as it is one of the few sources that has been compiled by a member of the Confederacy.

25. I chose *not* to use the word "our" here quite deliberately. Although education

systems do share some common values across cultures (such as the goal of preparing our children for the future as adults), I do *not* find that the values of an adversarial system of justice and Aboriginal systems of justice share any notable similarities. I am *not* yet certain that these similarities could not exist, just that they are not yet obvious. This is an area of study that requires further insight and research.

26. See Carter 1980, Deloria 1974, MacKinnon and Rhodes 1974, and Purich 1987.

27. For examples of this growing form of scholarship see: Hogg 1985: 551-567, Pentney 1988: 21 and 207, Slattery 1987: 727. The impact of this form of scholarship is apparent in the recent decision rendered May 31, 1990, by the Supreme Court of Canada in *Sparrow* v. *Her Majesty the Queen et al*, [1990] 3 C.N.L.R. 160. The ability to provide a place in Canadian law for the Aboriginal perspective is apparent in the discussion of the *Charter* and collective rights found in the minority judgment in the case of *Dumont* v. *Canada and Manitoba* (1988), 52 Manitoba Reports (2d) 291 (C.A.).

28. Scholars who are attempting to expand this vision include Lyon (1988), McNeil (1989), and Turpel (1989-90).

29. Coates, Robert. In 1994 *Canadian Lawyer* published a more progressive and understanding piece on the issues of Aboriginal legal education (by Bruce Livesey).

30. For a critical discussion of the situation regarding affirmative action admission standards and programs in the United States, see Ramsey 1980: 377.

31. In 1994, similar criticisms of the program (and all affirmative action programs were aired in editorials and articles in the *Financial Post* (Frum) and *The Lawyer's Weekly*. It is unfortunate that the energy of Aboriginal people is forcefully spent defending the few small gains we have made rather than building for our future. This is a troubling and constant re-occurrence. My concerns about this latest round of "criticism" can be read in 14(10) *The Lawyers Weekly* (Friday, December 15, 1994), 8.

32. Ronald G. Haycock (1972: 1) explains: ". . . there generally ranges three basic threads of conception (either singly or in some combination) about the Canadian Indian. The most obvious is a Darwinistic paternalism: the red man is doomed to assimilation by the incursion of Anglo-Saxons because he is unable to survive in competitive evolution. The White, however, is trying his best to make the death struggle of the primitive as soft as possible. The second view is that Indians are noble savages, children of nature who have prowess, cunning and dignity, yet tend to be ignorant and slothful in Anglo-Saxon eyes. The third conception is that the degenerate White has corrupted the Indian, but it is also an Anglo-Saxon virtue to raise the aboriginal to hitherto unprecedented levels of civilization and salvation, fashioned on the White model."

33. For a critique of liberalism as it applies to the context of Aboriginal issues, see Turpel (1989-90).

34. Ironically in the 1994 criticism of the Aboriginal access program, the same imagery was used. I believe this is an attempt to incite the reader.

35. Their letter as printed in the editorial column reads as follows:

> [This article] contains material, concerning fledgling attempts by Canadian law schools to combat racism in the legal profession, which is so twisted

in terms of fact and logic that it cannot go unanswered.

The article accuses Dalhousie and Osgoode Hall law schools of "relax[ing] academic standards" in their admission of minority students and this inappropriate charge colours the tone of the whole article.

The article does note that "most law schools" hold places for mature students whose admission qualifications differ from those of the undergraduate with typical educational profile.

[But the story's author] improperly raises the spectra of the "second-class degree" for minority students.

In fact, the point of the Dalhousie program for Indigenous Blacks and Micmacs is to ensure these students will perform well according to Dalhousie's traditional standards of excellence, while-supporting them in the environment of a legal profession that they have historically found to be indifferent, if not hostile, to their cultures and interests.

In the same issue, you print a commentary by George Jonas ("Back Page"). He suggests that those law schools attempting to provide members of visible minorities with the skills to assist others in their communities to participate in our liberal, pluralistic society are on the slippery slope to Nazism.

In publishing these two pieces, you provide grist for the mills of racism. . . . We are disgusted by it.

> Bruce P. Archibald
> H. Archibald Kaiser
> A. Wayne MacKay
> Mary Ellen Turpel
> Dalhousie Faculty of Law

36. It's time to air another pet peeve. We would not question that capitalization of "English" or "French" when referring to nations. Why is it that Black and Native so often appear without a capital?

37. The answers provided could easily have been shaped by a desire to encourage minority students who have experienced clear educational barriers and therefore have "weaker" academic records to consider applying. Access programs without applicants accomplish little. The tone of the editors implies they have "caught" the admissions office in some kind of untruth without recognizing that other plausible explanations exist for the way the answers were framed. In fact, the majority of people calling the admissions office are students seeking admission.

38. Concern has been raised that the Centre has not focused on nor been supportive of issues of Aboriginal law as Aboriginal Peoples define them.

39. This is evident from reading the list of publications found inside the cover of any volume of the *Canadian Native Law Reporter*.

40. In 1992, 25 Aboriginal people received law degrees. In 1993, 44 Aboriginal students graduated. Thirty-four Aboriginal students graduated last year (1994). In 1995, there are 48 possible graduates.

There are currently 175 program graduates enrolled in Canadian law schools. Of these, 23 are at the University of British Columbia (who no longer require that students attend the summer program). Thirty-four are at the University of Saskatchewan. At the University of Ottawa, 22 program alumni are presently enrolled. No other Canadian common law school has enrolled more than 15 program alumni this year.

41. This letter was in English only.

42. Although the Department of Law at Carleton University was forwarded a letter of inquiry, they did not respond. As they are not a degree-granting law school, I have excluded them from the results of my inquiry. There are three common law schools—Moncton, McGill, and Ottawa—which also offer programs in the French language or which also grant degrees in civil law. Ottawa has both a common law and civil law Dean. Only the common law Dean responded to my letter. McGill and Moncton were the two common law schools which did not respond. All schools which are solely an English language common law school responded to my inquiry.

43. Interestingly enough the Canadian Bar Association study of curricula reveals the same non-response pattern. See Canadian Bar Association 1988: 87-88.

44. The statistics I have do not indicate whether these students participated in the common law or civil law program.

45. One dean indicated that he would be pleased to respond to further specific questions but was having difficulty with the general nature of my request.

46. The reader should remember here the Native Law Centre at the University of Saskatchewan. As this program is of a different nature than the four other programs and given that I have already reviewed the nature of this initiative elsewhere in the paper I have not included further detail here.

47. Tutorial programs are, in my opinion, only a nominal solution to the struggles that many Aboriginal students face. They are not transformative solutions and often times Aboriginal students are criticized by their non-Aboriginal peers who are angry about the "special" treatment they are receiving.

48. Progress in course development remains slow. To provide one example, in January 1995, the University of Western Ontario offered its first seminar in Aboriginal rights after an intensive lobby by one Aboriginal law student (a woman). Her non-Aboriginal peers were critical of and hostile to both her efforts and the promise of the school to offer this course. The courage and wisdom of Bonnie Pelletier (Ojibwe, Fort William First Nation) has been an inspiration to me over the last two years as she has repeatedly challenged the law school she attends.

49. A single course in Aboriginal rights cannot properly prepare an Aboriginal student for a practice of law that is driven by the needs of an Aboriginal community where unique problems exist in areas of land, land claims, mineral rights, water rights, tax, corporations, child welfare and criminal law (to name only some of the obvious).

50. One hundred and eighteen of these are program alumni of the pre-law program at the University of Saskatchewan. In the academic year 1989-90, 91 pre-law alumni were registered at Canadian law schools. There were in the same academic year 30 to 35 First Nations   students registered who did not attend the Saskatoon program.

51. I wish to reiterate my initial caution on the interpretation of these results.

52. I prefer not to speak of minorities. The issue is not just one of numbers, as the gender literature would indicate. There are very real issues of power. For

Aboriginal Peoples, *we are not minorities* and that language hides the fact that we are the original inhabitants of the land. To characterize us as a group with racial minority status, perpetuates a lie which originates in colonialism.

53. For a discussion of my experiences as a law student see Chapter 1.

54. I attended law school at Queen's University in Kingston, Ontario.

55. Within the context of invigorating the intellectual law school environment, please see the suggestions of Mari Matsudi (1988).

56. Deloria (1974: 27) notes that the "greater the proportion of the funds that is provided by the university running the program, as opposed to the proportion drawn from outside sources, the greater the chances of success of the program." Funding is therefore an issue which should be critically assessed by those operating programs and monitored by minority communities who are the primary stake holders in these projects.

57. In 1995, I am still not aware of any Canadian law school that has taken seriously an individual complaint of racism directed at either an Aboriginal student or an Aboriginal professor. As there are a number of legal protections against discrimination (including the *Charter* and a number of human rights codes), I find this amazing. In each of the universities where I have taught, no internal rules protect professors from the racism of some of the students in a similar manner to the protection granted against sexual harassment. Racial harassment is no less ugly. During my tenure at the University of Ottawa an unsuccessful attempt was made to create such a code within the school.

58. Over the past decade, I know of three separate occasions when Aboriginal students requested their assignments in the Correctional Law Project to be Aboriginal focused. All of these requests were flatly refused. In the case of my own refusal, I was told I was welcome to accept additional clients (Aboriginal prisoners) as part of an extra workload. As a result I carried nearly twice as many files as my colleagues during that year.

59. Since the first writing of the article, both the University of British Columbia and the University of Ottawa have established clinical programs.

60. Since the writing of this article, the Department of Justice has cut out the amount of funding for "non-status" and Métis students attending law school. This is an issue of serious concern.

61. In the summer of 1994, the Program of Legal Studies for Native People offered the opportunity for Aboriginal students to receive credit for their summer studies. The materials studied in the summer now focus on property law rather than some combination of criminal law, torts, contracts and property. This accomplishes a number of goals, including the opportunity to hire Aboriginal law professors to teach property in a culturally relevant way. This should relieve some of the cultural distress that some Aboriginal students have felt in the past. It was this progressive development that created the media backlash in both the *Financial Post* and *The Lawyers Weekly* that was referred to earlier.

Some law schools have also made a committed effort to teach Aboriginal title as a significant part of the first year property course. The law school at the University of Ottawa teaches Aboriginal property for a full semester in some of its first year classes and has for the past five years. No other Canadian school can boast of this accomplishment.

62. See, for example Little Bear 1976.
63. See, for example Kline 1989: 122.
64. Detailed reviews of the application of the *Criminal Code of Canada* is provided in Mandamin et al. 1992 and Kaiser 1992.
65. Until 1985, 191 men had been admitted to the program and only 111 women. (See Purich 1987: 102). Statistics from the years 1985 to 1989 indicate that the gender disparity in admissions has been purposely or inadvertently corrected by the Centre.

    Sam Deloria (1974: 17) indicates that the program at the University of New Mexico operated without the need to establish a woman's affirmative action component. Men and women were equally represented.
66. See for example Backhouse (1990), Boyle 1986, McIntyre 1987/88, O'Brien and McIntyre 1986.
67. The 1986 census data analysis does not provide family composition statistics for Aboriginal families. The most current statistics available are drawn from the 1981 census data. Over 20 percent of Aboriginal families are single-parent families which are headed by women 80 percent of the time. Only 10 percent of non-Aboriginal families are single parent, 80 percent of those are headed by women. This percentage of Aboriginal single-parent families increases still further in urban areas (White 1985: 22).
68. Although Professor Matsudi is giving an American example, it is not difficult to borrow from it and bring it into the Canadian context. Reports such as the Marshall Inquiry, or those forthcoming in Manitoba and Alberta, should satisfy regarding the truth of this parallel.
69. For some insight into how men are responding to women's claims please see Feldthusen 1990.

Politics of Oppression

2. Women and Politics

A First Journey in Decolonized Thought: Aboriginal Women and the Application of the Canadian Charter

CHAPTER 7 WAS FIRST PRESENTED IN Whitehorse at Yukon College in March 1991. It was one presentation in a series hosted by the college on "Women and Equality." The purpose of this paper is to provide the reader with an introductory understanding of the right to non-discrimination protected in the Canadian Charter and the degree to which existing legal protection of equality is beneficial to Aboriginal women.

The reason that I was invited here was to speak to you on equality. That is an odd thing for me to be talking about because I do not think in terms of equality. I have not found it to be a relevant or useful concept. Equality is not a word that describes my experience in Canadian society or as an Aboriginal woman. I want to share with you why I have come to that conclusion. I only reached this conclusion after following a long and winding path which often seemed to go uphill only. I intend to retrace my steps on my equality journey for you. For me, equality talk resonates a particular kind of emptiness. I cannot relate to equality because I do not know in my heart what it is. Perhaps one of the reasons I do not know what it is, is because I have been trained in law. Law serves as the place where I began my journey in search for a meaning of equality which reflected my experiences as an Aboriginal woman.

Some people may find that this approach is arrogant, presuming that I can or should be able to find my own image within Canadian laws of equality. No individual is that important. It is not my personal image I seek (after all, I am only one Mohawk woman). What I seek is the image of myself and my sisters, my aunties, my grandmothers, my daughters and my nieces. Individualizing this equality journey as a story about what I have learned also respects the Aboriginal way of teaching about life. I can only talk about what I know and that is only myself.

Law as a discipline is rigidly structured. This structure contributes to maintaining the general inaccessibility of Canadian law. It has a particular set of rules to be followed by anyone searching for answers. Lawyers rely on two principle sources on which we base our knowledge. The first is the general written rules of law, including the constitution, statutes and regulations. The second source is also sometimes written and it is the previous decisions of judges. This is called the case law.[1] There is a clear relationship between these two sources of legal knowledge. The task judges are assigned involves the interpretation of the rules found in the constitution and statutes which are created by the legislatures. Students of law hear repeatedly that the first step toward answering any legal question is to read the statute.

In the case of my equality quest, several legislative instruments are important. All levels of Canadian government (provincial, territorial and federal) have enacted human rights codes. These codes guarantee against individual acts of discrimination.[2] Human rights codes protect against discrimination in the workplace or in housing, for example. Sexual or racial harassment are common examples of matters brought before human rights tribunals. The system of human rights law is intended to work in a complementary fashion with other sources of rights in Canadian law. In 1982, Canada repatriated[3] its constitution. Part of the repatriation package was the Canadian *Charter of Rights and Freedoms*. In section 15, the government of Canada guarantees a broad right to be free from discrimination.[4] Understanding the general structure of Canadian rights law as well as locating the specific *Charter* provision is the first step in my equality journey.

When disputes about equality rights have been brought before them, Canadian courts have examined the provisions found in the *Charter* and in human rights codes. The court's role is an interpretive one. It is often narrowly focused on a word or phrase found in a section of the legal provisions about non-discrimination. Because the work of judges is narrowly cast, what we as lawyers know about equality is also usually understood narrowly. Only by patching together a series of narrow court decisions can a broad definition of equality be found in Canadian law. Searching for a definition of equality in Canadian law is a complicated process involving the examination of many individual cases. This is another factor that contributes to the inaccessibility of Canadian law. Even the physical location of case law contributes to this inaccessibility. Law libraries are located in court houses, law offices and law schools. These places are both inaccessible places and foreign places to the majority of Canadians.

There is also a third layer of legal analysis that legally trained people recognize as important. Judges do not decide principles of law, including equality, in the abstract. The third layer of analysis is the examination of the facts of the particular case before the court.[5] Although lawyers and judges treat the examination of the facts of the case as an *objective* third level of analysis, it is important to remember that those facts are the real life experiences of individuals. This is one of the primary sources of dysfunction and dissatisfaction with the legal profession. Lawyers deal with facts (stories about peoples lives) as objective and neutral (that is, without emotion). This may work successfully in cases about corporations but does not work successfully when the stories are about the pain of discrimination.

The facts that contextualize judges' decisions in equality cases are usually painful and intense experiences of discrimination and this fact presents another complication for legal analysis. As litigation is costly, time consuming, and requires the engagement of experts (which means a certain amount of control over the individual's experience is given up), it can be assumed that usually courts hear only the most serious and offensive transgressions against equality standards. This negatively impacts on the courts' ability to define discrimination. Court cases do not provide detailed descriptions of the way individuals experience discrimination *throughout their lives*. Court cases examine the details of particular incidents only. These factors have a profound effect on how law, lawyers and judges are able to understand equality issues.

Equality issues will be litigated either under the *Charter* or human rights codes. Within the written rules of the law, there exists a hierarchy of sources where lawyers look to find the rules that guide their thinking and the arguments they place before judges. This hierarchy will impact on the decision whether to litigate under a human rights code or under the *Charter*. The constitution of Canada is the supreme law of the land.[6] This means that all statutes must conform to the rules set out in the constitution or they are of no force or effect.[7] For example, if a Canadian law discriminates against a group of individuals this law's validity may be successfully challenged under section 15 of the *Charter of Rights and Freedoms*. The *Charter* is about legal equality more than it is about individual acts of discrimination.

As the constitution is the supreme law of Canada, it is the obvious place to begin sharing my quest for a definition of equality. Perhaps this was not an obvious decision, just an easy decision given my legal education. On the path I followed in search of a meaning for equality this is the second stage I reached. It really has become an uphill climb now. Section 15 has already been introduced as an important recognition of the broad right to live free from discrimination. If you look at the *Charter of Rights and Freedoms,* searching for a home for your equality vision you will likely first rest at section 15.[8] Most women already know section 15 exists. The heading that runs right above section 15 is "Equality Rights." I have reached a peaceful plateau in my journey.

Being a Mohawk woman, I understand something special about equality rights. And I understand that whatever protection exists in section 15 today, it is more than just a few words that are written. Section 15 has a history. When I was younger I got a teaching from the Elders that says you have to know your history. You have to know what is behind you in order to know where you are going. If you do not understand that history, you cannot ever have any vision about where it is you want to go. When you think of the history of the section 15 protection, remember women in this country and the national political women's organizations had to fight, some might suggest tooth and nail, to secure the placement of women's rights within section 15 into the Constitution. It was in and out and back and forth and I think that experience was shocking for a lot of women (see, for example, Baines 1981). I know it shocked me. It must be understood that we live in a country where women's equality rights were not automatic. Equality rights were something that women had to stand up and justify. The fact that section 15 did not grow out of a kind, caring and nurturing relationship is something that is very important to me. Furthermore it did not grow out of respect. Its seeds were planted in a fight. I find that very disturbing.

A quick reading of section 15 identifies that there are four types of legal equality listed. Everyone in Canada has been guaranteed equality *before* the law and equality *under* the law. Also everyone will have equal *protection* of the law and equal *benefit* of the law. That is what section 15 says. This is the legal definition of equality. I suspect that these four forms of equality do not make much common sense. Each of the four parts to the definition of equality have been subject to the scrutiny of Canadian courts. Canada has lived with this style of non-discrimination since 1960 when very similar words were presented in a federal statute.[9] By examining two of the court's decisions under the *Canadian Bill of Rights* (which is the federal forerunner to the *Charter*), the meaning of these four types of equality can be understood.

As an Indian woman I remember very painfully the cases of Jeanette Lavell and Yvonne Bedard. Jeanette Lavell was from a community in Ontario located on Manitoulin Island. Yvonne Bedard is from my community, Six Nations. What happened to these two Indian women, one Ojibwe and one Iroquois, was they married non-status (White) men. That was their so-called offence or crime. I call their marriage a crime because they were punished for it. Both women were stripped of all their rights as Indian people because they were women who "married out."[10] The same thing did not happen to an Indian man who married out. Until 1985, his wife gained Indian status. Former section 12(1)(b) of the *Indian Act* specified that if a status-Indian woman marries a non-status (not non-Indian) man, she loses her entitlement to be registered under the *Indian Act*. Without this entitlement, Canada considers you to be a non-Indian. Many "Indians" by birth are non-Indians at law.[11] These two women took their cases to the Supreme Court of Canada. The judgment of the Supreme Court was reported in 1974 (*A.G. Can* v. *Lavell; Isaac et al* v. *and Bedard*, (1973), 38 D.L.R. (3d) 481). Their struggle before the court started some years before that.

In the case of Jeanette Lavell, her complaint was first heard by Judge Grossberg of the Ontario County Court in June of 1971 ((1971), 22 D.L.R. (3d) 182). The reasoning in this decision was very similar to the reasoning adopted several years latter by the Supreme Court. Judge Grossberg found that Ms. Lavell had equal rights with all other married Canadian women. Such a conclusion is based on a faulty assumption that Indian status is status less than the status of other Canadian women. He saw an elevation in personal status as a result of the disenfranchisement. He saw no cause for complaint. Jeanette Lavell had gained and not lost!

The decision of Judge Grossberg was appealed by Ms. Lavell to the Federal Court of Appeal in the fall of 1971 (188). Heard by three judges, they concluded that different rights existed for Indians based on their gender when a non-status person was married. The judges found this to be a violation of the guarantee of non-discrimination in the *Canadian Bill of Rights*. The Federal Court of Appeal was able to reason through a situation of discrimination that was concurrently based in gender and race. This is encouraging. Unfortunately, the saga continued to the Supreme Court of Canada.

In 1970, after separating from her non-status spouse, Yvonne Bedard returned to Six Nations to reside in a house left to her by her parents. As she was not a registered band member any longer, she was not legally allowed to be in possession of a home on the reserve. Yvonne Bedard was evicted by the band council. This rule about property "ownership" exists to protect Indian lands from White encroachment and originally appeared in the *Indian Act* to protect against the White settlement of Indian lands. The history of the rule applied against Yvonne Bedard is very interesting to me. It reveals a familiar pattern in the oppression of Indian people. Many of the rules developed to protect Indians are now used by Indians against Indians, particularly against Indian women. This is an indication that the colonized have accepted their colonization. As a result of the internalization of colonization, the colonizer can step back from the devastation caused by their acts. In all of the articles which discuss the *Lavell* and *Bedard* cases, little attention is paid to the impact of colonialism on the issue.

The *Lavell* case had already been decided by the Federal Court of Appeal when Ms. Bedard filed her action in the Ontario High Court (*Bedard* v. *Isaac et al.*, (1971), 25 D.L.R. (3d) 551). The decision of the Federal Court was followed in *Bedard* and the matter was easily decided. This is how the two cases were joined and were heard together by the Supreme Court of Canada in 1973. Immediately following the decision of the *Lavell* case in the Federal Court, the federal government announced it would appeal the decision to the Supreme Court of Canada. It is important to understand that it was the federal government that initiated the challenge to the highest court in the country; an appeal that should only be seen as allowing to continue the gender discrimination on the face of the *Indian Act*.

Chief Justice Ritchie gave the majority judgment in that Court. He broke a four-four tie amongst the other judges. And the Supreme Court of Canada held that Jeanette Lavell and Yvonne Bedard had not been discriminated against as Indian women. Ritchie's decision was based on his interpretation of equality before the law. Chief Justice Ritchie writing for the majority of the court states:

> "equality before the law" as recognized by Dicey as a segment of the rule of law, carries the meaning of equal subjection of all classes to the ordinary law of the land as administered by the ordinary courts, and in my opinion the phrase "equality before the law" as employed in s.1(b) of the Bill of Rights is to be treated *as meaning equality in the administration or application of the law* by the law enforcement authorities of the ordinary courts of the land (*A.G. Can* v. *Lavell; Isaac et al* v. *and Bedard*, (1973), 38 D.L.R. (3d) 495.

It was equality under the law (that is in the result) that the two Indian women sought. Unfortunately only equality before the law was guaranteed under the *Bill of Rights*.

I have read this case "megazillions" of times. It still does not make any sense to me. The best I can do at explaining what the Chief Justice said was to direct you to look at who is being discriminated against. Look at all Indians. All Indians are not being discriminated against. The men are not being discriminated against. Therefore, there is no discrimination based on race. Look at women (in the same way Judge Grossbeck did). All women are not being discriminated against because this does not happen to White women. Therefore, there is no gender discrimination. The court could not understand that this pile of discrimination (race) and that pile of discrimination (gender), amount to more than nothing. The court could not understand the idea of double discrimination. Double discrimination is not an acceptable legal category of equality. Grounds of discrimination are listed as separate entities.

This is a central reason why I am dissatisfied with legal definitions of both equality and discrimination. My life experiences are as both a Mohawk and a woman. I cannot say when I can name an act as discrimination, that it happened to me because I am a Mohawk *or* because I am a woman. I cannot take the woman out of the Mohawk or the Mohawk out of the woman. It feels like all one package to me. I exist as a single person. My experience is "discrimination within discrimination" (Kirkness 1987-88: 413). It is wound together through my experiences. This is very different from this idea of double discrimination. But the court could not even get to the first step, they could not see that two grounds of discrimination were occurring at the same time. In the court's view, discrimination is competitive. One form of discrimination must triumph.

The *Lavell* case fundamentally influenced the women's lobby around the entrenchment of women's rights in the *Charter of Rights and Freedoms*, such that both equality before the law and equality under the law are now protected in section 15 of the 1982 rights document. The legal advancement of the position of all women in Canada has been based on the struggle advanced by Indian women for Indian women. The result of the struggle advanced by Indian women is the betterment of the legal position for all women. Indian women, however, walked away with nothing tangible. Indian women still had section 12(1)(b).

The second case that profoundly influenced the women's lobby is similar to the "before/under" problem encountered in the *Lavell* and *Bedard* cases. It did not involve an analysis of race yet the outcome displays the same disturbing thought pattern. In *Bliss* v. *A.G. Can* ([1979]1 S.C.R. 183), a denial of unemployment insurance benefits to a pregnant woman was challenged. The decision of the unemployment insurance was in effect to deny pregnancy benefits because of a short period of employment while also denying "regular" benefits because the woman was pregnant. Like the *Lavell* and *Bedard* cases, *Bliss* involved some special magic—magic that erases obvious understanding. In *Bliss*, the court found that discrimination based on pregnancy was not gender discrimination. The court vanishes the knowledge that only women become pregnant because *not all* women are pregnant. There the Supreme Court of Canada held that the equal protection of law (the second *Canadian Bill of Rights* guarantee) did not extend to benefits of law but only to the imposition of penalties. The result of the *Bliss* case[12] is the knowledge that equal protection of law is insufficient to ensure a just result for women. The *Bliss* case is why benefits were also listed as one of the four types of legal inequality in the *Charter*.

Through the struggles of women such as Lavell, Bedard and Bliss, the four legal equality protections are more comprehensive now than what was found in the *Canadian Bill of Rights*. In section 15, the stepping stone to equality is the guarantee to be free from discrimination. The courts have spoke to the meaning of discrimination in the case of *Andrews* v. *the Law*

Society of British Columbia. This is what Justice MacIntyre says about the word, discrimination:

> The words, without discrimination, require more than *a mere finding of distinction* between the treatment of groups or individuals. Those words are a form of qualifier built into section 15 itself. And limit those distinctions which are forbidden by this section to those which involve prejudice or disadvantage. (*Andrews* v. *Law Society of British Columbia,* [1989] 1 SCR 141 at 145)

What discrimination means then, at law, is more than making a distinction. If you say men are different from women, that is not discrimination. That is a mere distinction. What the law requires for discrimination to exist is some kind of action based on the distinction. There has to be an unequal provision of benefits or some other form of disadvantage.

Section 15 has a particular way of describing the distinctions the court was referring to in *Andrews.* It sets out a list of prohibited grounds; they are sometimes called protected grounds or enumerated grounds. Those are the fancy words that you will hear lawyers tossing around. The list of enumerated grounds provides the distinctions that you are not allowed to make. The list of distinctions that are named are "race, national or ethnic origin, colour, religion, sex, age and mental or physical disability." This list is not complete. The way that section 15 is worded indicates that the grounds that are listed are important examples of common grounds of discrimination but they are not all the grounds that exist. The list of prohibited grounds of discrimination follows the phrase "in particular." It is those two words which give rise to the understanding that section 15 protects against forms of discrimination not itemized on the list. Lawyers call these other forms of discrimination non-enumerated grounds or analogous grounds.

It is as important to look carefully at the grounds of discrimination as it was to carefully consider the four types of legal inequality. The *Andrews* case that I quoted from earlier was a case that was based on citizenship. Citizenship is not on the section 15 list so this is a new ground of discrimination. It was about a man who wanted to be called to the Bar in British Columbia. British Columbia law requires that you must be a Canadian citizen to practice law in that province. Mr. Andrews was not. He was a British subject. In *Andrews*, the Supreme Court of Canada established the test that the courts will follow to determine if an analogous ground exists. Basically, the person complaining must show that whatever the form of discrimination they want to bring into the ambit of the *Charter* (be it sexual orientation or anything else) is comparable to what is already on the list. The courts will ask certain questions. Is it similar to those grounds that are listed? Is the discrimination based on a personal characteristic? In other cases the courts have held province of residency is an acceptable distinction (*Algonquin College* v. *O.P.S.E.U.* (1985), 19 L.A.C. (3d) 81 (Ont. Arb. Bd.). Murderers as a class of individuals are not a ground of discrimination (*R.* v. *Turpin* (1987), 60 C.R. (3d) 63 (Ont. C.A.)). These are not analogous grounds. The reason the court made these determinations is that province of residence or criminal conviction are personal characteristics. I am skeptical about whether or not the court would see status under the Indian Act as a personal characteristic or merely a legal distinction. However, it is not sufficient to show the discrimination is based on a personal characteristic, there is also a need to show some history of disadvantage based on the personal characteristic. Defining legal discrimination becomes a complicated matter.

It will probably be helpful at this point to state what I have thus far described about section 15. Regarding the broad guarantee to freedom from discrimination, the *Charter* establishes two criteria that must be met before any legal discrimination is found to occur. This is despite the broad protection provided by section 15 that every citizen is equal and has the right to be free from discrimination. First, the *Charter* does not protect against all discrimination but only transgressions of law. The *Charter* only guarantees equality before and under the law as well as the equal benefit and protection of law. If the discrimination does not fit within one of these four categories it is not legal discrimination. The next component is the enumerated and the analogous grounds. The broad guarantee of equality will not operate unless the individual complaining can demonstrate both the first (the four types of discrimination) and second elements (the grounds) which create the broad guarantee to equality. This means that the legal definition of discrimination may very well be narrower than the definition of discrimination held by those who survive discrimination. This concludes the discussion on the general legal meaning of section 15.[13]

The next level of analysis is my own personal analysis of the *Charter*. This is the third stage in this journey. It is the discussion that is most important in this journey and depends on what has already been discussed about section 15. It focuses on the list of enumerated grounds. The list is the place where I hope I can locate my own experience of discrimination as both an Aboriginal and a woman. When I read through the list of named grounds I see that several might apply to my experience. I see race on the list. I think I am a different race. I know I am different! My skin is a little browner than most people but who I am as a Mohawk woman does not stop at the end of this little brown nose. It is about who I am inside. Race does not capture the totality of the difference I live.

Colour is the next item on the list. Colour does not fully describe my experience as an Aboriginal person either. My concerns about the concept, colour, are similar to the ones I expressed about race. Both of these grounds are based on biological inference. But, my difference is really about who I am inside and not my genetic composition. It is about what I believe and why. My difference is really about culture. Culture is not on the list. This discovery is not a surprise to me. It is not on the list because the drafter(s) of the section were probably White and male and have no experience of surviving discrimination. It is not well understood that race and colour are incomplete and sometimes inaccurate categories.

National or ethnic origin is also equally incomplete and incapable of describing my experience. My experience is not just about origins and heritage although this is a part of it. This ground troubles me for a second reason. This is again the trouble about who has the power to do the defining. If you think about it, the meaning of national or ethnic origin, relies on the myth that Canada began in 1867 with the conquest by several European nations. It is belonging to one of these European nationalities that grounds this phrase. European (and time adds ancestors of Europeans born and raised in Canada to that list) is the norm. Others who come from a non-European heritage have different origins. This is a negative construction of difference. Yet, because European conquest resulting in confederation in 1867 is the time reference, then Aboriginal experience of this country thousands of years before conquest is vanished fully. In this category, Aboriginal heritage is non-existent. It is rare that Aboriginal experience is described as Aboriginal heritage or origin, which further demonstrates my point.

The next item on the *Charter* list is that little box called religion. This little box is conceptually different from the little boxes for race and colour that address only my biological differences. My people are a spiritual people. Maybe I can fit this concept of spirituality into religion. That does not work well either. Religion is more about institutionalized forms of worship. The way I was taught about respecting the Creator, I have to do every minute of every day. It is a total way of life. It is about how to walk through this world. I cannot separate "religion" from any other way of experiencing life. This probably returns to a discussion on culture. I know that I cannot fit what I experience as sacred (spirituality) into the four corners of the little box called religion.

I want to provide one example of the way in which I find religion and race or colour to be unacceptable and incomplete. I am a Mohawk woman. That is the way the Creator chose to make me. That is who I am, that is the way I walk. I am a traditional woman, and I try and live in respect of the laws that the Creator gave to the Haudenosaunee people when she put us here. And I use she on purpose when referring to the Creator and it is not just because I am standing in front of a group of women. I use she because when you make a lot of translations from Indian to English, it is very difficult. I do not speak, unfortunately, Mohawk fluently but our word for Creator is a word without gender. It is both male and female. When you have a respect for creation, you have a respect for both male and female energies. When you translate that into the English word and you get he, you are tipping creation to one side. Creation cannot be talked about out of balance all the time. I am trying to throw a little energy the other way. Whenever I refer to the Creator, I use she.[14] This teaching about creation is an example of the way that the fragmentation in law (lists and boxes) creates an experience of law that is away from both the way I have been taught and have experienced life.

The last ground of discrimination listed in the *Charter* that I might identify with is sex. I am a woman and obviously my experience can fit in here. Then I think of the *Lavell* and *Bedard* cases; how far am I going to get bringing a claim as a Mohawk woman under that box of sex? The way the list is constructed forces me to focus a complaint on gender to the exclusion of or prioritized over race, colour or national and ethnic origin or religion. In effect such a construction of my experience turns me upside down. I have a hard enough time walking on my feet without tripping over anything, without having to do life all upside down.

It is not just the *Lavell* and *Bedard* cases that have discouraged me about the way the courts interpret gender complaints.[15] Early litigation under the *Charter* indicates that Canadian courts have continued to have difficulty defining issues of discrimination within discrimination. In *Casagrande* v. *Hinton Roman Catholic Separate School District* ([1987] 4 W.W.R. 167 (Alta. Q.B.) an unmarried, pregnant school teacher challenged her dismissal. The court rejected her sex discrimination complaint as the "no intercourse" rule was equally applied to men and women (179). The courts finding fails to consider the fact that only women are likely to be detected for breaching this rule. The court also decided that the section 15 equality rights were over-ridden by section 29. Section 29 guarantees that nothing shall abrogate or derogate from any rights or privileges "in respect of denominational, separate or dissentient schools." This case as it involves multiple forms of discrimination (competing forms) is an indication that courts are still sometimes unsuccessful at this form of analysis.[16]

There is no single prohibited ground that captures my experience of life. I am forced to artificially separate my race (more appropriately my culture) from my gender. All of the categories within section 15 do not capture my experience. I have to twist and turn my understanding of the words to make my experience fit. This feels very much like one of the ways I experience discrimination—someone else does the defining, presuming I fit. I am left with the contortions. I am not very happy with section 15. Section 15 feels very much like the same old thing that did not work for me in the past.

Now I do not want to be interpreted as saying I prefer as a woman to totally discard section 15. As a woman, I would rather have some limited protection in section 15 than a total void. Perhaps legal complaints will not be successful but section 15 still establishes a general principle that Canada is a country now based on non-discrimination. But I do not want us resting around on our laurels, thinking our work is done. We have made the first step and it is a small baby step, just like a child learning how to walk. Maybe we are not even that far. We have just gone a little way and our work is not done. We have to put what we understand now, some thirteen years after the entrenchment of 1982 into the law and the interpretation of the constitution.

This brings us to stage four in our journey. Section 15 must also be understood from within that *Charter of Rights and Freedoms*. There are a number of other things that trouble me greatly about that *Charter*. When it first came out in 1982, Canada was celebrating about this wonderful new document and about the rights we had. When I went into Indian communities, people were excited about these rights. I did not understand the excitement. I was interested in law (but had not yet gone to law school) and had tried to understand on my own what the *Charter* meant. Read section 1. Any rights that have been demonstrated can be *limited* by section 1 when the government can show such a limitation is reasonable and justified in a free and democratic society. The legal process is not complete when one has successfully met the standard in section 15 (discrimination against a prohibited ground). If you have a government action that discriminates on its face against women or against Indian women, if they find under section 1 that it is a reasonable limit on the right, in a free and democratic society, the right can be limited. Well in my way of thinking about rights, rights are not something that you put on a plate and you are going to do a magic trick and take away with the other hand. A right is a right. You have it. You carry it with you. It is not something that can be taken away. What the *Charter* does is it takes away everything it is going to give before it even gives it! Section one comes first. That is a lesson for me in how much I will trust this new rights paradigm.

My position on the disappearing rights approach to issues of non-discrimination is a contentious one. Not everyone shares my opinion on section 1. I suspect some will find it harsh. My opinion is a result of my experience of Canadian law (and probably the result of my status as colonized). It is based on a knowledge of the *Lavell* and *Bedard* cases. It is based on the knowledge of Aboriginal over-representation in the criminal justice system. It is based on the knowledge that our ceremonies and dances were once prohibited by Canadian law. It is based on my understanding of the history of Canada and Canadian laws which is a history that has taught me not to trust easily.

Other scholars have managed to overlook the shortcomings in the *Charter* and have the ability to trust. Writing about both the *Charter of*

Rights and Freedoms and the recognition and affirmation of existing Aboriginal and treaty rights in section 35(1)—the first section directly following the *Charter*—Donna Greschner has this to say:

> The interpretation of aboriginal rights that I use in considering aboriginal women and the Constitution—that the rights are a promise of constitutional space for aboriginal peoples to be aboriginal—is the one that best exemplifies the *spirit* of the provisions, the one most consonant with their underlying purpose and harmonious with the Constitution as a whole. The method is not radical or revolutionary, although its results will be: namely, taking aboriginal peoples seriously. (1992: 342-43)

Part of this scholar's ability to trust in Canadian law is the fact that Canadian law is an experience of her own culture and not the experience of a foreign way of establishing relationship. Professor Greschner recognizes the fact that being a non-Aboriginal constitutional scholar impacts on her analysis. This is encouraging for me to see.[17]

Continuing with contextualizaton of section 15 as just one section of the *Charter*, there is also section 32 (as if section 1 was not enough). Section 32 talks about government.[18] The *Charter* is not an absolute document of rights. If someone discriminates against me because I am an Indian woman, and that someone is a private landlord and not the government, I cannot bring an action against the landlord under the *Charter*. (An action could possibly be brought under one of the human rights codes.) What the *Charter* does, is that it only protects those rights that are given to you against intrusion by the government. The courts describe the *Charter* as a fence around individuals where the government cannot trod. That is it.

It is section 32 that really causes me to be ambivalent about the possibility of securing gain for Aboriginal women through the application of the *Charter*. As an Indian woman centrally concerned about issues of abuse in Aboriginal communities, I understand that the *Charter* cannot be fully effective as a tool in reaching this goal. First, it took international action after the *Lavell* and *Bedard* cases[19] *and* the passing of the *Charter* to get the federal government to take seriously the overt discrimination against Indian women in the *Indian Act*. If overt discrimination required such heavy sanction to remedy what about some of the more subtle discrimination Indian women face such as the fact there are no matrimonial law regimes on reserve.[20] Second, abuse in Aboriginal communities— domestic violence to sexual abuse—does not fall within the scope of the *Charter*. It is not Indian governments that inflict this specific harm directly, but certain individuals in Aboriginal communities.[21]

We are not done examining the *Charter* yet. Read section 33. This is one of my favourites. It is the notwithstanding clause. If the government of the Yukon or maybe the province of Ontario decides to pass a law that knowingly will discriminate against somebody, all that has to be done is to state that this legislation is exempt from section 15 of the *Charter*. The federal government could choose to exempt the *Indian Act* from *Charter* review in a similar way that section 67 of the *Canadian Human Rights Act* exempts the *Indian Act* from those provisions. My ability to trust in and access *Charter* rights from this day forward is compromised by section 33. The supreme law of this land does not apply anymore. Section 33 is probably the biggest trap door I have ever seen in my life.[22]

We are still not done examining the *Charter*. Read the preamble. This is another one of my favourites. The preamble talks about the rule of law and the supremacy of God (probably "he" only). The rule of law causes me more concern than the second phrase. Both of these principles give stature to a particular view of the world. A view which is contradictory to the cultural beliefs of many Aboriginal people. It is important to consider the impact of these two principles. The most difficult to understand is the rule of law.

The rule of law means that both kings and beggars cannot sleep under bridges and cannot steal bread. Think about that for a second and see if you notice any contradictions; kings and beggars. Where are the queens? This is an example of how male specific Canadian law is (and note how invisible the male preference is). Think about it some more. How many kings and queens do you know that need to steal bread and sleep under bridges? I do not know very many. Really it was a rule about how beggars would behave. It is, therefore, a rule which in effect has little impact on kings (and queens). It is a rule about entrenching inequality! That must be seen as troubling. The preamble to the document that creates equality as the supreme law of Canada begins with a principle that entrenches inequality. This is another reason I have great disdain for the *Charter*. It is dishonest. Which Charter statement on equality will be honoured by the courts? Both equality and inequality are options that are available.

The rule of law also stands for the principle that there shall be a uniform application of all laws. This is also apparent in the kings and beggars example. And as in that example, uniform application of law cannot be said to ensure equality. Furthermore, the principle of uniform application of laws is not absolutely applied in Canada. If I were to assert (and I do) that the law of treaties were to be uniformly applied, Canada would shy away from this application of the rule of law. But if I engage in an act of civil disobedience to protect a treaty right, I can be sure that the criminal laws of Canada will be applied uniformly to me. The lack of implementation of treaty rights has been a central focus of Aboriginal litigation and this again demonstrates that the rule about uniformity has always been selectively applied in Canada.

There is one thing in the *Charter* that I find pleasing. That is section 25.[23] Section 25 is a shield (again that is lawyer talk). It says that if a dispute arises between a *Charter* right and Aboriginal and treaty rights then section 25 clearly resolves the dispute in favour of Aboriginal and treaty rights in a similar way that section 29 operated in the *Casagrande* case discussed earlier. Aboriginal Peoples have a notwithstanding clause in the *Charter*. The *Charter* creates a hierarchy of rights in which individual rights compete for superior status. I am powerless to change the fact that this hierarchy exists in Canadian laws of non-discrimination. I must be satisfied with the knowledge that the affect of section 25 should be to ensure that the many rights of Aboriginal Peoples have a superior position within that hierarchy.

Now we can walk away from that document, the *Charter of Rights and Freedoms*, because I think you probably understand now that at least one person does not believe it is the delightful little legal gadget that many people originally thought that it was. It is a total field day for lawyers but I am not sure of what it offers to the average Canadian or the average Aboriginal person. After looking in detail at the *Charter*, I came to a fairly simple conclusion. I am not going to find the answer there. At least I am not going to find a full answer to the problems Aboriginal people face nor am I going to find a vision of equality that reflects my experience as an Aboriginal woman. I can find maybe a few places to have a glimmer of hope. There are a few places where I can locate a partial image of myself (parallel to gazing in a fun house mirror). Enough to keep me saying, yes, I can work as a law professor and I can work at that law stuff as long as you give me that glimmer of hope. But we have a very, very long way to go.

Since the entrenchment of the *Charter*, there has been continued discussion about its value in a number of communities. This has continued to amaze me. The question of *Charter* application has created great divisions in the Aboriginal community, not necessarily along gender lines. I am amazed by the *Charter* application question because I have yet to see any clear and detailed arguments presented about how the *Charter* will benefit Aboriginal women. I hear lots of empty political rhetoric about how important the *Charter* is and the need to protect Aboriginal women from abuse. I have neither heard nor read any concrete examples of how we will be protected by the *Charter*. On the other hand, I have seen some clearly articulated concerns about the negative consequences of *Charter* application.

The majority of arguments that are made regarding the necessity of *Charter* application are emotional pleas. These rhetorical demands are prefaced on a single fact—Aboriginal women have been victims of abuse. There is no denying this fact. The Native Women's Association of Canada describes their demand for *Charter* protection in just this way:

> Since the release of the Canada package on the constitution, national Chief, Ovide Mercredi, has taken the position that the *Charter* ought not to apply to Native governments. . . . Experience has shown Native women what life is like without human rights protection. Native women lived under the sex discriminatory sections of the *Indian Act* for 100 years! The twenty year battle by Native women for the repeal of those sections was not without a price, but women have shown that they are willing to fight for their rights against the federal government and against Indian governments. (Letter to the Right Honourable Joseph Clark from Gail Stacey-Moore, Speaker, Native Women's Association of Canada, 1986)

What must follow such a line of reasoning is an accounting of the specific benefits that will accrue to Aboriginal women as a result of the *Charter* protections. Until the sound legal reasons about positive results from the application of the *Charter* are more than mere exceptions[25] then I will remain skeptical. I cannot imagine the way I would use the *Charter* to advantage Aboriginal women's rights.

Equally disturbing is the way in which the Native Women's Association of Canada (and at least two of their members are legally educated) passage reflects a fundamental misinterpretation of the role and scope of the *Charter*. The *Charter* is not human rights law. It cannot protect Aboriginal women from individual acts of abuse. The position of the Native Women's Association of Canada during the Charlottetown Round troubles me for a number of reasons. It cannot be said that Indian governments are responsible for the discrimination within the *Indian Act*. The discrimination against Indian women was the result solely of the actions of the federal government. The problem of gender discrimination in the *Indian Act* is a problem of colonialism. I see no expression or denial of colonialism in the *Charter*.

All of this is not to say that I fully disagree with the position of the Native Women's Association of Canada. In fact, I understand the source of their position and respect the heart-felt emotion of their response. Indian women through the *Indian Act* have been abused, because discrimination is a form of violence and violence is clearly abuse. As an individual, I have not suffered the pain of disenfranchisement. It still must be remembered that the author of the abuse was not Indian men but the federal government. For many years, band governments have been institutions whose offices have been occupied by men (in the same way that provincial and federal governments have). Many of the band governments have followed the lead of the federal government and have joined in the abuse of Indian women.[26] Indian governments have never had the power to amend section 12(1)(b) of the *Indian Act*. That is a power of the federal government only. Powerlessness and frustration is not a healthy state of existence. It is also a consequence of colonialism and colonization. As women involved in the healing of our nations we must remember this reflects the political way of the dominant society. I am yet to be convinced that any form of traditional Aboriginal government was *ever* based on a notion of gender inequality. We must take care to think with decolonized minds no matter how difficult the task may be.

I am also worried about the way that concerns such as those of the Native Women's Association of Canada can be manipulated within the larger Canadian political sphere. These arguments take on a purpose that Aboriginal women never intended:

> Concern for aboriginal women is piously invoked by closet opponents of aboriginal self-determination who reject the idea and practice of aboriginal sovereignty and use a new-found solidarity with women as an expedient and politically correct justification for their resistance. This belief in an inherent or irremediable chauvinism of Aboriginal men, worse than the chauvinism of non-Aboriginal men, must be shown for what it is: false, pernicious and racist. (Greschner 1992: 339).

Issues surrounding the politics of self-determination are very complicated. There are complications that arise within our relationships with the dominant political structure of Canada as well as within our own communities. When these sets of complications collide, confusion and struggle can be the only result.

The result of any abusive relationship, be it personal or political, is anger. I am not denying anyone's right to be angry. What has been done to Indian women is something to be angry about. I would in fact encourage the anger. Anger must be let before Aboriginal people can heal. Anger is a stage we must move beyond if we will ever again think as nations in a decolonized way. Remembering that anger is the reality of many Aboriginal women's experience, we must ask the men to respect our anger and work with us through it. We must collectively and individually move beyond this point if true progress toward self-government is to be made.

The anger that I carry as an Indian woman does not grow only in the abuse that women of First Nations have survived and continue to survive on a daily basis. The anger also grows from what I have learned about Canadian law. Canadian law is not my Aboriginal solution for many reasons. Discrimination in meaning or action in Canadian law does not reflect my experiences. I cannot be certain that a Canadian court will be able to successfully conceptualize a situation of discrimination within discrimination.

As an Indian woman, I am connected to the history of section 15 in a very profound way. The *Canadian Bill of Rights* was first passed in 1960. This is 1995. It has only been for thirty-five years in Canada that we have protected equality in the federal system of laws. It was the process of the civilization of our communities, largely through the *Indian Act*, forcing our people to a patriarchal style of government, where we women lost our status as well as the right to vote (until 1960 federally). It was only after contact with the European ways that women in my community were denied the federal franchise. Not only did women lose the vote in my community, but until 1960, if you were a status Indian, period, male or female, you could not vote. And I have asked myself many times, how I am supposed to recognize that as an advanced, progressive, democratic or equality seeking society? The federal government has thirty-five years of experience of aspiring toward equality. My people have hundreds and hundreds and hundreds of years of experience of successfully living in balance (you might call it equality).

I was so empty when I came to those understandings about Canadian law. And I had to think some more. And I had to think some more about what was the matter with the law and why Canadian law is not working for Aboriginal Peoples. It is simple why it is not working. It is because we have taken the *responsibility* out of it. Even more importantly, read some court judgments and hear them talk about impartiality and objectivity. It is not about your head. Where the answer lives is in your heart. Law is not about how you feel. And where is fairness? What is fairness? Fairness requires feeling. When you see something and it is unfair you get angry. It is in your heart, the standard of fairness. If fairness is in your heart and the law is not about feeling, then how are we going to get to fairness? How are we going to get to justice? Ask yourself who wrote down that law. It was men who wrote down that law. They took women out of it. Our responsibility as the women of this land is to see that they put the heart back in the law so that it starts to work for all of us. Then our relationship can start to be about fairness—about justice. And that is the legacy that I pray that we leave for our children, no matter what colour they are.

Notes

1. The decisions of judges are not all reported. There are a number of journals which report these cases and usually they have prominent lawyers and law professors who do the editing. Usually these editors are White and male. What they select as important does not also reflect a diversified view of the world. For example, many cases involving First Nations child welfare matters have not been chosen to be in these journals. Historically, there are few if any reported cases of *Indian Act* offences such as convictions for dancing or attending other ceremonies. The reporting of cases is one way which law does not reflect an Aboriginal view on what is important.

2. I am not satisfied with these definitions of discrimination. They do not fully capture what my experience has been. This discussion is complimented by the discussion in Chapter two.

3. The acquisition of full sovereignty for Canada was incomplete between the years of 1867 and 1982. For example, Canada could not independently (without Britain's approval) amend it is constitution prior to the 1982 repatriation.

4. Section 15 reads as follows:

   (1) Every individual is equal before and under the law and has the right to the equal protection and equal benefit of the law without discrimination and, in particular, without discrimination based on race, national or ethnic origin, colour, religion, sex, age or mental or physical disability.

   (2) Subsection (1) does not preclude any law, program or activity that has as its object the amelioration of conditions of disadvantaged individuals or groups including those that are disadvantaged because of race, national or ethnic origin, colour, religion, sex, age or mental or physical disability.

5. There are a multitude of legal rules which help lawyers determine which are the relevant facts.

6. The constitution has been the supreme law of Canada since the 1982 amendments. Section 52(1) reads:

   The Constitution of Canada is the supreme law of Canada, and any law that is inconsistent with the provisions of the Constitution is, to the extent of the inconsistency, of no force or effect.

   Prior to 1982, Canada was governed by the principle of parliamentary supremacy. That meant that any action of the Parliament was the supreme law. In 1982, the way Canada is governed was significantly changed. The Canadian system of government is now based on constitutional supremacy in addition to parliamentary supremacy.

7. This is just one task that is assigned to the constitution. The constitution also provides for the structure of Canadian government. In sections 91 and 92 powers to legislate are assigned to either the federal or provincial governments. If the authority to legislate cannot be found in section 91, then the federal government has no authority to act and laws enacted without legal authority are not valid. The impact of these sections on Aboriginal women are more fully discussed in Chapter six.

8. Section 28 of the *Charter* provides that all rights and freedoms are "guaranteed equally to male and female persons." This is an important section for women, but offers no certain assistance to women who also locate themselves centrally within other oppressed collectivities, such as Aboriginal people. Section 28, therefore, is not focused on in this discussion.

9. Section 1 of the *Canadian Bill of Rights* states:

   It is hereby recognized and declared that in Canada there have existed and shall continue to exist without discrimination by reason of race, national origin, colour, religion or sex, the following human rights and fundamental freedoms, namely,

   (a) the right of the individual to life, liberty, security of the person and enjoyment of property, and the right not to be deprived thereof except by due process of law;

    (b) the right of the individual to equality before the law and the protection of the law;

    (c) freedom of religion;

    (d) freedom of speech;

    (e) freedom of assembly and association; and

    (f) freedom of the press.

10. For a fuller discussion of the ramifications of the *Indian Act*, please see Jamieson 1978: 1-6.

11. What the *Indian Act* effectively did is disenfranchise a lot of our people and I will give you an important example of that. Before you are considered an Indian in this country, you have to get into these specific little boxes which are articulated by the federal government in the *Indian Act*. These two women were in those boxes. They married out. They married non-Indians, non-status people, and thereby lost their status. So the minute Lavell and Bedard said, "I do"— presto, like magic, they were not Indians anymore.

    I said I would give you an example about how extreme the question of registration becomes. One of the Mohawk communities that I am familiar with is Akwesasne. You may have heard about it because it was in the news a lot during the spring of 1990 because of the struggles they had regarding gambling. That community straddles an international border. If I lived on the Canadian side of Akwesasne, and I am marrying a man who lives three houses down, but he happens to live on the American side of Akwesasne, under that old *Indian Act* law, I am no longer an Indian. I would have married somebody from my community, a Mohawk man, but he is an American Indian so he does not have status under the *Indian Act*. The *Indian Act* only counts Canadian Indians. The *Indian Act* has caused turmoil in our relations in our communities and this is just one example. I could rant about the *Indian Act* all day (but will resist).

12. In 1989, even the Supreme Court of Canada had come to terms with the mistake in *Bliss*. See also *Brooks* v. *Canada Safeway Limited* (1985), 38 Man.R. (2d) 192 (Man Q.B.).

13. The discussion of the meaning of section 15 of the *Charter* is clearly not a full discussion of the scope, meaning and purpose of section 15. In 1989, the Canadian Advisory Council on the Status of Women released an analysis of 591 reported and unreported decisions based on section 15. This study considered decisions made within the first three years of litigation under section 15 (1985–1988) (Brodsky and Day 1989). Consider the vastness of the body of law the *Charter* has spawned if one section alone has initiated this many cases!

14. This is a teaching provided to me by Dr. Art Solomon, Ojibwe Nation. Art has written down many of his ideas, 1990 and 1994.

15. The Native Women's Association of Canada challenged their exclusion from the constitutional process known as the Charlottetown Round. This litigation also discourages me for a series of complicated reasons. These reasons are complex enough to require a separate article and I have left this topic alone on the list of many things I may write about.

16. I am not suggesting that some courts have not gotten it right. As long as one court gets it wrong, it is a problem. See also the discussion in Brodsky and Day 1989: 52-53.

17. In her own words:

   As a non-aboriginal constitutional lawyer, I approach the topic of this paper—aboriginal women, the Constitution and the criminal justice system—aware of the limits of my cultural experience and the necessity of intense and detailed sensitivity to aboriginal peoples. My cultural experience as a non-aboriginal person precludes direct and intimate understanding of aboriginal cultures and gender traditions. I have also been spared the devastating experience of racism that injures aboriginal peoples daily and deeply. My responsibility is to understand aboriginal peoples as best I can, recognizing and attempting to overcome my cultural biases and accepting aboriginal understandings without misinterpretation or patronization. I may not fully succeed, but if I fail to try, I will not be showing the respect for aboriginal peoples that must underlie and permeate this study of the criminal justice system. (339)

18. Section 32 reads:

   (1) This Charter applies
   (a) to the Parliament and government of Canada in respect of all matters within the authority of Parliament including all matters relating to the Yukon Territory and Northwest Territories; and
   (b) to the legislature and government of each province in respect of all matters within the authority of the legislature of each province.
   (2) Notwithstanding subsection (1), section 15 shall not have effect until three years after this section comes into force.

19. *Lovelace* v. *Canada.* U.N. Dox. CCPR/C/Dr (XII)/R.6/24, 31 July 1981; 2 *Human Rights Law Journal*, 158.

20. For a discussion of this topic please refer to Montour 1987 and Turpel 1991b.

21. Indian governments have participated in silencing this issue. The act of silencing *as a government* could be a possible *Charter* challenge but it would be a very difficult one. Legal remedies usually direct that an action be stopped rather than directing any government to do something positive about abuse.

22. Now in fairness to section 33, there would be severe political consequence to the inappropriate use of section 33.

23. Section 25 reads:

   The guarantee in this Charter of certain rights and freedoms shall not be construed so as to abrogate or derogate from any aboriginal, treaty or other rights or freedoms that pertain to the aboriginal peoples of Canada including
   (a) any rights or freedoms that have been recognized by the Royal Proclamation of October 7, 1763; and
   (b) any rights or freedoms that now exist by way of land claims agreements or may be so acquired.

25. *R.* v. *Daniels*, [1990] 4 *Canadian Native Law Reporter* 51 (Sask. Q.B.). This decision was overturned by the Saskatchewan Court of Appeal.

26. For a discussion see Silman 1987.

Constitutional Renovation: New Relations or Continued Colonial Patterns?

CHAPTER 8 WAS ORIGINALLY PUBLISHED under the title, "Seeking My Reflection: A Comment on Constitutional Renovation," in Conversations Among Friends: Proceedings of an Interdisciplinary Conference on Women and Constitutional Reform, *edited by David Schneiderman. (Edmonton: Centre for Constitutional Studies, 1992).*

I was asked to this conference to speak about Aboriginal women and the Canadian constitution. Such a venture always make me nervous. I speak only for myself as a Mohawk woman, one woman. There are many Aboriginal women with a multiplicity of views. My views are often in opposition to the views held by political organizations of Aboriginal women. This is a difficult place to negotiate. I also recognize that my legal education is a privilege, and this education plays a central role in shaping my views on constitutional amendment. I do, however, have a purpose in sharing this paper in this collection. My legal education is a privilege but the understanding that it brings about Canadian laws is a skill that needs to be shared in Aboriginal communities. Canadians also need to begin to understand how and why their laws have not been the solution for Aboriginal Peoples—but are a very real part of the problem. Canadian laws are a central source of the oppression Aboriginal Peoples continue to survive.

There exists a fundamental contradiction in the way I experience law. This contradiction has many sides and many angles. Examining the constitution of Canada exposes one face of the contradiction. Others seem to have a regard for the constitution as the supreme law of the land and accept that it is a good place to begin a discussion on the inclusion of Aboriginal Peoples within Canadian state relations. This constitutional conversation usually proceeds along a path that assumes we all share a single definition of law. Much of my work has involved explaining how this single shared definition of law is really a myth. Many Aboriginal Peoples do not share the Canadian view.

When I first presented this talk at the Edmonton conference, I attempted to dispel this myth about the universality of law. After my presentation, a Métis woman brought me a gift, a collection of Elder's stories. I sat in the hallway and read this book for awhile, rather than returning to the conference room immediately. I was still unsettled and not entirely happy with my conference presentation. I had gone on and on and on during my conference presentation about Aboriginal women and the constitution, constructing what I hoped to be a compelling argument to equitably remedy Canada's historic constitutional failure(s). I argued that we must set aside current political choices such as federalism and parliamentary sovereignty and instead determine what Aboriginal Peoples' visions are. What I had done in forty five minutes, Rolling Thunder expressed in a few words. Rolling Thunder captured the essence of the contradiction, and I had only been able to talk all around it. Rolling Thunder said:

> To bring about the healing of an individual or nation depends on respect for all things that have life including the rocks, the mountains and the waters. We should show our respect for all things and all people. And we should respect the differences. We call on the animals, the four-leggeds, the two-leggeds, the lightning, the thunder, the wind, the eagle—we call on all these spirits in order to attain these healing powers. (Garnier 1990: 64)

The contradiction is about the unspoken constitutional aspirations and dreams of both Aboriginal Peoples and this country. Aboriginal people seek healing and health. Aboriginal people seek a return to balance in our relationships. This is, perhaps, a new expectation for Canadian law. This chapter examines the process I followed to come to understand the constitutional dilemma Canada continues to try to resolve.

I quite like the phrase "constitutional renovation," but have forgotten whose words I am borrowing. First, I am attracted to the phrase because it does not commit us to the notion of merely amending Canada's constitution. I am not concerned (yet) with the structural process of amendment[1] or what form it would take, because I do not believe that we are properly prepared for the process of renovation. I think we require fundamental change to both the constitution as a document and also to the principles which ground Canadian constitutional law. It is only in this way that Aboriginal Peoples will be able to choose to confederate (or not) with the rest of Canada.

Second, I like the phrase because what we usually renovate are houses—and consider here what makes a house a home. Homes are safe places. Creating a place for each individual should be the fundamental nature of a constitution. But it is not enough to create a place. We must create a place that is safe—a place which respects the fundamental worth of each individual, both man and woman, a place where every individual has the opportunity to be who they are and to become all that they can be. What is important to consider in this context is who exists in the family of Canada's constitution and who does not? The more important question arises when we honestly confront the obvious constitutional exclusions—how do we make the constitution a home for all?

It is not difficult to determine who has been excluded from full participation in the constitution of this country. Clearly, Aboriginal Peoples and women have both been excluded. The contours of the exclusion are not identical for women and for Aboriginal Peoples. The contours of the exclusion among Aboriginal Peoples are not identical either. Aboriginal Peoples are legally recognized as the Indian, Inuit and Métis. Indians have the *Indian Act* regime which grants a number of rights (which often feel like a series of burdens). For example, registered Indians did not receive the federal franchise until 1960. The Métis exist at the opposite end of this legal spectrum. They survived as people and as nations within a full constitutional silence—the Métis were excluded. This exclusion of the Métis operated expressly until 1982. The Inuit exist somewhere along this legislative continuum of complete exclusion to oppressive statutory inclusion.

The exclusion of women from Canadian political relations was challenged by a group of women in 1930. In that year, the Privy Council[2] considered whether women were persons capable of being summoned to the senate.[3] The highest Canadian court had decided that women were not persons. The Privy Council overturned the Supreme Court of Canada and decided that persons was an ambiguous term and could include women. Both Aboriginal Peoples and women have struggled against their constitutional exclusion since confederation in 1867. From the two examples I have cited, it is obvious that the history, timing and amelioration of the exclusions have not been identical. Nor will the future solutions be identical.

Once the initial recognition about exclusions is made, it begins to get complicated. As a Mohawk woman, the exclusions that shape my reality are grounded in both my gender and my race/culture. The experience is not as simple as my own bifurcated experiences of race/culture and gender. Aboriginal women also experience discrimination based on their sexual orientation and their disability. Language is also an area of concern. Canada is a bilingual country, that is, comprised of French and English. Anyone speaking an Aboriginal language really faces a requirement that they become trilingual. This failure to recognize the contribution of Aboriginal languages to the development of Canadian society is not acceptable. (Just consider the names given to many Canadian cities and the impact of Aboriginal languages in Canadian development becomes apparent.) We must not only recognize all the exclusions but we must make meaningful efforts to overcome *all* obstacles to participation. Exclusions of identifiable groups occur in a variety of ways. Encouraging participation means more than ending legal obstacles.

It does not appear to me that the goals of Canada and Aboriginal Peoples are harmonious when engaged in processes of constitutional amendment. Rolling Thunder speaks to us about healing. Part of the healing that Aboriginal men and women must do is to heal the wounds of exclusion (that is, oppression and colonialism). This is the reason that healing is a constitutional issue for Aboriginal Peoples. Healing is an issue that Canada has never had to deal with as a matter of constitutional discussion. However, Canadian constitutional scholars respect that the constitution "must recognize and reflect the values of a nation" (Hogg 1985: 1). The recognition and reflection of new and agreed upon constitutional values represents what I consider the content of creating the ideal of a "constitutional family." The challenge that lays before this country is to respect that any constitutional amendments which hope to end the historic exclusion of Aboriginal people must have the effect of embracing our central value, which is to heal our nations. I think this asks Canadian parliamentarians and legal scholars to twist their thinking around significantly. This means that the most important constitutional question is not, "What do Aboriginal Peoples want?" but "What is Canada doing to end the constitutional exclusion of Aboriginal Peoples?" The reason is that this exclusion is a significant source of the pain that Aboriginal people seek to heal from. The answer to the second question is disturbing. Canada has not been willing either to fully examine its role or assume its responsibility for the state of Aboriginal communities today.

Many but not all Aboriginal people understand that our legal relationships under Canadian law are a significant contributing factor to our experience of oppression and colonialism. This understanding is finely developed as a result of surviving an oppressive legislative regime (the *Indian Act*) for more than one hundred years. The link between the *Indian Act* and Canada's constitutional arrangements does not necessarily present itself clearly to all people. The *Indian Act* is seen as colonial and oppressive in many Aboriginal communities but somehow the constitution is not always seen in this same light.

The *Indian Act*, a single statute, controls almost every aspect of the life of a registered Indian person. For all other Canadians, there is no parallel experience. No single statute controls every aspect of non-Indian life.

Canadians (non-Indian) can therefore look first to the constitution for a vision of what Canada means to them. For Indian people the *Indian Act* obscures our access to the supreme law and the vision we see of ourselves there. It is almost as though the *Indian Act* replaces the authority of the supreme law in our daily experiences and eclipses the legal order that operates for all other Canadians. This entrenches inequality and the subordinate status of Indian people (that is to say, oppression and colonialism).

Several times in recent history, the choice has been made to place the constitution at the centre of our attempts to re-define Aboriginal legal relationships with Canada. This is not the only available course of action for Aboriginal Peoples. We can re-claim our old laws and live in a self-determining way in our communities. This choice can be exercised at either the individual or community level. This action can have a serious consequence— it can incur the wrath of the federal Indian Affairs bureaucracy and funding to our communities can be jeopardized. The ways in which colonial relations are continually forced on Aboriginal people are numerous.

I have been examining the constitutional framework of Canada while searching for my own vision or reflection in the text of the Canadian constitution and/or the current constitutional discussions (the 1992 Charlottetown discussions). I undertook a similar journey through the Canadian *Charter of Rights and Freedoms* in the previous chapter. Finding my vision or my reflection within the constitutional text, even though such a task strikes me as a strange kind of venture, seems to be important for at least one reason. Constitutional amendment is one significant way of re-casting history in a way that includes Aboriginal Peoples.[4]

Constitutional inclusion alone is insufficient to ensure Aboriginal inclusion. The contours of the exclusions that presently exist must be noted. The notion of two founding nations obliterates Aboriginal Peoples, our histories and our relationship to the development of this country. Our absence is not solely due to our absence from the constitutional text. Even when we are expressly mentioned, such as in the case of the Métis in the *Manitoba Act* 1870 (which brought the province of Manitoba into confederation), the country manages to govern in such a way that Métis involvement, contributions and lives are marginalized. The truth is the Métis were the founders of the province of Manitoba. This example illustrates that what Canadians have written in their constitution does not necessarily reflect the values they will live by.

It is worth remembering that the constitutional exclusion results both from the fact that Canadian leaders over the decades have chosen to vanish Aboriginal Peoples from the constitutional text but also as the choice of Aboriginal Peoples to remain outside the Canadian constitutional fold. This is more true of some Aboriginal nations, such as the Mohawk, than it is for others. This recognition is important because it identifies that the solution is greater than simply having those who are in positions of recognized Canadian political power write us in. This may not be sufficient to secure the consent of Aboriginal Peoples to the inclusion. A constitutional inclusion of Aboriginal Peoples without consent is just as oppressive as the exclusion. The offer to include must be meaningful to Aboriginal Peoples as well as satisfactory to Canadians. This dual standard of acceptability must always be maintained.

The threshold issue for many Aboriginal Peoples in the quest for constitutional renovation is the recognition of the inherent right to self-government. To say this right is *inherent* means respecting that Aboriginal Peoples have always been self-governing. Self-governing simply means that "we are able to carry ourselves."[5] Inherency is the Aboriginal standard and can be contrasted with the federal view which seems to always favour delegated powers. Delegated means that the source of the power is Canadian sovereignty. In this view, Aboriginal government powers are given to Aboriginal Peoples by Canada. Canadian sovereignty has historically operated as a way to deny Aboriginal experience and understanding of our rights to self-determination. The extent to which the Aboriginal understanding is reflected in Canada's present constitution is subject to continued controversy. There is not a single Aboriginal view about how to proceed. The simplest way to share the understanding I have come to is to examine the existing provisions in Canada's constitution.

In Canada, 1982 was a remarkable year. The country repatriated its constitution. This action began more than a decade of intense constitutional struggles in this country. These are struggles which are likely to resurface again. The repatriation ended the dependency on England's parliament for matters requiring constitutional amendment. Included in this package were a *Charter of Rights and Freedoms*, an amending formula,[6] a commitment to move from parliamentary supremacy to constitutional supremacy,[7] and a protection of existing Aboriginal rights and treaty rights.[8] The new constitutional recognition of Aboriginal rights is a logical place to start examining the impact of Canada's constitution on Aboriginal Peoples. It is the high point in my analysis.

Section 35(1) of Canada's constitution recognizes and affirms existing Aboriginal rights and treaty rights. This section is broadly worded. It provides no specification about what the contents of Aboriginal rights or treaty rights might be. Both Aboriginal rights and treaty rights are separate legal categories of rights possessed by Aboriginal Peoples. The general uncertainty about the meaning of section 35(1) is what leads to the generation of hundreds of thousands of words of academic comment and judicial reasoning. The constitutional package of 1982 provided for a process to reach agreement about the scope of the rights recognized in Aboriginal Peoples. As part of this process, from 1982 to 1987, four first ministers' conferences (including the Prime Minister and the premiers) were held. Little was accomplished that clarified the meaning of Aboriginal and treaty rights (such as self-government) during these four meetings. Two amendments were made in 1983. Section 35(3) provides the certainty that land claims agreements negotiated in the future are "treaty rights" within the meaning of the constitution. Section 35(4) protects gender equality.[9] Despite the failure of the talks from 1982 to 1987, sound legal arguments can be made that the inherent right to self-government for Aboriginal Peoples is already "recognized and affirmed" in the Canadian constitution. This is my firm position.

Although the section has generated thousands of words regarding its application, the legal argument about inherency is very simple. The words found in the constitution which protect Aboriginal rights and treaty rights are Canada's "solemn promise"[10] to *recognize and affirm*" the rights. Guarantees (such as the rights found in the *Charter*) are sourced in the authority of Canadian governments to legislate.[11] *Charter* rights are granted not "recognized and affirmed." The *Charter* is a guarantee of rights from Canada to Canadians. Section 35(1) is not a grant of rights. The wording of section 35 is vastly different. To understand this difference, the meaning of the phrase "recognized and affirmed" must be considered. Both a recognition and affirmation when understood in their common usage imply that whatever is being recognized or affirmed already exists—in the case of section 35, that is Aboriginal and treaty rights. As section 35 implies these rights were pre-existing rights; the section affirms the inherency of Aboriginal rights. The recognition and affirmation made in section 35 strongly suggest that Aboriginal and treaty rights are pre-existing rights and do not come from any order of Canadian sovereignty. Therefore, they are not granted rights. This is so important because it entrenches in Canada's constitution a respect for the way Aboriginal Peoples see ourselves, a respect that has been missing from the Canadian legal and political perspective since confederation.

Immediately following the failure of the fourth first ministers' conference, the 1987 talks which were intended to "codify" or list the specifics of Aboriginal and treaty rights, Canada, under the direction of then Prime Minister Brian Mulroney, turned its attention to another pressing constitutional problem. It was a problem of a relationship which is as old as the country itself. Quebec[12] failed to ratify Canada's new constitution in 1982. Immediately following the failed Aboriginal talks, Canada negotiated a package that would gain Quebec's signature on the 1982 document. The package gave to Quebec greater powers in the areas of immigration, senate appointments, courts and spending, as well as recognized the francophone population as belonging to a "distinct society." The phrase "distinct society" was undefined.

Canada's willingness to accommodate Quebec's distinctiveness just weeks after the fourth failure to implement Aboriginal Peoples' distinctiveness (that is to define self-government) raised the ire of many Aboriginal people, including the leadership. Canada's politicians could not agree to a meaning of the term Aboriginal self-government and insisted that it be clearly defined. A cynic would suggest that the process of defining self-government was really a process of limiting the broad recognition of Aboriginal and treaty rights that had been placed in the constitution in 1982. Within a few weeks of the failed Aboriginal talks, Canada could agree not only to recognize the distinctiveness of Quebec society but also hand out only to Quebec new provincial powers. The irony was immense and could be seen in the immediate Aboriginal resistance to the Meech Lake Accord, which was the document that proposed the new changes. The Meech Lake Accord was defeated in June 1990 largely due to the resistance of Manitoba politician Elijah Harper, a Cree MLA from Red Sucker Lake.[13]

The empowering resistance by Aboriginal Peoples to the Meech Lake Accord because of its failure to recognize us in any substantive form signifies that constitutional recognition must be important to Aboriginal Peoples. It is also testimony to our strength and resourcefulness. Aboriginal people are no longer willing to accept exclusion or marginalization. This is not to deny the importance of the issues that Quebec brings to the constitutional table. However, in a search for a specific constitutional recognition of any constituency's inherent, linguistic or human rights, the rights of others cannot be vanished.

Aboriginal people cannot be asked to wait in turn for their opportunity to "negotiate." This is the point of principle at the heart of Aboriginal People's resistance to the Meech Lake Accord. The resistance was not a rebuke of Quebec desires but an affirmation of the respect we have for ourselves as nations. The fact that Quebec's desires are pitted against Aboriginal aspirations is a consequence of how Canadian politicians have chosen to proceed on constitutional questions. It is not necessarily inherent in the relationship between Quebec and Aboriginal people. The fact that Aboriginal people have been forced to carry the consequences of the federal approach to constitutional amendment is important and should not be disappeared.

Constitutional renovation was necessary prior to 1982 and it may still be necessary. The rights affirmed in section 35 remain to be specified. Furthermore, there is a great gap between the position of Canada and the position of Aboriginal nations to the itemization of those rights. The implications of amending Canada's constitution to include Aboriginal Peoples are still uncertain. Some of the uncertainty is being resolved through litigation initiated by Aboriginal people. Engaging the courts as the principle process of reaching a certainty about the meaning of Aboriginal and treaty rights is an incremental one and it will be slow. That is the nature of the judicial process.

What I understand about the constitution must be filtered through how I understand myself as a Mohawk woman with a legal education. I cannot deny that my desire to even seek an image of my people within the principal document of Canadian nationhood is shaped by my personal experience which includes my legal education. I do not believe that the majority of Aboriginal people would engage in such an activity. I still believe that real change can be affected through Canadian law (although on some individual days this is a difficult belief to maintain). This discussion is, therefore, not one that focuses on the merit of any general constitutional renovation, as it appears we are already committed at least to having the constitutional discussion.[14] This is easy to say as I believe it is legally possible to create a constitution which respects the true Canadian national identity. That identity is not only about two founding peoples, but also about the original peoples and more recently, a commitment to multiculturalism.[15] To accomplish such a constitution will require all the wisdom and creativity that we as a country possess.[16]

That much said, a caution also seems necessary. The Canadian constitution is founded on principles such as the rule of law, parliamentary sovereignty, federalism, separation of governmental powers between two levels of government, and so on. Some of these political choices (and they were choices in 1867 or perhaps earlier), foreclose certain recognitions that Aboriginal Peoples may seek. For example, because Canada is a federal state, it seems impossible to imagine a construction of Aboriginal self-government that is not affected or compromised by the fact that the federalist choice has already been made. The federal government has certain powers as do the provinces. In all of the constitutional discussions with Aboriginal people the federal nature of the Canadian state has never been put on the table for negotiation. This means Aboriginal people have always been required to shape our relationship with Canada in any gaps between federal and/or provincial powers. This is not an ideal choice but it has been the only choice (assuming that the delegated powers route is rejected).

The majority of Aboriginal nations proceed to any constitutional discussion with the view that our rights are inherent. Aboriginal Peoples believe that our right to self-determination is not just an issue of human rights but is a right that involves our unique cultural beliefs. The Creator is the one who established the legal order that we followed long before the Canadian state was ever imagined. Our respect for our inherent view of Aboriginal rights is a respect for the source of our Creator-given rights. These rights to self-determination exist completely independent of the Canadian state and its right to self-determination sourced in a way that seems right to that state.

In the past Canada has only been willing to delegate rights of government to Aboriginal Peoples (primarily registered Indians living on reserve). Delegated rights to self-determination are really rights to a minimal form of self-government that does not challenge the existing Canadian state relations. Delegated rights of Indian government are sourced in Canada's sovereignty, a sovereignty that prior to 1982 did not recognize inherent Aboriginal rights. Delegated rights to self-government are an affront to the beliefs and values of Aboriginal Peoples. It requires Aboriginal people to compromise our principles in an unconscionable manner. Delegated rights are a modern way to ensure that colonialism continues to be reproduced in Canada. This is a pattern which Aboriginal people seek to disrupt.

It is important to understand the agreements that Canada is already committed to and that we can learn about by examining other sections of Canada's constitution. The nature of Canadian federalism and the manner in which federal/provincial relations are defined is a necessary consideration in any discussion about constitutional reform. It is a union of a national government and regional governments called provinces. The totality of Canadian sovereignty is divided between these two levels of government, federal and provincial. How these powers have been shared since 1867 is itemized in sections 91 and 92 of the constitution. The parameters of this division of powers has a profound impact on the choices available to Aboriginal Peoples. More importantly, the way Canadian sovereignty is divided causes a barrier to be erected around the application of section 35. This barrier can only be understood by thinking about sections 91 and 92 together with section 35.

All of the major concerns that Aboriginal People have, such as education, child welfare and justice relations, already exist as either a federal or provincial power.[17] In particular, many of the issues that Aboriginal people are concerned about are provincial spheres of legislative activity. These powers of the federal and provincial governments generally operate to the exclusion of the other level of government. The existing structure of the division of governmental powers (found in sections 91 and 92) must likely be challenged if Aboriginal Peoples' governments will be any greater than a delegated power. This does not require a re-ordering of existing federal and provincial relations. It merely requires the recognition that this ordering does not affect Aboriginal people unless Aboriginal people consent to that ordering. Such a simple solution has not been introduced in any proposed constitutional reforms.

The manner in which sections 91 and 92 structure the political powers of federal and provincial governments obviously cannot escape amendment if the aspirations of Aboriginal Peoples are to be met. This problem is also a simple one. It only requires constitutional amendment that states sections 91 and 92 do not apply to Aboriginal governments. This suggested amendment is required in the wake of the *Sparrow* decision. Prior to Sparrow, it could be strongly argued that section 35(1) constitutionally mandated the re-ordering of section 91 and 92 in such a way that the inherent right to self-determination of each Aboriginal nation was recognized. In a paragraph with too many themes, the unanimous Supreme Court states:

> There is no explicit language in the provision that authorizes this Court or any court to assess the legitimacy of any government legislation that restricts aboriginal rights. Yet, we find that the words "recognition and affirmation" incorporate the fiduciary relationship referred to earlier and so import some restraint on the exercise of sovereign power. Rights that are recognized and affirmed are not absolute. *Federal legislative powers continue, including of course the right to legislate with respect to Indians pursuant to s.91(24) of the Constitution Act, 1867.* These powers must, however, now be read together with s.35(1). In other words, federal power must be reconciled with federal duty and the best way to achieve that reconciliation is to demand the justification of any government regulation that infringes upon or denies aboriginal rights. Such scrutiny is in keeping with the liberal interpretive principle enunciated in *Nowegijick, supra* and the concept of holding the Crown to a high standard of honourable dealing with respect to the aboriginal peoples of Canada as suggested by *Guerin* v. *The Queen, supra.*[18]

Since the Supreme Court has affirmed the power of the federal government in section 91(24) to legislate over Indians, a fundamental contradiction exists with the powers entrenched in section 35(1). As it stands now, section 35(1) protects an inherent right, but there is no mechanism to channel this right into actual government powers. The problem is really one of implementation.

This is not the only reason that sections 91 and 92 are of paramount importance. Prior to 1982, the only constitutional reference to my people[19] was to be found only in section 91(24) of the *British North America Act* (as it was then). This is a section of the constitution where I cannot locate a healthy image of myself. That section provided the federal government with the authority to pass laws regarding "Indians and Lands Reserved for Indians."[20] Effectively, Aboriginal status in Canada is a subject matter of federal authority. We are numbered 24 in between "copyrights" and "naturalization and aliens." We are not equals, merely subject matters.[21]

This must be disturbing for a country that asserts it prides itself on a respect for principles of equality. Section 91(24) is unacceptable as it entrenches inequality.

It is section 91(24) that provides the authority for the federal government to pass laws pertaining to Aboriginal Peoples.[22] This is the constitutional basis for laws such as the *Indian Act*. One of the many problems with the *Indian Act* regime is that it denies basic democratic rights to Aboriginal Peoples. Elected band officials are responsible to the Minister of Indian Affairs and his[23] department.[24] Responsible government demands that elected officials be answerable to their electorate *directly*, not to another body or individual. And it makes sense not to forget that the Department of Indian Affairs is *not* a system which operates on or reflects Aboriginal cultural values. Quite the opposite is true—it operates on the principle that these Aboriginal values are worthy of only extinction.[25] When section 91(24) is understood to be the source of authority for the *Indian Act*, then the oppressive nature of Canadian constitutional law is in full view.

It is more than the government structure established by section 91(24) and the way the federal government has exercised its authority over Indians that causes me concerns. One of the essential elements required to understand the Aboriginal view of our rights is our relations to the land. I am of the land and it is of me. Section 91(24) seems, ironically, to envision this as it recognizes both "Indians" and "Indian Lands." This is an odd twist of fate because the Indian lands referred to are not lands envisioned in an Aboriginal way. The irony lies in the fact that the connection in section 91(24) between Indians and land is not a recognition of how we see ourselves as being of this land. It merely creates two *separate* subjects of federal authority to legislate. It also does not require that any level of government exercises that authority or exercises it in a particular way. Rather, it exposes the reason why we gained constitutional recognition—the land *not* the Aboriginal People were of central importance to the settlers. This recognition is obviously *not* based upon respect.

Some Aboriginal people have tried to creatively interpret section 91(24) and believe that it entrenches the "nation to nation" relationship Aboriginal people have with the Government of Canada (to the exclusion of provincial governments). I understand that the "nation to nation" belief is a fundamental principle of the treaty view of Aboriginal/Canadian relations. I understand that the desire to read section 91(24) broadly as a protection of the "nation to nation" relationship is located in a desire to protect an important Aboriginal belief in the nature of Canada's relationship with Aboriginal nations. There was no other constitutional source to protect this view prior to 1982. I know that this view is also located in the vulnerability that Aboriginal people feel in our relations with Canada. While I respect the "nation to nation" position and the need to protect this view, such a construction of section 91(24) is based on a total reconstruction of Canadian constitutional arrangements contained in the two "division of powers" sections. It is a dangerous construction when the legal purpose of section 91(24) is understood. Section 91 only authorizes federal legislative authority. This authorization is in fact contrary to the "nation to nation" view. Sections 91 and 92 do not define the nature of those powers or any form of relationship other than the relationship between the federal government and the provinces.

What I have learned about the law in turn affects the way I am able to understand who I am within the structure of Canadian society. I recognize that I am Mohawk. But I must also recognize that the world understands my Mohawk identity as being capable of being controlled (governed) by a foreign and colonial state (the federal government). It is this section of the constitution that is a paramount source of the denial of my people's beliefs that we are self-governing. Perhaps many people without legal education or an interest in constitutional law have never recognized that this is one of the seeds from which the subordinate status of Aboriginal Peoples flows. Although the affect of Canada's constitutional structure on the oppression of Aboriginal Peoples as individuals is not direct, it is in my mind a relationship of great importance. The Canadian constitution establishes the possibility that Aboriginal Peoples can be viewed as *less than* (as opposed to distinct but equal) other residents of this territory.

It may seem crazy to some people to try to locate an Aboriginal vision or image in Canada's constitution. What I am really trying to accomplish on this guided journey through the constitution of Canada is to discover the ways in which and the extent to which the constitution is a tool of the colonization of Aboriginal Peoples. 'Primitive,' 'sub-human,' 'uncivilized,' 'savage,' 'backwards,' 'without law or government' and so on is still the language of the courts in Canada when discussing Aboriginal rights and claims. Section 91(24) is part of the problem as it reinforces the subordinate status and inequality accorded Aboriginal nations. Section 91(24) creates that possibility. The first step that Aboriginal litigants are forced to make is to prove to the court that they exist and then show that they lived in "organized societies."[26]

The philosophical underpinnings of section 91(24) rest on the European doctrine of discovery. Aboriginal Peoples were less than human because the territory "discovered" was then *terra nullas* (empty lands). The European state could then claim title by virtue of their discovery. Section 91(24), as long as it stands as part of Canadian constitutional law, entrenches an ethnocentric (at best) view of the history of this country. All of these historical myths that must be corrected if we are to proceed as a country, from here, in a good way.[27] And it must be considered who clings to these myths. It is difficult being colonized, but it is more difficult to be a decolonized colonizer.

Sections 91 and 92 are essentially a part of the discussion we must have for a number of reasons. The powers divided between federal and provincial governments cannot be a component of the constitution which escapes our notice in the current (or any future) constitutional discussions. I have provided six reasons for why it is essential to amend sections 91 and 92 of the constitution. I would simply categorize these reasons as follows: 1) dispelling historical myths, including the doctrine of discovery, 2) ending the denial of Aboriginal participation in the creation of this country, 3) recognizing the reality that Aboriginal Peoples were historically and continue to be self-governing, 4) dispelling the narrow view of the relationship between people and land, 5) removing the source of the divide and conquer strategy, and 6) ending the legitimacy for legislative regimes such as the *Indian Act* which are non-democratic. It must be recognized that sections 91 and 92 as they now stand are a major obstacle to Aboriginal aspirations— both our aspirations for equal status and for governmental powers that are anything greater than delegated powers.

Failure to address any one of these individual reasons precludes recognizing and respecting the inherent nature of the rights of Aboriginal Peoples—a commitment in 1982 that received the status as the supreme law of the land. Canada has not made significant process since 1982 in implementing this commitment. In the pages of discussion on the meaning of section 35 little mention is made of the impact that section 35 necessarily has on the established Canadian ways of doing business with Aboriginal Peoples. The beauty of section 35 is that it creates a new way of viewing the responsibility of Canada to Aboriginal Peoples.[28] Since 1982, this means that Canada is failing to govern itself in a constitutional way with regard to their dealings with Aboriginal Peoples.

This is not meant to be a full discussion of the federal proposals. However, it is obvious at the outset that the federal proposals are clearly unacceptable to Aboriginal Peoples. It seems to be more logical to create our own proposals and not merely react to someone else's agenda. The fact that Aboriginal involvement in constitutional negotiations has always occurred in response to Canada's initiation of such talks for a purpose other than resolving the relationship with Aboriginal people is disturbing. Canada's constitutional discussions on Aboriginal people have only occurred as a collateral package attached to another goal that Canada sees as worthy.

Notes

1.   Several possibilities exist including amendments such as those contained in the federal proposals, *Shaping Canada's Future Together* (1991); or composite

amendments, or a national treaty (to list but a few options). I firmly believe that the process of renovation must be equally as creative as the vision of Canada that Aboriginal People's possess.

2. Until 1949, the Privy Council (in England) was the last court of appeal for Canada. Since 1949, the Supreme Court of Canada is the court of last resort.

3. *Edwards v. Attorney General of Canada*, [1930] A.C. 124.

4. My preference has previously been to speak of First Nations. Here, as I am focusing on the Canadian constitution alone, I have adopted the language of the constitution in the interests of clarity. Unlike the constitution, I pay my respects to the citizens of the many First Nations by capitalizing the words Aboriginal Peoples.

5. This is a literal translation of the Mohawk word for self-government. In my language the word is *tewatatha:wi*.

6. Section 38(1) states:

   An amendment to the Constitution of Canada may be made by proclamation issued by the Governor General under the Great Seal of Canada where so authorized by

   (a) resolutions of the Senate and House of Commons; and

   (b) resolutions of the legislative assemblies of at least two-thirds of the provinces that have, in the aggregate, according to the then latest general census, at' least fifty percent of the population of all the provinces.

   It is important to note that Aboriginal Peoples or governments have no constitutional certainty that their consent will be required to any amendment (even if the amendment fundamentally affects Aboriginal lives). The amending formula agreed upon in 1982 is another example of the way inequality is entrenched in Canada's constitution.

7. Section 52 is fully discussed in the previous chapter.

8. Section 35(1) states:

   The existing aboriginal and treaty rights of the aboriginal peoples of Canada are hereby recognized and affirmed.

9. This section states:

   Notwithstanding any other provision of this Act, the aboriginal and treaty rights referred to in subsection (1) are guaranteed equally to male and female persons.

10. *R. v. Sparrow*, [1990] 3 C.N.L.R. 163-188 at 163.

11. Canada has a federal system of government. It is comprised of two distinct levels of government, the federal and the provincial. The full sovereign powers of Canada are shared between these two levels of government under the parameters set out in sections 91 and 92 of the *Constitution Act, 1867*. The federal powers are found in section 91 and the provincial powers in section 92. Canada also has territorial governments and municipal governments. Their powers are not constitutional but delegated.

12. Quebec is one of Canada's ten provinces. It houses the largest francophone population in the country and operates under a system of civil law. The rest of the country follows the common law tradition.

13. Please refer to Turpel and Monture 1990 and Comeau 1993. Public discussion

on the Meech Lake Accord had been initiated by the release of the federal proposal, *Shaping Canada's Future Together*, 1992.

14. At the time of the writing of this article, Canada had embarked on a new round of constitutional amendment to become known as the Charlottetown Round.

15. This commitment is recent *only* on the part of the founding nations. Aboriginal Peoples have always welcomed all races and all nations to the shores of what we call Turtle Island.

16. Although I do not consider myself to be a Canadian, in the interest of unity, I am using language in this paper which suggests that we have already accomplished the difficult task of meaningful inclusion of Aboriginal Peoples.

17. I am not overlooking the territorial governments. The source of their exclusion is constitutional, based on the status of those territorial governments. Under the *Northwest Territories Act*, R.S.C. 1970, c. N-22 and the *Yukon Act*, R.S.C. 1970, c. Y-2, both of the territorial governments' legislative powers are subordinate to the federal parliament. Effectively, there are four tiers of government in Canada; federal, provincial, territorial and municipal. It is only the federal and provincial powers that are constitutional. The powers of territories and municipalities are subordinate. This is a fact that territorial governments are not satisfied with. It is *not* the will of the majority of Aboriginal people to secure subordinate legislative powers. This violates our principle of inherent rights.

18. *R.* v. *Sparrow*, [1990] 3 C.N.L.R. 163-188 at 181.

19. For Métis people, the same cannot be said. Their vision and image was disappeared within the constitutional document up until the 1982 entrenchment of "Aboriginal rights."

20. The meaning of the word Indian shifts when the discussion moves from the *Indian Act* to section 91(24). Indians in the *Indian Act* definition is a narrow term and refers to only those Indians entitled to be registered. This is not the same Indian that appears in section 91(24). As the constitution is the supreme law, its authority is greater than any statute. The constitution cannot ever be changed by unilateral political action (such as any legislature passing a statute). This rule of constitutional interpretation is the first legal indication that there are different legal meanings for the word Indian (which confuses matters of language even more). In section 91(24) Indians includes Inuit people (see *Re: Eskimos* [1939] S.C.R. 104). Similar arguments are easily made to show that Métis are Indians within the meaning of section 91(24).

21. I owe the clear articulation to this concept to my legal colleague Moses Okimaw.

22. Although the federal government has exercised its authority in s.91(24) only to Indians, it does not follow that an equal authority is not present in s.91(24) with respect to the Inuit and Métis. I, therefore, use the term, Aboriginal Peoples in my discussion.

23. The use of the male pronoun is intentional. I have only heard tell of one female Minister of Indian Affairs. This post never been held by an Aboriginal person.

24. Section 3(1) of the *Indian Act* provides that the Act is to be administered by the Minister who is the superintendent general of Indian Affairs. Section 81 provides for making of band by-laws only when they are *not* inconsistent with the Act or any regulation. Section 82(2) specifies that every band by-law must be forwarded to the Minister and comes into force forty days after forwarding.

Further, the same section provides that the Minister may disallow any by-law within the forty-day period. No by-law can come into force until the Minister's approval is secured!

25. By this I mean that the Department as well as all current "Indian" legislation was established to meet the purpose of first controlling and then assimilating Indian people. For a discussion see Frideres 1988: 25-38.

26. See, for example, *Delgamuukw et al* v. *The Queen* [1991] 3 W.W.R. 97 (B.C.S.C.).

27. Nowhere in the federal package, *Shaping Canada's Future Together*, are there any express recognitions for the need to amend section 91 and 92 in such a manner that the types of concerns that have been thus far articulated in this paper are addressed. Furthermore, there is an eerie silence with respect to Aboriginal nations in the section of the report that deals with sections 91 and 92. It is clear that the federal proposal does advance amendment of these two sections. In particular, the report suggests that the federal government is willing to turn over responsibility to provincial governments a number of heads of federal power, such as tourism, forestry, mining, recreation, housing and municipal/urban affairs. Some of these matters are of deep concern to Aboriginal Peoples and Aboriginal Peoples will be profoundly affected if these matters are turned over to provincial governments. Yet, nowhere in the federal proposal do I see this recognition let alone respect for a transfer of powers that holds the potential to have a negative relationship on Aboriginal lives.

The thinking in this document about Aboriginal Peoples remains hauntingly familiar. The report makes it clear that the federal government will continue to recognize its own responsibilities. Aboriginal Peoples are recognized as one of those responsibilities (that is, subject matter only). I trust this means that Aboriginal people will remain a head of federal power. This means Aboriginal people will continue to be subjugated and oppressed. This remains an unacceptable way to entrench what we believe is an historical relationship based on a principle of "nation to nation" respect. This is haunting because it is not the first time that Aboriginal people have seen proposals that do not go to the heart of Aboriginal concerns. The federal proposal was only a reorganization of Canada's existing colonial relations with Aboriginal Peoples.

28. Only nominal attention has been paid to examining the impact of the fiduciary relationship that exists between the Crown and Aboriginal Peoples. Even less litigation has occurred under this legal concept.

Organizing Against Oppression:
Aboriginal Women, Law and Feminism

CHAPTER 9 HAS NOT BEEN PREVIOUSLY published. It is for Kate, my girlchild. May you never carry the thunder in your soul that grows as a result of violent relationships and experiences. This is my mother's dream for you, girlchild.

Women have organized for many different reasons. We have organized to resist our political oppression and to rebel against it. We have also organized to resist the way in which our work is marginalized and all the forms of socially sanctioned violence against us. We have organized along racial and cultural affiliations. Women have organized around our philosophical positions as well as our professional associations. To suggest there is a single women's movement is ludicrous. Similarly, there is not a single Aboriginal women's perspective or movement. Aboriginal women are women of many different nations and many different experiences.

I have a particular interest in understanding the organization and political relationships of the Indigenous women's movement.[1] It is not just an academic interest. It also stems from the fact that I am a survivor of violent relationships. My definition of violence includes the effects of both racism and colonialism. Especially, I am interested in the relationship or patterns between violence against women and violence against Aboriginal people. Women's organizing has often also focused on an anti-violence platform.

I started writing this paper with the idea of reflecting on the 1992-93 constitutional round (fondly referred to as the Charlottetown Round) and the way violence against Aboriginal women was a topic of that debate. This idea was formed in response to a request from a feminist press that was editing a collection of papers focusing on women's organizing. As has happened too often, I was called at the last minute to fill an unacceptable gap in the text—a gap left by the exclusion of Aboriginal women's voices. In a very short timeframe, no more than several weeks, I prepared this paper to fill in the token space left for an Aboriginal woman's voice. My involvement with that project came to a sudden and never explained end after I forwarded an early draft of this article to the editor. I never heard anything back. In preparing my own book, I decided it was important for me to revive this paper. In the two years that have transpired, I have lost the desire to speak anymore about constitutional renovations. In the re-working of this paper for inclusion here, the constitutional theme seemed artificial and no longer very important. I am not sure whether this merely reflects the passage of time or some form of personal change.

During each of the various constitutional rounds, I was very much an observer. The work I did for the Assembly of First Nations was very much peripheral.[2] I did not sit in on any of the negotiations. My views are definitely outsider views. I am not sure than anyone benefits from the further discussion of outsider views (mine or anyone else's). There are good Indian stories to tell of the constitutional rounds; Indian survivors of that process are the ones to tell those stories.

It is likely that Aboriginal women experience violence in their lives with greater frequency than any other collective of women in Canadian society. Only one form of this violence is physical. Frequently, Aboriginal women are battered, raped, and sexually violated from the time we are only children. One study (Task Force on Federally Sentenced Women 1990), discovered that unlike non-Aboriginal[3] women our experience of violence is not incidental (that is, it is not one rape *or* one battering partner *or* incest). Many Aboriginal women move from the violence of our childhoods—which is often an experience of the violence our mothers survived layered over the violence we ourselves have survived—to violent relationships with men, including both rape *and* battering. Violence is not just a mere incident in the lives of Aboriginal women. Violence does not just span a given number of years. It *is* our lives. And it is in our histories. For most Aboriginal women, violence has not been escapable.

Violence is not just physical. Some women recognize that psychological battering is a devastating component of the battering relationship.[4] For Aboriginal women, the psychological battering in a violent relationship is twinned in our experience of the social and political reality. Racism and colonialism are psychological violence with the same effects as overt physical violence. I have not experienced either racism, colonialism or political oppression differently from the physical violence I have survived. Political oppression is a form of racism. Racism holds the same potential to erupt in physical violence as the battering relationship. Consider the experience of the Mohawk people attempting to leave Kahnawake in the summer of

1990, stoned by their White neighbours at Chateaugay—one man died as a result. The media did not avidly follow this death in the same way or with the same velocity that they covered the death of a White police officer. This is the graphic image of Canadian "freedom" that I carry with me. My experience of violence transcends my gender and also includes my experience of the state.

When the experience of Aboriginal women is fully understood on these terms, it seems to make little sense to report on the incomplete statistical evidence that documents that eight of ten Aboriginal women currently live in situations of overt physical violence—the violence of their male partners (Ontario Native Women's Association 1989: 18). Focusing on a moment in time or incidents of violence, abuse or racism, counting them—disguises the utter totality of the experience of violence in Aboriginal women's lives. This distinguishes Aboriginal women from the organizing-against-violence and political action that often occurs in the women's movement. Organizing against a single form of violence—men's—is not a "luxury" I have experienced. The general definition of violence against women is too narrow to capture all of the experiences of violence that Aboriginal women face. This narrow definition, relied on by dominant institutions, structures and groups, constrains my expression of my experience of violence and the reality within which I live in a way that is most counter-productive. In fact, this constraint feels very much like ideological violence. The fragmentation of violence and the social legitimation of only the wrong of physical violence results in a situation where I am constrained from examining the totality of my experience within a movement that is advanced as offering the solution to that violence. The simple truth is feminism as an ideology remains colonial.

The majority of organizations of Aboriginal women have as one of their focuses the abuse that exists in Aboriginal communities. These efforts have been instrumental in securing both national recognition of this crisis as well as acceptance of it as a crisis at the community level. At the same time, the image of the women's associations receives national attention as a result of the crisis conditions of our community. However, the efforts of Aboriginal women and Aboriginal women's organizations to expose the intolerable levels of violence in our communities has not occurred without internal struggle.

When the Ontario Native Women's Association released their 1989 study of violence against women in their locals, some chiefs and chief's organizations were quick to criticize the statistical reliability of the report and the overall findings, disavowing that a problem of such magnitude exists. The chiefs were correct that this study was methodologically flawed. However, focusing on the method of study and the process of study instead of the very real problem of violence against Aboriginal women is unacceptable.

Many Aboriginal women are hesitant to speak out about the abuse they have survived. It is not just the overt violence against women in Aboriginal communities that is the problem. The silence surrounding this issue is equally problematic. The commissioners of the Aboriginal Justice Inquiry of Manitoba state:

> The unwillingness of chiefs and councils to address the plight of women and children suffering abuse at the hands of husbands and fathers is quite alarming. We are concerned enough about it to state that we believe that the failure of Aboriginal government leaders to deal at all with the problem of domestic abuse is unconscionable. We believe that there is a heavy responsibility on Aboriginal leaders to recognize the significance of the problem within their own communities. They must begin to recognize, as well, *how much their silence and failure to act actually contribute to the problem.* (Hamilton and Sinclair 1991: 485, emphasis added)

We know little about the reasons for the silence that surrounds the issue of violence in Aboriginal communities. It is easy to note the gendered nature of the relationship and blame the pervading silence on patriarchy. I think this answer is too simple.

Violence against women must be understood as just one of the many challenges Aboriginal communities face. These community crises include: substance abuse among our youth, inadequate housing, poverty and starvation, alcoholism, suicides and attempted suicides. There are so many crises in our communities requiring the attention of Aboriginal leaders and politicians. When your life is always lived on crisis mode, it is difficult to sit down and prioritize your activities. Are the consequences of violence against women more severe than poverty and alcoholism? At least some of the failure to address issues of abuse in Aboriginal communities is a failure to resource communities in a way that they can address the multiple crises they face. I would assert that the failure to adequately resource Aboriginal community healing is another level of violence Aboriginal people survive. I also understand that silence is sometimes an expression of helplessness— helplessness learned through colonialism and oppression. If we need to blame, then we must seriously consider who is to blame—the colonized or the colonizer, who still controls essential elements of our lives.

The problem of the silence around issues of violence in Aboriginal communities is compounded by residence in remote or northern locations. The usual strategies will not work in small and isolated communities. Consider for a moment just how small and isolated some Indian, Inuit and Métis communities are—200 or 300 people. Can you really afford to further marginalize yourself or alienate yourself from the people who provide *all* the housing and social support systems in your community? Does the impact of the women's movement and their initiatives, political or otherwise, reach into Grassy Narrows, Davis Inlet, Hay River or Norway House? How do you build a safe house with a protected location in a community of not even twenty homes? Ensuring the right to live without violence in your life as an Aboriginal women requires a degree of creativity that the women's movement has never been required to fully imagine.[5] What is known about violence against women cannot be assumed to fully explain the violence that Aboriginal women survive.

In our communities (here, I am referring to "Indian" reserves),[6] when an incident of child sexual abuse is disclosed, investigated and reported, and the perpetrator found, the process has only just begun to unfold. That perpetrator, young or old, changes faces from the perpetrator we can be ever so angry at and has his (gender specificity intended) own story of victimization to tell. After an initial disclosure, this process repeats and repeats itself, like a web falling over the entire community. Every individual is touched. If not directly, you are touched because one of the "victim"/perpetrators is your relative.[7] Again, remember just how small and isolated many Indian communities are. Also notable is the direction in which the disclosures all eventually point. The disclosures unfold in such a way that residential schools, foster care, government and the church are all centrally implicated.

Indian communities do not experience the process of disclosure as incidental anymore than the experience of abuse is lived as a single episode. Where to place your anger is difficult to determine.[8] Residential schools are behind us. Who will carry that anger? Apparatus and individuals of the state are far away and inaccessible. How do you deposit that anger? The perpetrator is victim too (and may be someone you love). How do you see this person as a criminal with whom you can (or should) be angry? When you are angry at that person, what can you do? How do you trust in a criminal justice system that is foreign (colonial) and based on values that you do not share? The anger and frustration of Aboriginal individuals and Aboriginal communities swirls and swirls and all too often there is no channel for release. It is a cyclone of pain. It is a cyclone of pain that has no parallel in urban communities. I am able to understand why some people, faced with that cyclone of pain, may prefer to choose silence.

Indian communities are also the poorest in the country. All too often, we have few fiscal or human resources. Mainstream remedies often do not help us as our communities are different and the way the pain of violence is experienced is different. Once in crisis mode, it is difficult to find the time to sit and write funding proposals (assuming you even have access to such expertise) to establish the programs that are so necessary to address issues of family violence and sexual abuse. Blaming existing band council governments does not provide a solution to violence. It does provide an outlet for the pain and anger. But that outlet is false and dangerous as it masks the real source of the oppression, violence and pain. It creates a layer of alienation between men and women in our communities that is also dangerous. In no way should anything I have said be seen as an excuse to defend against any act of violence, overt or subtle. I am merely trying to understand all the layers of overcoming violence. Violence is never right, nor is it ever a solution. Instead, I speak to break the silence that I survive as an individual. It is through individual acts of strength (breaking the silence) that our communities will become re-united and we will be able to re-claim for Aboriginal Peoples the healthy communities and lives we once had.

As someone who has been legally trained, my search for solutions often involves an examination of both Canadian law (including laws about Aboriginal and treaty rights) and Aboriginal law. I have learned that by examining Canadian law I am not likely to encounter viable solutions to the oppression, the violence and the pain I seek to remedy. In fact, over the years of study, I have noticed a distinct pattern. Canadian law is most likely at the centre of the problem I am examining. For example, residential schools were mandated by Canadian law. Many incidents of abuse (physical, sexual and psychological) were perpetrated against Indian children in these schools. The Canadian government either did not know or did not care what happened in those schools after the law established them and government money supported them. Canadian officials were only concerned with the colonial imperative of those schools, to teach Indian children to be non-Indian.

The residential school system leaves our people with a long legacy, a legacy of dysfunction, that spans generations. In particular, the residential school system disrupted the learning and parenting skills across several generations of Indian people. One chief explains how his residential school experience impacted on his family life.

> Because of the treatment in residential schools, I didn't understand how to raise my children. I didn't know how to love my children, how to hold my children. It's an awful feeling when you let children grow up in your midst and you cannot hold them in your arms, with the warm tender love that you are capable of. I lacked all that information, all those skills.[9] (First Nations Circle on the Constitution 1992: 7)

It is also important to retrace our steps here. Band council governments have been criticized for their failure to act on issues of abuse, but it is entirely possible (perhaps more than likely in some areas of the country) for our

Aboriginal leaders to themselves be survivors or victims in denial. Breaking personal silence and denial cannot be demanded.

The residential school system is, however, not the sole legacy left by the state. The state signed treaties and forced people onto small pieces of land called reserves. It is not just the initial ordering of reserve life that impacted negatively on Indian people. The establishment of reserves is more than just a story about the taking of Aboriginal lands. The establishment of reserves was one of the original ways in which our family lives were disordered. Indian family life survived a round of disruption prior to the residential school legacy. And the legacy continues. The state-controlled system of reserves is one significant source of the poverty Indians face today. And poverty is also a form of violence.

The patriarchal nature of the state has different meanings and consequences from the vantage point of Aboriginal Peoples. Understanding how patriarchy operates in Canada without understanding colonization is a meaningless endeavour from the perspective of Aboriginal people. The Canadian state is the invisible male perpetrator who unlike Aboriginal men does *not* have a victim face. And at the feet of the state I can lay my anger to rest. Being able to name the state as my oppressor has allowed me to sit outside the personal cyclone of pain that once raged out of control in my life.

Current thought must recognize that Aboriginal women do not fully share the history of legally sanctioned violence against women with Canadian women. Violence and abuse (including political exclusion) against women was not tolerated in most Aboriginal societies.[10] This is rarely incorporated in feminist analysis or the principles of the women's movement. This is an example of where colonialism must be incorporated in feminist analysis. Many of the laws of Canada have sanctioned only disrespect for women. The women's movement has never taken as its *central* and long-term goal, the eradication of the legal oppression that is specific to Aboriginal women. The differences in the historic experience of Canadian law by women has helped me to understand my dissatisfaction with both the women's movement and feminist ideas.

The way in which the aspirations of Aboriginal women are often characterized in the academic literature, including feminist writing, is often problematic. It is necessary to point out that many Aboriginal women do not have access to this literature and are often unaware of how they are talked about. Two facts substantiate this observation. Statistics indicate that the majority of Aboriginal people do not complete high school or access post-secondary education. Second, some Aboriginal people reside in remote areas and do not have easy access to places where books can be readily purchased. The result is that academic writing on Aboriginal women fails to reach people in many communities and an important function of accountability is lost.

Writing in 1994, Margaret Jackson, a professor at Simon Fraser University, draws the following conclusions:

> The various positions taken by Aboriginal women and Aboriginal groups are not significantly different in their basic assumptions. For the most part, the social values they seek to entrench are the same: sexual equality, freedom of speech, etc. The differences lie in the paths chosen to secure those values and in the speeds safest to achieve them.[11] (195)

These conclusions ignore or misinterpret the work of many Aboriginal women. Aboriginal society is not ordered around the same values, such as sexuality, equality and especially freedom of speech, as Canadian society. Expecting Aboriginal society to be ordered around the same principles as Canadian society ignores the possibility that difference can exist. It also ignores the fact that Aboriginal societies have survived colonization (and that Canadian society colonized). This is a fundamental difference between the two communities. Professor Jackson participates in perpetuating this colonial tradition and exercises the power of the colonialist by selectively recognizing only the values that the Canadian system aspires to.

The history of "White" women's organization is not always a history that should be recounted with pride in the respect demonstrated for racial and cultural diversity.[12] In fact, women in the 19th century who respected Aboriginal women are probably the exception, not the norm. In 1879, a group of Christian women in the United States organized the Women's National Indian Association. A great majority of women in this organization were *not* Aboriginal. The executive of the organization certainly was non-Aboriginal. The organization toiled for seven decades in an effort to teach domestic skills to Aboriginal women claiming their efforts would continue until:

> The Indian women and home *are permitted* to rise from pagan darkness, degradation, destitution and suffering into the light of Christian faith, nobleness, comfort and independence. . . . (Mathes 1990: 8)

The Christian women believed in their path of reform in which they were the chosen teachers. In the hundred years since the Women's National Indian Organization was formed, progress has not been made in disrupting the ability of the mainstream to interpret the reality that Aboriginal women should aspire to.

The inclusiveness of early women's organization has not been the subject either of retrospection within the women's movement or of rigorous academic inquiry at any point in history. Although it is reported that the women of the National Indian Women's Association conducted extensive research (obviously not with the objects of their inquiry), they concluded that law, citizenship and education were the answers. More disturbing, the women asserted:

> ... treaties which hindered their civilization process should either be altered or abrogated and that Indians should hold their lands in severalty. (5)

Colonization of Indigenous nations is not a process that is unique to governments but was supported by the majority of social institutions at the time. The process of contact and colonization from an Aboriginal perspective is not yet commonly understood. Analysis of the early women's movement and their relationship with Aboriginal women is scant. This is an area of rigorous inquiry that needs to be completed by academics. The current relationship of Aboriginal women with the women's movement cannot be understood without an understanding of the past. Non-Aboriginal academics would do better to pursue their own historical responsibilities rather than continuing try to explain Aboriginal women's aspirations today.[13] For example, the assumption that Aboriginal women's organization began in the 1970s is an historical error. It is based on the failure to incorporate the impact of colonialism on women's ideology. It relies on a definition of organization that belongs to mainstream women. It is about the power to define what organization is and is not.

I do not consider my position to be anti-feminist. I just do not see feminism as removed from the colonial practices of this country. I do not believe in a single truth. My position is a reaction to the exclusions and intrusions I have felt from within the women's movement and feminist academia. I remain very woman-centred. Some would call it Aboriginal feminism but I have no use for a label that has no meaning for me. My view is simple. It is the view of a single Mohawk woman who has experienced more than a decade of study of Canadian law and before that a decade of overt physical violence in my life.

Some Aboriginal women have turned to the feminist or women's movement to seek solace (and solution) in the common oppression of women. I have a problem with perceiving this as a full solution. I am not just woman. I am a Mohawk woman. It is not solely my gender through which I first experience the world, it is my culture (and/or race) that precedes my gender. Actually if I am the object of some form of discrimination, it is very difficult for me to separate what happens to me because of my gender and what happens to me because of my race and culture. My world is not experienced in a linear and compartmentalized way. I experience the world simultaneously as Mohawk and as woman.[14] It seems as though I cannot repeat this message too many times. To artificially separate my gender from my race and culture forces me to deny the way I experience the world. Such denial has devastating effects on Aboriginal constructions of reality. Many, but not all, Aboriginal women reject the rigors of feminism as the full solution to the problems that Aboriginal women face in both the dominant society and within our own communities.

Over the years I have come to believe that one of the reasons why Aboriginal women were not forced to survive violence in their homes until the present century is the power we had to define what was a "crime" (unaccepted behavior). Included in that definition of wrongdoing was the failure to respect women (and I think this is a greater standard than merely not abusing women). It has often been said to me, "Grandmother makes the rules; Grandfather enforces them"[15] (First Nations Circle on the Constitution 1992: 62). The state's involvement in the historic oppression of Aboriginal women and the denial of our individual and collective rights has not been incidental or accidental. It at times may have been without intent but that does not excuse the devastating impact it has had on our communities. The state is fully implicated in the violence that exists in Indian communities today. The state constructed the *Indian Act* and saw to its implementation, which has continuously stripped Indian women and our children of basic rights such as citizenship. In the 1876 *Indian Act*, women were entitled to be registered based either on their marriage to an Indian man or because of their birth to an Indian man. Women were men's property. This was not an Aboriginal tradition.

In my experience (and documented in the first part of this chapter), the woman's movement must come to terms with Aboriginal women's diversity *as we define it*. The same can be said for the political organizations and structures of Canada.[16] The recognition of distinct Aboriginal ways of being is the minimum precondition of my involvement in mainstream relations such as the women's movement. I cannot come to any discussion while at the same time always having to explain and defend why I am different and deserve different treatment. This places an oppressive burden on Aboriginal women.

I am brought again to a paradoxical conclusion. My involvement in the women's movement (or other mainstream political movements) carries with it the very real threat of racial and cultural discrimination (or oppression). My involvement in the Aboriginal movement carries with it the very real threat of gender and/or sexual discrimination. Again, in confronting this paradox of my existence, I realize how much of my life is spent negotiating contradictions and exclusions. I can only conclude that the development of a strong Indigenous women's network (which is purposefully not to say organization) is essential. Within this imagined Aboriginal women's network, it is essential that we construct our relationships based upon the respect for diversity across Indigenous nation lines (that is to say, the Mohawk, Cree, Dene, Mi'kmaq, Métis, Inuit and so on) and upon respect for our diversity in experience (that is to say, of violence, poverty, residency, colonialist patterns, sexual preference, ableism, language, education and so on).

Striving at all times to re-claim[17] the traditions of my people, the respect and power women once held, is the single most important reason why I cannot accept a feminist construction of reality. My ability to re-claim my position in the world as Haudenosaunee woman is preconditioned on the ability of our men to remember the traditions that we have lost. These traditions are not found in the European roots of the feminist movement or the present day idea that women's oppression will be eradicated when women assume male-defined positions of status and power. The status of Aboriginal women is at times documented (and envied) in the early years of feminism and the women's movement, but the stories are there only because they have been borrowed.[18] Involving myself deeply in the women's movement, including locating my quest for identity there, means being willing to accept less than the position accorded to women of my nation historically. Equality is not a high standard in my way of thinking.

The impact of colonization on the present day experience of Aboriginal Peoples cannot be minimized. The idea of Indian experience defined by the four corners of a piece of land called an Indian reserve, a fraction of our original territories, is of central importance. It is also violence. It is violence of a different kind. In the Aboriginal worldview, the Creator put each of our many nations down on a separate territory. We still know how to delineate those territories. That land that supports and nurtures our lives is Mother. We have to live in a foreign system of drawing lines on our Mother, dividing her up, just in the same way pornography exposes various parts of a women's anatomy for the pleasure and gratification of the male sex. I refuse to continue to think in terms of Canada, Ontario, Quebec, and so on, or this reserve or that reserve. I know which First Nation territory I live in. I also know I am from Grand River Territory. I married into the Cree Nation, Treaty Six. Recognizing in thought the true relationships which govern my life is one small way I try to reclaim the integrity of my people and the earth.

The construction of reserve-based "Indian" experience as somehow more legitimate or absolute fosters false divisions among Aboriginal people, including the way Aboriginal women have chosen to organize. The Native Women's Association of Canada organized itself around provincial boundaries, with each province or territory having a representative organization. In my mind such an organizational choice forces us to accept a certain degree of colonialism as legitimate. The same problem occurs within the political organization of the chiefs and the Native Council of Canada (now the Congress of Aboriginal Peoples). The Assembly of First Nations is organized on the concept of chief found in the *Indian Act*. There is nothing truly Indian about the *Indian Act*. It was not written by us or for us or about us. It is a foreign system of ideas and beliefs about governing that was forced on us. The *Indian Act* is about imposition. The source of authority for the political leaders in our communities is illegitimate as that source is someone else's system of law and belief. It is from within this ultimate contradiction that our leaders are expected to negotiate and mediate our futures.

Over time, reserve residency has come to be equated with "true" Aboriginal experience. The affect of this presumption is far reaching and impacts on Aboriginal and non-Aboriginal thinking about the problems confronting Aboriginal communities. There are numerous examples of this conceptual difficulty. For example, in a recent work on self-government, one scholar makes this statement:

> While difficult to judge, it may be that the harm done to customary Aboriginal ways of being is already too great for a return to spiritual balance without the imposition of structure and process. . . . there are many Aboriginal people who are no longer in touch with their Aboriginal roots. *What of the overwhelming proportion of Aboriginals who have become urbanized.* What meaning does a healing circle have to someone born in a city where concrete, and concrete poverty, provide the surround. (Jackson 1994: 194, emphasis added)

This scholar concludes that Aboriginal aspirations require the "imposition of structure and process." This conclusion is based on the mis-assumption that urbanization *only* results in assimilation. This is colonial thought (as well as patronizing and simplistic). This conclusion cannot be maintained when it is based on such a gravely faulty assumption. Non-reserve residency is seen by the mainstream as less real or less legitimate Aboriginal experience.

Unfortunately, some of our own people have embraced this false dichotomy. This construction is problematic for a number of reasons. First, my experience as an Aboriginal (Haudenosaunee) woman is not necessarily negations of or opposite to mainstream experiences. I am not a negation of Canadian culture, but I am citizen of a distinct cultural enclave. That cultural history and experience is just as meaningful and legitimate as the mainstream equivalents. Second, not all Aboriginal experience is Indian experience. Remember, Indian status is merely a legal construction and has no distinct cultural meaning. It is only registered Indians who hold the "right or privilege" to reside on reserves. By inference then, reserve residency as a criterion for legitimate or authentic Aboriginal experience excludes by definition many enclaves of Aboriginal people, including the Métis. The second inference is that off-reserve residency somehow equates to assimilation (or no longer Indian). At most my experience is bi-cultural, not non-Aboriginal (that is, assimilated).

The ideas that people have about reserve residency need to be modernized. When reserves were first established, they were very much part of a plan to control Indian populations. Land for reserves was therefore granted in isolated places. Indians were once prohibited from traveling off these reserves without a pass secured from the Indian Agent. The seclusion of Indian peoples on reserves was an important aspect in understanding Indian/White relations *historically*. Today, Indian people have also had access and benefit from new technologies. This has had an impact on the isolation of community life. It is now possible to work in a city hours from your reserve. The idea that Indian people experience *either* reserve life or urban life is a great fallacy. Many Indian people have found creative ways of experiencing both. The situation is no longer either/or.

This idea that being raised on an Indian reserve and/or maintaining your residency on reserve is a requirement of legitimate Indian experience also has particular consequences for women. Because section 12(1)(b) of the *Indian Act*—the marrying out clause—impacted disproportionately on women, Aboriginal women are statistically more likely to reside in cities (or off-reserve). This means that women have less opportunity to claim the legitimacy that is granted because of reserve residence. This means that the parameters of legitimacy surrounding "Indian-ness" are likely to reflect a male bias and a male view of the world.

The first personal memory I have of Aboriginal (Indian) women organizing is the battle against the *Indian Act* provisions which stripped a woman of her Indian status if she married a non-status Indian.[19] The efforts of Indian women across the country coalesced into the formation of a national women's organization, the Native Women's Association of Canada.[20] It is interesting to understand that the first *formal* (that is to say, under the corporate laws of Canada) organizing of Aboriginal women[21] occurred around the issue of state oppression and *not* around so-called women's issues (violence against women and children, rape, custody, daycare, employment equity and so on). This is paralleled in the women's movement during the late 1800s and early 1900s in North America.[22] Early feminist efforts focused on securing for women the right to vote. There is, however, a difference. Members of the women's movement have always wanted access to the existing political structures; many Aboriginal women continue to just want out of that mainstream political structure. This recognition is so essential. It is one of the biggest sources of conflict among Aboriginal women.

Not every Aboriginal woman feels well-represented by the Native Women's Association of Canada.[23] The simplest answer would be to blame the leadership of that organization in the same way that we blame chiefs for the many problems in our communities.[24] I was uncomfortable with the idea that *Indian Act* governments ought to be blamed, and chiefs in particular, for the epidemics of violence against women in some of our communities. This same courtesy is naturally due to the political leaders of the Aboriginal women's movement. The source of the conflict amongst Aboriginal women is often the misconception by the mainstream that we are all alike. That misconception is racism. As Aboriginal women we have tried not to disturb that misconception because our access to a voice in Canada has been prefaced on our ability to put forward a unified front. Aboriginal women have benefited from "acting" all the same. Rather than lose the little voice Aboriginal women have, we have often turned ourselves inside out trying to project that image of "sameness."

The effects of former section 12(1)(b) of the *Indian Act* cannot be minimized. It is a significant source, if not the primary source, of the opposition that exists between Aboriginal men and women (at least in formal political spheres). The *Indian Act* replaced Aboriginal forms of government with non-democratic[25] and hierarchical government institutions which were unfamiliar to the people of our communities. The imposition of the band council governments met the opposition of many communities.[26] Ironically, the source of much of the political opposition between Aboriginal organizations and the two genders does not belong to us but is found in the continued failure of the federal government to implement a full recognition of the inherent right to self-government. Unfortunately, there are those Aboriginal people who embrace our oppression in such a way that we blame each other rather than the oppressive state institutions and structures who have authored our situation. It is for this reason that the 1985 amendments to the *Indian Act* are an important point of inquiry.

The 1985 amendments to the *Indian Act* (commonly referred to as Bill C-31) did not result in true equality for Indian women. They do not even establish the lesser standard of gender parity. I see gender parity as a lessor standard because it does not take into account difference. This fact is not obvious on the face of the statutory provisions.[27] Speaking to the Joint Parliamentary Committee on Indian Affairs and Northern Development in June of 1984, Chief Wally McKay stated:

> ... the witnesses for the Assembly of First Nations made it very clear that we are in favour of the federal government's ending its

discrimination against Indian women under section 12(1)(b) of the Indian Act. We made the point that it is not within our Indian tradition and ethics to practice discrimination. We regard that discrimination as a wantonly unjust act. We cannot, therefore, agree to a continuation of discrimination, and we want to see justice done and the total restoration of the Indian status of those persons of Indian ancestry who lost their status as a result of the operation of section 12(1)(b).

That is why we advocate that all such persons be entitled to reinstatement. If this Bill confines reinstatement to the first generation only, it will perpetuate the discrimination and its effects. (*Hansard*, June 28, 1984, vol. 19: 87-88)

Despite the objections of the Native Women's Association of Canada and other national Aboriginal organizations, Bill C-31 was passed into law in June of 1985 with the second generation cut-off intact. The effect of this is to treat men and women differently under the current *Indian Act* status regime.[28] The grandchildren of a woman who "married-out"[29] are not eligible for re-instatement or registration. Yet, the grandchildren of a man who "married out" are eligible to be registered. Effectively, brothers and sisters (and their children) can be differentially affected by this regime. This does not remove gender discrimination from the *Indian Act*. The second generation cut-off can only have the affect of increasing gender resentments in our communities.

The efforts of Aboriginal women against the oppression of the *Indian Act* have only succeeded in achieving a more equal access to the existing system of band membership and Indian registration for women previously enfranchised. It has also created a system of registration that undermines the future population. Status is now hierarchical. Only children with parents registered at the same band are entitled to "top status." This status used to accrue prior to the 1985 changes to a single parent registering a child. It is impossible for me to construct this as some form of meaningful progress.[30] Aboriginal women's identity has not been re-claimed through the "Bill C-31"[31] amendments. What was secured at the cost of a cumbersome and illogical system of registration was a more equal access to the system of laws which have successfully oppressed our people since the advent of the *Indian Act* in 1876. Equal access to oppressive laws (colonialism) is not progress. I do not see this as a failure of the organizing and politicking of Aboriginal women but as a demonstration of the helplessness and powerlessness of Aboriginal people in Canadian society and the inability of Canadian law makers to respond to the issues in the way that Aboriginal Peoples experience them.

I have heard it suggested that the compromise position of "Bill C-31" results from the inability of Aboriginal organizations to agree on the substantive issues. Given our great diversity, where does the requirement for unanimity arise? This is a standard that no other level of government in Canada is held accountable to. Aboriginal organizations, however, did all agree that section 12(1)(b) was unacceptable and that the inherent right to self-government included the right to define citizenship. The requirement for a compromise amendment results not from gendered Aboriginal tensions but the failure of the federal government to accept the inherent Aboriginal right to define our own citizenship. The decision to separate band membership and Indian status is in no way predicated on any position taken by Aboriginal political organizations. It is a compromise position that the Canadian government could deal with. It is a compromise position forced on Aboriginal Peoples that continues to have grave consequences in our communities.

In the recent constitutional debates, the media emphasized the alleged chasm which exists between Aboriginal men and women largely resulting from the s.12(1)(b) debates. It was exemplified there by the alleged gendered positions on individual (the women) and collective (the men) rights. The traditional understanding that has been shared with me indicates that this construction of individual *versus* collective rights is a false one. Individual rights exist within collective rights, and the rights of the collective exist in the individual.[32] Any hierarchical ordering of either the notion of collective rights or individual rights will fundamentally violate the culture of Aboriginal Peoples.[33] Such a violation, whether it favours or prioritizes the individual or collective, can only result in one thing—the further destruction of Aboriginal cultures. It must also be remembered, especially by Aboriginal individuals, that the roots of our oppression lie in our collective loss of memory.[34]

There is a further problem with placidly accepting the construction of Canadian law as a solution for Aboriginal people. Aboriginal societies are not ordered around a conception of rights. Early in my legal education I went home to talk to the Elders about what exactly a right was. I had become confused and overwhelmed by the number of rights I had discovered at law school. What I learned when I went home is that I have one right, the right to be a Mohawk woman because that is how the Creator made me.[35] The rest of what I have are responsibilities. Even today, when I think too hard about rights, I become confused. Responsibilities, however, I understand. It is necessary to understand how rights discourse impacts on my Aboriginal perceptions of the world and of law.

A lot of Aboriginal political activity, including the energy of Aboriginal women, has focused on the politics of resistance. I think being preoccupied with rights ideology is related to being able to live in resistance only.

Someone else sets the agenda and Aboriginal people respond to it. This can be seen in each round of constitutional negotiations Aboriginal people have engaged in over the last two decades. In the early 1980s Canada decided repatriation, a home-grown amending formula and a *Charter of Rights and Freedoms* were necessary components of Canadian state organization. Aboriginal people responded, not wanting to be left out of the constitutional renovations because Aboriginal people knew that our exclusion from these areas of reform would have a negative impact on Aboriginal lives and well-being. When Canada was concerned with leaving Quebec out of the constitutional fold, again, Aboriginal people responded with resistance.

Perhaps it is my dissatisfaction with resistance that inspires my dissatisfaction with women's politics as the standard that I am expected to be content with. Resistance is not a healthy condition. Resistance is a mode of life that is cultivated in the seeds of Aboriginal oppression and more than a century of living under and with colonialism. I expect that it is this dissatisfaction with resistance as *the* mode of life that is the realization that leads me to conclude that constitutional negotiations with Canada are *not* something I really want to write about anymore. Canadian laws are not an Aboriginal answer. In the future, I do see solutions on the horizon. For me they are located in the collective memory of my people and our ancestors, and not in constitutional reform. Our survival as a peoples has always depended on our own creativity and not on a political power-sharing relationship with the federal government. And Aboriginal women have special responsibility within that creativity.

Notes

1. I use the term Indigenous when I wish to refer to the global situation of all original peoples. I use the term Aboriginal Peoples to refer to the peoples who live on the territory now occupied by Canada.
2. I co-ordinated four constituent assemblies (women, youth, Elders and urban) for the First Nations Circle on the Constitution.
3. I am uncomfortable with this construction of race. I am also uncomfortable with the word "White." So far, I have not been able to discover English words that are comfortable to me when I wish to refer to non-Aboriginal people. This is just one example of how inadequate the English language is, especially for individuals who wish to bring a different cultural or gender perspective to the discourse. I think this problem of language is a reflection of the disempowered status of both Aboriginal Peoples and women.
4. For a full discussion, please see Walker 1979: 71-77.
5. This is not to suggest that political action and securing resources for the protection of women has even been easily gained in mainstream society. The point is that particular places within the struggle are more privileged. This privilege can come in a number of forms, race, wealth, familiarity with mainstream structures and institutions of government (such as funding applications), language and residency to name a few.

6. I refer only to Indian communities here because this is what I have experienced. The same may be true for other Aboriginal communities but I will leave this for those women to speak about.

7. I also have a degree of discomfort around the images of helplessness that the victim label imposes sometimes for the lifetime of the individual. Initially, there is a period of victimization but after that a time comes when you first become a survivor. Once you have matured in your healing you come into a position where the horrible acts committed against you become strength and compassion and you are woman warrior. I owe the last insight to Deborah Hanly (Métis Nation, Alberta) with great gratitude.

8. Anger is one of the first responses to the memories of abuse.

9. First Nations Circle on the Constitution. For a fuller discussion of the impact of residential schools please refer to Knockwood 1992.

10. For a discussion of criminal behaviors amongst the Iroquois at the time of contact, please see Newell 1965. Quoting from the journal of Mary Jemison, "a white woman who spent 68 years of her life among the Iroquois," Newell provides:

    "From all history and tradition it would appear that neither seduction, prostitution, nor rape, was known in the calendar of this rude savage, until the females were contaminated by the embrace of civilized man. And it is a remarkable fact, that among the great number of women and girls who have been taken prisoners by the Indians during the last two centuries. . . not a single instance is on record or has ever found currency in the great stock of gossip and story which civilized society is prone to circulate, that a female prisoner has ever been ill-treated, abused, or her modesty insulted, by an Indian, with reference to her sex."

11. Jackson, Margaret 1994. Professor Jackson relies on my work and fundamentally misinterprets my views.

12. After locating Valerie Sherer Mathes' article (1990) I rushed home in great anticipation to read, looking for confirmation that Aboriginal women's organizing began earlier than 1970. The confirmation I had been looking for was not what was located.

13. For example of the work that can be done please see Backhouse 1991.

14. I have also discussed this experience in "I Know My Name: A First Nations Woman Speaks" Monture 1993 and in "The Violence We Women Do: A First Nations View" Monture-Okanee 1992b.

15. I have also been told this many times by my Elders.

16. In Canada, the Department of Indian and Northern Affairs is not an Aboriginal organization. It does not provide service to Aboriginal Peoples, it provides service in the form of administrative ease for the federal government. The organization is structured around creating easy relationships for the federal government. Its form of organization has never been the choice of Aboriginal Peoples (nor were we ever consulted about its creation), but has been forced upon us.

    Another example of the point I am trying to make is the suggestion that there is an area of law that is about Aboriginal rights. There is nothing Aboriginal about these laws, they are Canadian laws forced on Aboriginal

Peoples. As an Aboriginal woman who is legally trained, the majority of my work focuses on understanding Canadian law in an effort to make space for Aboriginal aspirations.

17. I want to again emphasize that this reclamation project is risky business. It is dangerous to accept historic accounts without considering the possibility and impact of gender, racial and cultural bias born by the authors.

18. These ideas are more fully discussed in Chapters 7 and 11.

19. Please refer to section 12(1)(b) of the *Indian Act*, R.S.C. 1970, C. 1-6. For an historical legal discussion of these issues please refer to Sanders 1975.

    I am not suggesting that this was the first time Aboriginal women organized in a political way. See also Jamieson 1978 and Krosenbrink-Gelissen 1991.

20. Two Aboriginal women's organization were originally formed. The women present at the first national Aboriginal women's conference in Edmonton in 1971 and the second conference in Saskatoon the following year, could not come to agree on the importance of the status question and the explicit sexual discrimination in the *Indian Act*. In particular, the Alberta women felt a strong loyalty to their treaties and their chiefs. Indian Rights for Indian Women had a single political mandate and that was to address the injustices created by the operation of section 12(1)(b) of the *Indian Act*. The Native Women's Association of Canada had the broader mandate including everything but the status question. In 1981, Indian Rights for Indian Women was disbanded as a national organization and became an Alberta-based group. The Native Women's Association of Canada became the only national organization which had members from each of the three classifications of Aboriginal Women (that is, Indian, Inuit and Métis). In 1975 Inuit women began to organize in a national organization. There is still no Métis women's national organization. Several Métis women's organizations exist at a provincial level.

    For a full discussion please see Krosenbrink-Gelissen 1991: 84-87, 95, 99.

21. I am not suggesting that Aboriginal women did not organize historically. There were women's societies prior to contact with European nations. It is interesting to note that Aboriginal women are only recognized for organization when that organization resembles the way in which mainstream social organizations are structured. This is an excellent example of the ethnocentrism which exists in the feminist literature.

22. Further research into the relationship between the early women's movement and Aboriginal women must be encouraged. Little is known about Aboriginal women's involvement and influence in the formative years of the women's movement. Constance Backhouse has made an admirable contribution to the literature in her work.

23. My thoughts here are based on experience. I am the former Vice President of the Ontario Native Women's Association. I held that office from June 1988 to October 1989.

24. The leadership of the Native Women's Association of Canada has changed since the Charlottetown Round.

25. For example, section 82(2), of the *Indian Act*, R.S.C. 1985, c. 1-6 provides that elected chiefs and band councillors are accountable to the Minister of Indian Affairs, not to the members of the communities they are supposed to represent.

26. The story of one community's opposition to the *Indian Act* governments is told in the cases of *Logan* v. *Styres*, [1959] O.W.N. 361, 20 D.L.R. (2d) 416 (Ont. H.C.) and *Isaac* v. *Davey*, [1973] 3 O.R. 677, 38 D.L.R. (3d) 23 (Ont. H.C.) and discussed in Johnston 1986: 19-24.

27. For a full discussion of the effects of the C-31 amendments please refer to Native Women's Association of Canada 1986a and Ontario Native Women's Association 1987.

28. For the purposes of clarification, some Indian peoples did not support the amendment of the *Indian Act* because they believe that "Indian" nations have the inherent right to define citizenship (and note citizenship is different from membership). As a point of principle, these people called for the abolition of state control over the governmental functions of "Indian" nations.

    For an interesting discussion please refer to Native Women's Association of Canada 1986b.

29. It is only the women who were affected by the membership provisions in the *Indian Act*. Men who married out did not lose their status. More incredibly, the non-status women (sometimes "White" women) acquired status.

30. Perhaps I do not fully understand the robes of exclusion of a person with "no-status." Through the luck of birth I have always been entitled to be registered.

31. When a bill is passed it becomes law. Once it is law the bill does not exist anymore. Anyone referring to Bill C-31 Indians is making a reference to something that no longer exists.

32. Interestingly enough, the Assembly of First Nations (who are often accused of representing only men) understands this at least at a philosophical level. In resolution 34/92 passed unanimously by the chiefs (without discussion or one word of opposition from the floor) at their Annual General Assembly held from June 23 to 25, 1992, in Fredericton, New Brunswick, it is said:

    . . . the laws of Canada have actively oppressed the women of the First Nations, diminished their traditional roles and responsibilities, and compromised the respect for women in our communities; and,

    . . . it is recognized that housed within the notion of collective rights of First Nations, are the individual rights of all our citizens . . ..

33. For a discussion of this topic with specific reference to Charter rights please see Turpel 1989-90.

34. Paula Gunn Allen originally speaks of this need to remember in *The Sacred Hoop: Recovering the Feminine in American Indian Traditions* (1986: 213-14). This idea of collective memory loss is also discussed by Sally Roesch Wagner (1990).

35. I have come to understand that this one right is all I need. I am indebted to Jacob Thomas of the Cayuga Nation for his time and patience in helping me to understand.

Politics of Oppression

3. Justice

10

A Vicious Circle:
Child Welfare and the First Nations

THIS PAPER WAS WRITTEN IN 1988 and 1989. It was first published in Volume 3, Number 1, Canadian Journal of Women and the Law, *1-17.*

A t the age of nineteen, Cameron Kerley brutally murdered his adoptive father. The murder followed years of sexual abuse. The child welfare systems of both Canada and the United States had clearly failed this First Nations child. Before he was taken into "care" by child welfare officials and before he was placed for adoption in the United States, Canadian social workers took no preventive measures to keep Cameron with members of his own extended family. After he was placed in the United States, no social workers assessed his placement nor the suitability of his adoptive father nor completed a progress summary of Cameron's adoptive home despite a marked decline in his school achievements. No one in authority ever questioned the placement of a Cree child who resided in Canada across an international border—until a man was dead. The judge and lawyers who participated in his trial never got to the bottom of the matter. They never knew about the sexual abuse nor of the frustration of being an "Indian"[1] in a foreign environment.

It is only Cameron Kerley who must bear the legal and moral responsibility for the life he took. Today, he sits in his prison cell, alone:

> Cameron Kerley looks older than twenty-two, and wearier than a young man should. On bad days he wishes he'd never been born. On good days he dreams of another life, "a house, a job, a car, some quiet place in the country." He's convinced that someday, somehow, he'll find a place where he belongs. (Aboud 1986: 39)

191

When social institutions and legal processes fail, where do we place the responsibility? This is only the first question that must be asked about the Cameron Kerley case. Who stops to ask how many other First Nations children there are like Cameron Kerley?[2]

Statistical data indicates clearly that the situation for First Nations children in Canada is bleak. The most recent comprehensive data available was collected in 1977.[3] It is estimated that there are 15,500 First Nations children in the care of the child welfare authorities (this includes status Indians, non-status Indians and Métis children). Twenty percent of the total number of children in care in Canada are First Nations children. The First Nations population in the western provinces is larger, and the over-representation of children in care is also greater. Thirty-nine percent of the children in care in British Columbia are First Nations children; the figures are 44 percent in Alberta, 51.5 percent in Saskatchewan and 60 percent in Manitoba (Hepworth 1980: 112).[4] In contrast, the First Nations population of Canada is approximately 3.5 percent of the total population (Asch 1984).[5] First Nations children are clearly over-represented within the child welfare system. There are no indications that the situation is improving.

Not only are First Nations children more likely to be apprehended but, once they are taken into care, they are less likely to be either returned to their parents or placed for adoption. If a First Nations child is placed for adoption or placed in a foster home, it is unlikely that such a home will be a First Nations home. Only 22 percent of such placements are with First Nations (Johnson 1982: 176). The effect of the child welfare process is to remove and then seclude First Nations children from their cultural identity and their cultural heritage.

The historical failure of legislative bodies and the courts to protect or respect the cultural identity of First Nations children has been identified in the literature as a disregard of the "indigenous factor." The unique character of First Nations children as members of a specific class is under-emphasized, undervalued or ignored in child welfare matters. This situation requires a response that is particular to the needs of First Nations children, rather than one that is general to the needs of all children (Carasco 1986: 111).[6] The disregard of the "indigenous factor" within the Canadian child welfare system is merely a reflection of the position of First Nations within Canadian society. The pressure to assimilate (i.e., to disregard the importance of the "indigenous factor" in your own life) is immense. This places tremendous psychological burdens on First Nations children, families and communities. First Nations communities believe that their future and the survival of the traditional ways depends on children. When children of original ancestry are removed from their homes and communities:

The traditional circle of life is broken. This leads to a breakdown of the family, community, and breaks the bonds of love between the parent and the child. To constructively set out to break the Circle of Life is destructive and is literally destroying Native communities and Native cultures. (Hill 1983: 55)

Removing children from their homes weakens the entire community.[7] Removing children from their culture and placing them in a foreign culture is an act of genocide.[8]

The failure to recognize the importance of the "indigenous factor" is not limited to the child welfare system and the corresponding legal decisions. The "indigenous factor" is ignored throughout the entire judicial system in matters which involve First Nations people or issues. First Nations people are also over-represented within the criminal justice process. Criminologists have long recognized the relationship between family breakdown and delinquency. Troubled children get involved in the criminal justice process. In a study of a single community where probation and court records were examined, it was found that 39 percent of the sample were First Nations children, even though the total First Nations population in the area was only 10 percent (LaPrairie 1983: 343). The over-representation of Native people does not end with juvenile justice statistics. In Kenora, Ontario, the waiting list of fine defaulters convicted of liquor offences could fill up the local jail four times over (Jolly 1983: 58). Sixty-six percent of fine defaulters are of original ancestry, and First Nations people are twice as likely to default on fines as are Euro-Canadian people (Hagan 1977: 172). The incarceration of First Nations people is reaching crisis proportions. Quite expectedly, studies of the federal penitentiaries reveal that 10 percent[9] of inmates are of original ancestry (Frideres 1983: 182-83 and Ponting and Gibbins 1980: 58).

Indeed, the over-representation of First Nations peoples within institutions of confinement—be they child welfare institutions, provincial jails or federal prisons—is part of a vicious cycle of abuse. Cameron Kerley was trapped in this vicious cycle, and he is but one example of how the dominant culture in Canada is grinding down the people of the First Nations.[10]

This vicious cycle of abuse is the subject of the Canadian Bar Association's report entitled *Locking up Natives in Canada* (Jackson 1988). The report does not focus principally on criminal justice institutions or even on First Nations prisoners. It is a detailed analysis of the models available to establish tribal courts. The conclusion of this report is simply that the jurisdiction and the control over matters of criminal justice must be meaningfully assumed by First Nations. It is in this way that the over-representation of First Nations citizens in Canadian institutions of incarceration will be alleviated. The report traces the problem of over-incarcerating First Nations citizens to a failure to recognize the sovereignty of the First Nations in any meaningful way.

I am deliberately connecting child "welfare" law with the criminal "justice" system. From the perspective of a traditional First Nations woman, I see the child welfare system as being on a continuum with the criminal justice system. The child welfare system feeds the youth and adult correctional systems. Both institutions remove citizens from their communities, which has a devastating effect on the cultural and spiritual growth of the individual. It also damages the traditional social structures of family and community. Both the child welfare system and the criminal justice system are exercised through the use of punishment, force and coercion.

As a First Nations woman, my worldview[11] does not revolve around the acceptance of punishment or the validation of force and coercion. Instead, it revolves around balance. The spiritual ceremonies and traditional teachings given by the Elders[12] involve instruction about who we are as individuals and as members of a nation. These holistic teachings involve education, spirituality (religion), law (living peacefully), family and government. Holistic means to be connected. The earth is mother. The sky is father. Woman is earth and earth is woman. They are inseparable. The traditions in no way involve a hierarchical ordering. There exists a natural balance between women and men in the way of creation. It is the woman who stands at the centre of the nation because women are the caretakers of children. The children are women's responsibility first. Before this can be understood, the role and meaning of caretaker must be understood.[13] Spiritually, women are more fortunate than men, especially in this modern society where the role of provider has substantially dwindled in importance or been confused through social welfare programs and women's developing economic power.[14] As women, we know who and what we will be when we grow up. We will be mothers, and mothers have even today primary responsibility for children.[15] It is in this way that Aboriginal women's roles remain clearer than the roles of our men.

The structure of First Nation's society is based on cooperation and consensus. When difficulties arise within a community, the community responds by attempting to bring the person who is the source of the difficulty back into the community. This process naturally involves all parties—the parents, the child, the relations and the Elders. In a criminal matter, the offender, the victims and the Elders are all naturally involved. The aim and the result is to restore balance in the community, which includes balance in the relationships among the individuals involved. In the case of child welfare, no parent is left believing he or she is a "bad" parent—nor is any child alienated from the family or community. In a community which operates on norms of consensus and co=operation, the collective's rights are the focus. However, balance of the collective cannot be accomplished without the well-being of the individual. By contrast, the structures of the dominant society, where the philosophy of punishment is paramount and force and coercion are validated, there are winners and losers. As the dispossessed people of this land, First Nations citizens will continue to be the losers.

Whatever the issue, be it child welfare, criminal justice, family violence, alcohol and drug abuse, or lack of education or employment, the same path can be traced to a conflict in the basic values of the two societies—force and coercion versus consensus and cooperation. This realization, then, can take us to only one conclusion: First Nations demands for self-determination (sovereignty)[16] must be realized. Drastic reforms are necessary both within the legal system and child welfare policy regimes as they affect First Nations citizens. What is not generally recognized is that to accept and advocate only legislative changes to the laws of child welfare is not the final solution.[17] To advocate only piecemeal changes to legislative structures is effectively to accept that the lives of First Nations individuals who fall prey to the instruments of the child welfare system will not substantially change. There has been only nominal change in the statistics reflecting the involvement of First Nations citizens in both child welfare process[18] and the criminal justice system[19] over recent decades. The failure to fundamentally shift the situation is the first indicator that piecemeal legislative reforms are not the singular solution. Failure to meet this challenge will continue to result in further piecemeal legislative reforms. The inevitable consequence will be the genocide of First Nations people.

If the premises presented thus far are correct, and I believe they are, they necessitate a reconstruction of the way in which we understand what has happened as First Nations have come in contact with dominant institutions. We must peel back the layers of misunderstanding of both the dominant culture and First Nations culture which currently shape our cross-cultural (mis)communications. This requires an extensive examination of the meanings underlying dominant social structures, including legal institutions and their traditions. It is also necessary to recognize how the concepts of the dominant society conflict with or contradict those of First Nations social structure as well as where there is common ground. If individuals who belong to a specific group are unable to accept the underlying values—such as force and coercion—of the dominant social system, they will never be able to participate fully in it.

Inviting people of the First Nations to the table to discuss the definitional structures and assumptions which underpin the dominant social systems is not a new idea. In 1966, the Hawthorne Report examined the plight of First Nations people in Canada in search for a solution. "The public concern about the Indians and the public knowledge of their problems that would demand a change are scanty and uneven. Public knowledge does not even match public misconception. Not enough is known of the problems to create a call for their solution" (Hawthorne 1966: 6). In 1980, a conference on social development cited as a "national tragedy" the plight of First Nations children within the child welfare system. Further, the situation of First Nations children was cited as the single greatest problem confronting the child welfare system in Canada in the 1980s. Federal government officials also agree, calling the access to child welfare and preventive services for First Nations people "grossly inadequate by any recognized standard" (Johnson 1982: 175).

Between the 1960s and the 1980s, little meaningful change has been accomplished. More than twenty years of First Nations children continue to suffer. That truth is a reality that First Nations women carry, for we are the ones who continue to watch the children suffer. If we have not yet arrived at a place where there can be an appeal to the general public for a solution, then education of the general public must be part of the solution. It is just part of the solution. We must also educate all individuals employed within the field or reach of the child welfare system. This must include, at a minimum, lawyers, judges, social workers, policy makers, academics, scholars and politicians. It is not just *for* First Nations that this commitment is necessary. It is for all of us in this society.[20]

I can best participate in this process by exposing the racism inherent in our legal systems. The devaluation of the "indigenous factor" in child welfare cases has already been mentioned. What has not been said is that the "indigenous factor" is a soft way of referring to the racism inherent not only in child welfare structures, but in the laws and cases regarding child welfare. It is necessary to understand the racism identifiable in legal processes and institutions. The case law of child welfare is only one example. Piecemeal reforms to legislative structures without changing the fundamental racist notions which underpin these laws only allows for a significant change in the *manner* in which racism is constituted and implemented within legal structures—it cannot eliminate it. This is a massive undertaking because racism extends across all of our legal relations. Yes, racism is a hard word. But racism (perhaps colonialism better expresses the problem) is woven into our legal system. I have chosen to start with child welfare because First Nations people are taught that our children are our future. It is also the logical starting place for me, as a woman who accepts responsibility for the traditional teachings which show us that we are responsible for seven generations yet to come.

Through the late 1970s and early 1980s, a great deal of the child welfare literature focused on the grave situation which First Nations children were surviving. This academic impetus reflected the lobbying efforts of First Nations coalitions and political bodies (undertaken within the larger society) to effect change in child welfare regimes. The cumulative efforts of these First Nations individuals were successful in securing a number of initiatives meant to address the crisis in child welfare. The Spallumcheen Indian Band By-Law, the most well known of the initiatives, was secured by the hard work and dedication of members of that specific Band.[21] Both the federal government and numerous provincial governments have been involved in the negotiation of bipartite and tripartite agreements which primarily resolve disputes between levels of government and their respective financial and constitutional responsibilities.[22] These negotiations and agreements, secured by the lobby of First Nations, principally addressed the complete void of prevention services available to First Nations. The services secured by these efforts had been made available to all other Canadian parents and their children for many years. First Nations were excluded from receiving prevention services because of a jurisdictional dispute between federal and provincial governments which resulted in the provision of emergency services only to all children resident on Indian reserves. It must be wondered how many child apprehensions would have been unnecessary if preventive services had been provided to First Nation families.

The history of child welfare and First Nations has been fundamentally shaped by the jurisdictional disputes between federal and provincial governments. The resolution of the jurisdictional dispute merely released First Nations children who were trapped in a void between the federal government and individual provincial governments as they argued over legislative and financial responsibilities. It did not, however, improve services for First Nations children.

The outright denial of child welfare services to the First Nations except in "life threatening" (Carasco 1986: 116) situations precipitated the outcry which is reflected in the literature of the 1970s and 1980s. The outcry was further fueled by the removal of children from their cultural community when they were deemed children in need of protection—children such as Cameron Kerley. The denial of services except in emergency was sustained by the "jurisdictional dispute."[23] "Indians and Lands Reserved for Indians" is a head of federal authority under section 91(24) of the *Constitution Act, 1867*. Child welfare is a responsibility of provincial governments. Indian child welfare spans both these areas of government responsibility (the federal government is responsible for Indians, the provinces for child welfare). Each level of government has been able to point at the other as responsible while denying their own accountability. Instead of receiving twice as much attention, Indian child welfare matters received none.

Both levels of government have historically exploited the contradictory distribution of their legislative powers to voice only their own lack of responsibility for child welfare services to the First Nations. In some provinces, individual judges[24] have been effective in resolving the unwillingness of either level of government in initiating responsibility. In a Manitoba decision, Judge Garson is explicit in citing the provincial government as the body responsible for Native child welfare.[25] He lays the foundation for his judgment with this quotation from the Hawthorne Report:

> An evaluation of Indian status and the consequences which have been attached to it by governments make crystal clear that there is a remarkable degree of flexibility or play in the roles which have been, and in the future could be, assumed by either level of government. For the entire history of Indian administration, this play has been *exploited to the disadvantage of the Indian.* The special status of Indian people has been used as a justification for providing them with services inferior to those available to the Whites who established residence in the country, which was once theirs.[26]

Judge Garson follows the strong words of the Hawthorne Report with strong words of his own:

> [T]he court would fail in its special responsibilities if it did not bring to public attention and scrutiny action or conduct by government allegedly justified by constitutional law that is *in reality, in truth and in law, unfair, discriminatory and unlawful.* (238, emphasis in original)

Judge Garson concludes that it is absolutely clear that child welfare services to treaty Indians are a provincial service which must be offered to treaty Indians in the same manner as all other residents of Manitoba.

The case demonstrates that First Nations people will indeed turn to the judiciary for resolution of issues when the political process and Canadian governments willfully fail to address them. With the entrenchment of Aboriginal rights in section 35(1) of the *Constitution Act, 1982,*[27] the role of judges will be of even more importance. Assuming that judicial intervention will be fair, will it be enough? Ironically, the strong position that Judge Garson took on the jurisdictional issue in this case did not return the children to the care of their mother (or her family). The mother's parenting skills were so deficient that not even preventative child welfare counseling and parental skill development would now help. One wonders whether this would still have been the case if the jurisdictional dispute had not prevented the provision of services since the birth of the child.

A second irony becomes apparent when the Manitoba case is put into historical perspective. The Hawthorne Report, commissioned by the federal government, was published in 1966. It condemned government policies which effectively precluded the First Nations from receiving child welfare resources that are available to all other Canadians. Some thirteen years later when this Manitoba case was decided, the jurisdiction issue was still not resolved, and First Nations still did not receive child welfare services. This failure to provide child welfare services is an important historical fact which should not be easily forgotten or brushed aside. It would be a mistake to ignore the negative manner in which the jurisdictional dispute has shaped our present. In reality, it will take child welfare authorities many years to heal the damage created by the denial of jurisdiction by both levels of government, in both the minds of the First Nations and in the real lives of First Nations children.[28]

First Nations distrust the child welfare system because it has effectively assisted in robbing us of our children and of our future. The distrust is further complicated by the adversarial process itself, which is antithetical to the First Nations consensus method of conflict resolution. Judicial decisions on child welfare reinforce the status quo by applying standards and tests which are not culturally relevant. This is a form of racism.[29]

These racist standards and tests of child welfare law were developed by judges. The most important test is the "best interests of the child." The racist content of this test is not difficult to see. In *Racine* v. *Woods* (1983 S.C.R.), Madame Justice Bertha Wilson wrote for the Supreme Court of Canada: "the law no longer treats children as the property of those who gave them birth but focuses on what is in their best interests." This is the first level of misunderstanding in the laws regarding Canadian children. First Nations laws never were constructed on a view that saw children as property. What is viewed as progress in Canadian courts and law is a source of bemusement for First Nations.

The case of *Racine* involved a status Indian child who was made a ward of the Children's Aid Society of Manitoba, with the consent of the mother. At the time of trial, the child was seven years old, and the non-Indian[30] foster parents had applied for her legal adoption—against her mother's will. Since the time the mother had given custody of her child to the Children's Aid Society, she had left an abusive relationship, recovered from alcoholism, re-educated herself, established a home on her reserve and begun a teaching career. The mother believed that her daughter should grow up within her own culture and tradition. The Supreme Court of Canada effectively refused to take this belief seriously and based their decision on the "best interests of the child" test.[31]

Psychological evidence was presented at trial. The position of the adoptive parents was advanced by testimony which concluded the child's best interests are met by the bonding which occurs with parents and the security of the established home. The natural mother's position was bolstered by psychological testimony which indicated the importance of cultural ties, especially during adolescence.[32] After balancing both sets of interests, Madame Justice Wilson concluded:

> In my view, when the test to be met is the best interests of the child, *the significance of cultural background and heritage as opposed to bonding abates over time.* The closer the bond that develops with the prospective adoptive parents the less important the racial element becomes. (188)

There is evidence that the importance of heritage does not abate over time.[33] The assertion that the importance of heritage abates over time really reflects a belief in the value and certainty of the assimilation of First Nations. This belief is not grounded in First Nations tradition and culture but is a reflection of both government policy and "White" values, which are the values that Canadian courts are constructed upon.[34] It is a belief that conceptualizes and prioritizes the rights of individuals (adopting parents) over collective rights (the right to culture). And it is a test that effectively forces the assimilation and destruction of First Nations people. The issue of inter-racial adoption affects the entire First Nations population in this country. Courts, however, as a result of the structure of the law only view the question in individual cases. This eclipses important issues that First Nations communities wish to see addressed. This is all racism.[35]

The evidence relied on in the *Racine* case to resolve the issue of race is instructive. Madame Justice Wilson relies on the expert testimony of Dr. McCrae to validate her position; the words she chose to rely on are very telling:

> I think this whole business of racial and Indian whatever you want to call it. . . . It doesn't matter if Sandra Racine was Indian and the child was white and Linda Woods was white. . . . It has nothing to do with race, absolutely nothing to do with culture, it has nothing to do with ethnic background. It's two women and a little girl, and one of them doesn't know her. It's as simple as that; all the rest of it is extra and of no consequence, except to the people involved of course.[36]

In her Supreme Court judgment, Madame Justice Wilson said essentially the same thing:

> I believe that interracial adoption, like interracial marriage, is now an accepted phenomenon in our pluralist society. The implications of it may have been overly dramatized by the respondent in this case. The real issue is the cutting of the child's legal tie with her natural mother. . . . While the Court can feel great compassion for the respondent, and respect for her determined efforts to overcome her adversities, it has an obligation to ensure that any order it makes will promote the best interests of her child. This and this alone is our task.

Compassion and respect do not excuse or make acceptable the court's inability to contextualize the decision made in *Racine*. The texture of the decision rests on a construction of the world which respects the culture and worldview of only one of the parents.

The *Racine* case is not an isolated instance of the suppression and misinterpretation of First Nations culture. In *Re Eliza* (1982, 2 C.N.L.R.) the court benevolently recognized the importance of recognizing "community differences." But the judge used ethnocentric stereotypes of the "drunken Indian" to shape the definition of "community differences." Provincial Court Judge Moxley referred to habits such as "acceptance of widespread drinking and even drunkenness" and "tolerance to violence while drunk." These are not "habits" that are "tolerated" by First Nations communities— they are some of the *realities* of racial oppression. Value judgments such as these reinforce the "blame the victim" approach to First Nations people. Yet judges treat these value judgments as self-evident truths.

Another example of the devaluation of the First Nations tradition and the willingness to blame the victim is found in *John* v. *Superintendent of Child Welfare*:

> Here we have a young Indian girl, born and brought up among her people. She became pregnant. She was upset, confused and worried. One would expect that she should be entitled to feel that she could turn to her own people for help, or at least for some understanding and compassion. But what happened? Her own mother was not interested. Her father did not lift a finger to help her. Her own sister gave no assistance. MacDonald's sister came to see her, but offered her no help. The father of the child was indifferent or worse. That was the time for him to show that he had fatherly instincts. There is no evidence that one single member of the Indian community offered her a helping hand. Not a relative, nor a counselor, not an Indian chief, no one. One has to feel very sorry for the girl.
>
> If her plight is an example of what happens when one is in

trouble, it leaves one considerably unimpressed with the value in such circumstances of the togetherness of the Indian community.

If it is true that an Indian child has a better chance in life by living among his relatives and among others of his race, then I should have thought that it ought to be possible to demonstrate that this is so, by way of some cogent evidence, with particular reference to this child. (1982, 1 C.N.L.R.: 49)

The racism in this case stings. The judge has no idea of the context in which to place his judgment. He can see only the inadequacy of the response but does not recognize that the inability to take control is a learned response to racism, colonialism and oppression. There are many teen pregnancies in Indian communities, so many that they are not seen as unusual or a cause for particular concern. One of the consequences of colonialism and oppression is that dysfunction begins to look normal after you have been surrounded by it for several generations. Part of this must also be contextualized in the value attached to children, which is very different than in the dominant society. The judge's understanding must be contextualized in the poverty and alcoholism that exist on reserves. When everyone is suffering and struggling, it is difficult to set aside your own struggle to assist another. It is clear that the judge uses as his standard that which is experienced in his community. This is particularly disturbing as he proceeds as though he understands the Indian community.

A further line of cases applies the best interest test to justify the removal of special needs children from the reserve community when those needs cannot be met fully there. These children were found to be in need of protection simply because they had "special needs."[37] The health or education needs of children should not be denied on the basis of race. However, both medical and education needs are responsibilities of the federal government under Aboriginal rights, treaty rights and section 91(24) of the 1867 *Constitution Act*. What is omitted from these discussions is any comment on the requirement of the federal government to meet these children's real needs, which would include the right to reside in their home community.

Judges seem to "regret" removing First Nations children from their communities.[38] They express "compassion and sympathy" for the mother (1982, 1 C.N.L.R.: 47). Judges feel compelled to indicate that in previous cases they have ruled "that it was the best interests of the native child to be raised with his or her own native people" (*Re C.J.W.S.*, [1982] 1. C.N.L.R. 47). But these comments do not reach the real harm that is being done by forced assimilation and the removal of our children. Instead, they are patronizing[39] and are sure flags of racism.

Possibly because disproportionate numbers of First Nations children have been removed from their homes, legislative initiatives in Ontario in 1984 have attempted to reconstruct the best interests of the child test (see *Child and Family Services Act*, S.O. 1984, c.55, section 37(2)-(4)). The legislative reform is described in a discussion paper published by the Ontario government as follows:

> The *Child and Family Services Act* also represents a significant and historic breakthrough in services to Indian children and families in Ontario. There are many provisions in the Act specific to Indian children and families. These are unparalleled by any other jurisdiction in Canada. No other province has so clearly recognized the importance of maintaining the cultural environment of children coming into care. The Act provides clear instructions to the court and other persons making orders or determinations in the best interests of the child, that where the child is an Indian person, the person making the order or determination shall take into consideration the importance of preserving the child's cultural identity. The Act also explicitly instructs the court and children's aid societies to place the child, if the child is an Indian person and removal from the home is necessary, with a member of the child's extended family, a member of the child's band, or another Indian family, unless there is substantial reason for placing the child elsewhere. (Ontario Ministry of Community and Social Services 1985: 2)

These are innovative provisions. They are also intrinsically problematic. Certain protections are offered to "Indian" children and their families. But, the definition (section 2(15)) adopted is the *Indian Act* definition which excludes Métis, urban and disenfranchised people.[40] This definition is unacceptable and it is another barrier to reuniting our families. This is the now familiar strategy of divide and conquer: First Nations people are separated from each other and are thereby unable to put forth a common political front. This is another way of perpetrating racism.

Under the auspices of the Ministry of Community and Social Services, Children's Services Branch, the provincial government is currently soliciting the comments of First Nation's groups on proposed amendments to the *Child and Family Services Act*. One of the suggested amendments will bring the definition of "Indian and Native" into line with section 35 of the 1982 *Constitution Act*. Other amendments suggested by the Ministry include funding, band representation and status reviews (Ontario Ministry of Community and Social Services 1988: 1-4). This Ministry has taken some initial positive steps, but further reviews of the implementation of this legislation, especially in the absence of reported court decisions, need to be conducted.

Legislative enactments require the cooperation of judges to facilitate the implementation of the intent of legislative reforms. The existence of the reforms alone is insufficient to secure change. This is illustrated in the only reported case involving the amendments to the *Child and Family Services Act*, the provincial court judgment in *Re Catholic Children's Aid Society of Metropolitan Toronto and M* (1986, 57 O.R. (2d)). In that decision, the judge merged sections 53(4) and 53(5)[41] of the legislation in order to emphasize the alternative of wardship over adoption in the case of Indians and Native children. This has effectively shifted the burden in the best interests test[42] from bonding and forced it directly onto racial heritage. On appeal, the district court set aside this wide reading of the child protection provisions even though it affirmed the decision of the lower court on the facts (1987, 62 O.R. (2d)).

If the legislative intent behind these amendments was to shift the balance in the best interests test, this judgment nonetheless relies on the old standards and thereby reaffirms the status quo. As such, it is just one in a long line of examples of a pattern familiar to First Nations people. Judicial reaffirmation of the status quo not only nullifies the intent of the new legislative regime, but also emphasizes that legislative reform is not, in itself, sufficient to solve problems that have been caused by centuries of domination.

•••

Post Script

There have been a number of articles written on Aboriginal Peoples and the child welfare system since 1988.[43] There have been inroads made in the opportunities for First Nations to rightfully assume greater control in matters of child welfare. I know that there have been a number of important cases decided by the courts (any case that removes a child from his or her family and home community is an important one).[44] There are two reasons why I believe this article could not be published again without a few current comments.

The first concern I have with the republication of this article is an academic one. From a legal perspective, articles are generally dated within ten years of their publication. This is because new cases are always being decided that modify the existing rules of law. In the situation of Aboriginal child welfare, this is not entirely true. Canadian courts have failed to address concerns raised regarding the bias inherent in the best interest of the child test. This is evidenced in the following discussion of the *Sawan v. Tearoe* case (48 *Reports of Family Law*(3d), 392) decided by the British Columbia Court of Appeal in 1993.[45] Even though this chapter was written in the late 1980s, it is still reflective of the current situation.

The second reason I feel the need to comment on this chapter is a personal one. It is harder for me to find the proper expression for this reason. I simply did not feel "right" about republishing this article without being honest about the way child welfare agencies, policies and practices have impacted on my life and my family over the last four years. It has been a real struggle to confront this pain in such a way that it could be put down on paper in the kindest way I knew.

Issues of child welfare and First Nations have remained important to me over the years. These issues, however, are not just of academic interest. As with many areas I have studied formally, issues of child welfare affect my life in a personal way because they are often issues I have survived. Nothing in Native Studies or law has ever been only a matter of academic inquiry for me. It has not been objective. This failure to succumb to the standard of objectivity is not a personal fault of Aboriginal scholars. It is a fault that is inherent in the structure of academic inquiry into the lives of Peoples. In fact, it is the standard of objectivity that is falsely elevated. Often academic inquiry regarding issues pertinent to Aboriginal Peoples is the study of my own life or the life of others whom I care deeply about. Perhaps it is this painfulness that is one of the reasons why I have never made the time to write another child welfare article, even though I often find myself thinking about these issues.

The patterns that I traced in the *Racine* case are apparent in many of the cases that have been more recently decided. This is evidence that the concerns I raise in this chapter are still pressing. Sadly the article is not dated. This passage of Madame Justice Wilson's judgment is often cited:

> In my view, when the test to be met is the best interests of the child, the significance of cultural background and heritage as opposed to bonding abates over time. The closer the bond that develops with the prospective adoptive parents the less important the racial element becomes (*Sawan* 1993: 403).

The clear majority of cases, particularly reported cases, that involve Aboriginal children result in the validation of the removal of Aboriginal children from both their immediate and extended families. The problem is *not* that the courts are misapplying Canadian law. They are not. The problem is much more insidious. The problem is in the exclusivity of Canadian law generally. It reflects a single (cultural) way of resolving disputes. Canadian law excludes any consideration of the worldviews, philosophies and childrearing practices of Aboriginal Peoples. This situation is acute in the child welfare (removal) cases.

Canadian law is a central source of the marginalization of Aboriginal

Peoples. This marginalization does not occur only in the formal components of the Canadian legal system such as courts. It also exists in the secondary institutions of law, such as institutions of legal education. The marginalization includes a fundamental disrespect towards Aboriginal scholarship and the unique contributions made by Aboriginal scholars. Sometimes this is even greater than mere disrespect; often Aboriginal scholars are personally trivialized.[46]

One particular case, recently decided, documents the nature of the marginalization of Aboriginal worldviews and philosophies by Canadian courts. In the *Sawan* case[47] the natural mother, a Cree Indian, gave up her child for adoption when he was two months old. Several days after signing the adoption agreement the mother, Cecilia Sawan, verbally revoked her consent. The social worker in the Peace River office of Alberta Family and Social Services advised Ms. Sawan that this revocation of consent must be given in writing. Some time later, the adopting (non-Aboriginal) parents sought legal affirmation of their custody, despite the fact that Ms. Sawan had contacted them on more than one occasion about the return of her child. The British Columbia Court of Appeal over-ruled a lower court decision which returned the child to his natural mother. Under British Columbia law, a natural parent can only revoke their consent to adoption when that revocation is determined to be in the best interest of the child.

When I first heard about this case I was horrified. Ms. Sawan clearly communicated to the appropriate individual at the appropriate child welfare office in Alberta that she had changed her mind regarding adoption. She did this within the ten-day period allowed by law. The response she received was "write it down." In my mind, this is obviously a wrong answer. The decision a young mother faces in keeping a child or placing a child is a difficult one and it is obviously an emotional one. The response, "write it down," at minimum, is insensitive to the totality of circumstance surrounding this issue of placement. What were the other possible responses? What would the kind response have been? Was there a way to facilitate Ms. Sawan legally communicating her decision? Is it reasonable to expect child welfare workers to act in the best interest of an Aboriginal family? What is obvious is that if the social worker in this matter had acted differently, it would not have caused the degree of grief that was inflicted on both the Sawans and the Tearoes. It would not have been a case that found its way to the courts.

The fact that Ms. Sawan is a Cree woman must also influence the way the actions of the social worker and the court's decision are understood. The information about Ms. Sawan that is reported in the judgment indicates that she has plans to return to school. This knowledge must inform the consideration of the social worker's demand for Ms. Sawan to "write down" her revocation. The ability to write things down is not a universal one. It is a task that some find easy and others find difficult. Second, Ms. Sawan is an Aboriginal woman. She comes from a worldview that represents the spoken over the written word. Against a cultural standard, a spoken revocation of consent is more serious than a written one. To an Aboriginal person, and perhaps to Ms. Sawan, the legal obligation to write down the revocation may very likely seem nonsensical.

Even more troubling than the failure of the child welfare agency to take account of Aboriginal culture is the clear misapplication of culture that is exposed in the British Columbia appeal court's decision. Justice Proudfoot's emphasis of several facts clearly indicates that the judge's perception of "Indian-ness" is based on biological criteria. Biological criteria are insufficient to explain differences between Aboriginal and non-Aboriginal worldviews. Justice Proudfoot notes Ms. Sawan is only "half-Indian." Indian-ness is not something that can be part done — it's quite like being pregnant. Either you are Indian or you are not. Only biological constructs of race can be mathematically dissected. Culture cannot, and culture is the relevant criterion. In a similar way, the court emphasizes that Ms. Sawan was not raised and does not currently reside on the reserve. The court uses this fact to undermine the mother's assertion of the importance of the child having access to his culture by insinuating that the mother herself does not have access to her culture. However, non-reserve-resident Indians are no less Indian. Consider the fact that the reserves are constructs of Canadian law and not of Aboriginal culture or tradition. Yes, it is easier to live within your culture on an Indian reserve because you are surrounded by people who share at least similar cultural values. This does not foreclose the possibility that Indian culture can be transmitted in other environments. The court's reasoning on these issues exposes the same pattern of cultural misunderstanding that was seen in the *Racine* decision more than ten years previously.

As I have indicated, it is usually difficult to think through the pain surrounding the "academic" interests I have in child welfare. To explain the envelope of painfulness regarding matters of child welfare, I must choose to disclose another layer of my private self. I do this with some trepidation. In November 1993, my husband's niece came to live with our family. It was a difficult struggle over more than a year to convince the child welfare workers in Alberta to send her to our home despite provincial guidelines which place a priority on family placements. The non-Indian foster parents in which my niece had been placed were prepared to adopt her. That fact established that the repatriation was going to be difficult. I am hesitant to tell more of this story because this little girl will one day have to face my words in black and white. Maybe when she is older and can decide for herself how she feels about my telling her story (or our story because the two are undeniably entwined), I will write more. Because of her experiences, it has been painful for our family—a family that has a history (as do many Indian families) of child abuse allegations and apprehensions. My husband was raised in foster care and the struggle to regain a place in his family for this girl has been difficult for him. It took him back to a time and place he usually chooses to forget. What is important to understand are the layers of rippling experience that a single child welfare contact today creates.

There is another story that is even more painful for me to speak about. My son Blake was taken from us for eight days in the late summer of 1991. He had fallen and broken his arm while practicing his walking around some furniture when he was just eleven months old. The file that child welfare and the police opened at the insistence of the hospital was eventually closed. I found it unexpected that the local Children's Aid Society supported us. I think that is a rare experience for a First Nations family. It was the doctors at the hospital who vigorously pursued the abuse allegation. For example, most laughed when they heard my professional credentials while others continued to question me on how frequently my husband beat me. I had only been married six weeks! My experience of the hospital was of layer upon layer of racist treatment. I have not yet accepted that the doctors or the hospital have done nothing to set this right. Even telling this little of a long story ties my belly in knots and I am afraid. Eventually they discovered my boy had a bone disorder and could not prove their case in court (which is not to say that we were ever vindicated.)

The most difficult layer of my son's story for me to accept is not the allegation of abuse so much. I do admit to feeling very vulnerable to another allegation because I know how simply it can happen again. It is still terrifying to take my children to the doctors. It is sad that the actions of a few doctors have tainted my perception of an entire profession. It was this brown face and an unexplained broken arm of a particular nature and the process rolled on its own all over its path. It is an unkind process, not one that offers any hope of building or bettering human life let alone true, human caring about the "clients." It is the sheer lack of responsibility of the system, of those with the power (power sanctioned by the state) to level that charge of abuse, to take a look at the consequences of their actions as well as the consequences of their non-actions. I am not saying anything that suggests that child abuse ought not to be a pressing social concern. It is. However, the actions of some of the professionals involved in my son's case caused at least as much harm to my family (two other children were also affected) as the broken bones my son suffered. I watched my small son learn fear for those eight days in the hospital. He had never slept alone in a crib and was terrified of the experience. He did not know pain inflicted by another, until they started running test after test. There are times when I still see that same look of fear in his eyes that I first saw in the hospital and nearly three years have passed (and thankfully he has never broken anything else). I felt so crazy because no one could see my mother's pain for what it was. I was helpless to keep those people from abusing my son.

My experiences of the child welfare system have not been pleasant. It is not a welfare system at all. I have a hard time thinking through the pain that I have experienced as "client" of the child welfare system. I have experienced that system as a child, as a parent accused and as a "foster parent." I really do not think of myself as a "foster parent." I was only ever an Indian auntie exercising my traditional responsibilities for my sister's child. I also understand that my experience of that system is somewhat unique — through my educational privilege I hold the power of the pen. One day I will tell all. In the meantime, however, the truth remains that I have little good to say about this system of so-called child welfare except for a few rare and unique caring individuals employed in that system.[48] But for every individual I encountered who exercised their responsibility to care, I found a dozen who did not. The loudest lesson I hear is that if my family has struggled so desperately against this system when I am educated in that system of rule manipulation (law), and we have a sound income and a safe and secure home—things that are sadly not found in every First Nation's home — then there are stories of pain and terror more grave than I could bear to hear.

Notes

1. The 1982 Constitution Act defines Aboriginal Peoples as the "Indian, Inuit, and Métis." Tracing the linguistic roots of the word *Aboriginal* indicates that one meaning of *abo* is "away from." (This was brought to my attention by Professor Nicholas Deleary who at that time was teaching at the University of Sudbury.) We are not people who are away from the original. We are the original peoples, the First Nations of this land. "Indian" has a strict legal definition as it is found in the *Indian Act*. However, as I grew up the word we used was "Indian." Shortly after I began my academic studies, I learned that even deciding what to call myself was a dilemma in itself. Am I Aboriginal, Native, Indian? As a matter of personal preference, I will use "First Nations" or "original peoples." This dilemma is not only symptomatic of the "divide and conquer" colonial mentality (with Columbus "discovering" America), but also illustrates the dimensions of our struggle, even, to be.

    As this article deals specifically with "Indian" child welfare matters unlike other papers in this collection, I have not changed the language from First Nations. Issues of child welfare are also important in Métis and Inuit communities. However, the legal framework has unique elements for each of the Métis, Inuit and Indian.

2. Please refer to York 1990 and in particular Chapter 8, "From Manitoba to Massachusetts: The Lost Generation." The author tells the story of a young Métis woman who is located by her family in Boston. It is a long way from

Camperville in northwestern Manitoba to the eastern sea coast of the United States. But this is Lisa's child welfare journey. There are many similarities in the stories of Cameron and Lisa including the sexual abuse they survived at the hands of their adoptive fathers (at page 201).

3. In 1995, it is still difficult to locate comprehensive national statistics.

4. It was impossible to locate complete statistics more recent than 1980 on the issue of First Nations and child welfare. Is this an indication, in itself, of the importance Canadian social agencies place on this problem?

5. As Michael Asch indicates, this is a difficult figure to calculate. Not only is there confusion as to the definitional limits of who is Native, as indicated above, but census figures only recently (1981) included questions regarding Native ancestry. Michael Asch relies on figures provided by the Secretary of State and claims that the 2 percent figure determined by the 1981 census is too low. He estimates that there are approximately 840,000 Native people in Canada.

6. Emily Carasco introduced the term "indigenous factor." I am indebted to her work on race discrimination in the child welfare system.

7. At a recent conference, a woman from British Columbia spoke about her experiences and the impact of residential schools. She asked us to imagine a community without children for thirty years. She asked us to imagine the pain of her grandmother. This image has stayed with me.

8. Genocide is a crime at international law. See the *Convention on the Prevention and Punishment of the Crime of Genocide,* 78 UNTS 277. The convention was adopted by the United Nations General Assembly, 9 December 1948. It was entered into force on 12 January 1961. Canada signed this convention on 28 November 1949. The United Nations definition of genocide requires there to be an intent to destroy the culture of a people before an act of genocide is recognized. That lack of intention completely excuses this offence in the eyes of the law is completely unsatisfactory. Genocide is a situation where a people's way of life has been destroyed. This is the reality that justice must now begin to address. This is also the position of the British Columbia Native Women's Society. See Johnson 1982.

9. Personal experience indicates that this figure is probably low. In the Ontario region, the federal penitentiary population may be as high as 20 to 25 percent original ancestry. About thirty of the one hundred and twenty women in the Prison for Women are First Nations women. Statistics cited are likely low due to the failure of the court process to regularly consider the "indigenous factor" and cultural identity as relevant factors at trial or sentencing. Thus First Nations people are not identified. Second, once in prison, being a First Nations individual carries additional costs, and many chose not to identify themselves officially to prison authorities as First Nations people. The common difficulties with collecting data on First Nations people also operates here.

10. The degree of harm being inflicted on First Nations citizens as our plight is made visible is to effectively make invisible the private lives of those individuals who bravely speak out. We must make public our private lives. No amount of social change discounts the pain those particular individuals carry who become the symbols of our struggle. To Cameron Kerley, an apology for this further invasion into his private life.

11. I recently attended a workshop where I had the opportunity to discuss philosophy, tradition and culture with Lee Maracle, the author of *I Am Woman*. In her view, culture is the way we do things. Philosophy is what we carry around inside us (the values of consensus and co-operation) that shapes our culture. This philosophy is what First Nations individuals are born with. This points then to the fallacy of the assertion that one's culture can be destroyed or one can be truly assimilated.

12. It is impossible to capture the essence of traditional ways in a moment or on paper. It is a lifelong commitment to learn these ways. For fear of being misunderstood, or worse, it is with great hesitancy that I speak of ceremonies. What I have given is a simplistic rendition of ceremonies because I have not earned the right to conduct any ceremony. What is given are my views and feelings.

13. The way in which First Nations see our relationship to land is very different from western concepts. Land is not "owned"—the Creator put the people of the First Nations here to be the caretakers of the land. Considering our relationship to land will help bring a simple understanding of women's role as caretakers.

14. In today's society our roles and responsibilities as given to our nations have become confused and forgotten as we become more involved in the structures of the dominant society where sex roles have become de-gendered. My comments are not intended to de-value the important, positive and necessary accomplishments of women in this country.

15. This is a source of political conflict between First Nations women and the larger women's movement, which in my experience tends (I am generalizing) to minimize the role of mother as well as the responsibilities of women. I do recognize that the distance between the contemporary women's movement and First Nation's women has narrowed as the women's movement has begun to grapple with the concept of White privilege. Black women were instrumental in forcing this shift. See hooks 1981.

16. Traditional Mohawk people assert that we have never lost or surrendered our sovereignty. Sovereignty has a meaning that is not synonymous with the western definition. To be sovereign is one's birthright. It is simply to live in a way which respects our tradition and culture. Sovereignty must be lived, and that is all. The traditional Mohawk perspective on sovereignty cannot be simply understood and accurately explained in a few words.

17. There are two levels at which change must be effected. Legislative changes over the last decade which legitimize the First Nations control of child welfare have begun to alleviate the suffering of our First Nations children, families and communities. But the long-term picture has not changed. The structural effects of the systems of the dominant society on First Nations must become part of our analysis and solution. For an examination and discussion of the child welfare initiatives which have taken place, see James 1987, Johnson 1982, and MacDonald 1985.

18. In discussions with a representative of the Child Services Branch of the Ministry of Community and Social Services, it was agreed that recent statistics on child welfare are not available or accessible. For status Indian children who are Crown wards, the number of adoptions has decreased from eighty-six in 1980

to thirty-five in 1987. It cannot be assumed this is a clear indicator that the situation is improving, because these figures do not include Métis, Inuit and non-status adoptions. Adoptions of non-Crown wards (i.e., those adoptions informally arranged between consenting parties) are also excluded. The Ministry provides that there is "no guarantee that's what happened." The proportion of status Indian children adopted into status Indian families has increased from 27 percent in 1980 to 37 percent in 1987. The Ministry is not satisfied with this increase, claiming it is still not a satisfactory situation. The same cautions to the interpretation of these statistics also apply.

19. The disproportionality of First Nation's federal prisoners is also increasing and the situation is expected to intensify given the higher birth rate in First Nations communities. See Correctional Law Review 1988: 3.

20. An example which is easily understood and demonstrates this point is the environmental crisis the world now faces. All nations must work together for this resolution or we will all face destruction. If the First Nations teaching that all life is to be valued (the trees, animals, birds, plants are all my sisters and brothers) had been followed, we would not be facing the potential destruction of the earth, our mother.

21. A discussion of the by-law is contained in MacDonald 1983.

22. The most rigorous source which examines the situation in each province is Johnson 1983. For an example of a tripartite agreement, see the Canada-Manitoba-Indian Child Welfare Agreement, [1982] 2 *Canadian Native Law Reporter*, 1-33. The Manitoba agreement led to the creation of a number of Indian controlled child welfare agencies. The establishment of Indian controlled agencies has not fully solved the problem, please see Cox and Fox-Decent 1993.

23. The resolution of the jurisdictional dispute required judges to interpret and finalize the legal meaning of section 88 of the *Indian Act*, R.S.C. 1970, c.I-6. Section 88 states that provincial laws of general application apply to status Indians, subject to exceptions which give precedent to treaty guarantees and the provisions of the *Indian Act*. The case of *Natural Parents* v. *Superintendent of Child Welfare* (1975), 60 D.L.R. (3d) 148, provides a detailed discussion of the possible interpretations of section 88 and its potential ramifications on the situation of First Nations child welfare. This case, however, did not finally resolve the interpretation of that specific provision. The Supreme Court of Canada in *Dick* v. *The Queen* (1985), 23 D.L.R. (4th) 33, provides that section 88 incorporates provincial laws which would otherwise not be applicable to status Indians because it touches on their "Indian-ness," which would otherwise be a head of power under federal authority. This issue is already adequately presented in the literature. See Carasco 1986: 115-121, Johnson 1982, and McNeil 1984: 1-2 and 4-11. Kent McNeil's article also contains a useful and comprehensive review of the jurisprudence on child protection and adoption of First Nations children.

24. The manner in which the British Columbia courts resolved this issue, as discussed by the Supreme Court of Canada, can be found in *Natural Parents* (see footnote 23).

25. This contradicts the view of many First Nations. Over the years, various National First Nations groups have repeatedly requested the federal government legislate national standards.

26. H.B. Hawthorne 1966: 253, cited in the *Director of Child Welfare for Manitoba* v. *B.*, [1979] 6 W.W.R. 229 (Man. P.J.C.), 238.
27. The Supreme Court of Canada at the time of original writing of this article had yet to provide any clear guidelines to assist lawyers and legal scholars with the meaning of this section. In May of 1990, the Supreme Court articulated its view of section 35(1) in *Regina* v. *Sparrow* (1990) 70 D.L.R. (4th) 385.
28. For a similar type of analysis involving hunting and property cases, see Mandell 1987. Perhaps the most eloquent rendering of First Nations understanding of law and legal relations is found in Lyons 1985: 19-23. It is interesting in child welfare matters to note that notwithstanding the jurisdictional dispute, provincial governments have very willingly asserted their authority under section 88 to limit the hunting and fishing rights of the First Nations. This contradictory position has not previously been commented on in the legal literature, but it has not been missed by First Nations.
29. This article is not intended to be an ideological analysis of racism. I do not view racism as behaviour or attitudes which require intent or ill-will. Allegations of racism do not call into question the integrity of the individuals involved, but merely reflect a state of not knowing. My purpose is to expose racism and secure personal examinations of the privilege conferred by merely having white skin.
30. Since originally writing this article, I have been reminded in conversation with a relative of the adoptive parents that one of the parents (the father) who adopted this child was Métis. The race and culture of either of the adoptive parents is barely mentioned in the case. I have recently re-read the case as I am struggling to deal with another complexity in it. I understand that there is a differnce in culture between Indians and Métis, yet not a comment in the Supreme Court's judgement recognizes the complexity of the cultural issues. Granted, Indian and Métis cultures are more similar to each other than to "Canadian" (White) culture. I am not certain what conclusions to make regarding the disappearance of the adoptive parents' culture and race. I do not know at what stage of the legal process this is disappeared. It could have been a decision of the adoptive father or the adoptive father's lawyers to not mention his cultural background or it may have been overlooked at any level of the court's decision-making process. From reading the case, it is impossible to determine the connection the adoptive father has to his cultural identity and this is one of my difficulties in processing this renewed information. I also have learned that the adoption was not a "successful" one. The child in question has had problems with substance abuse and has been in conflict with the law. I do not know if she is in contact with her mother or her home community.

    I have thought a lot about this disappearance of the cultural identity of the adoptive father since first learning of it in the summer of 1994. It lends itself to two other very interesting discussions. In both Canadian culture and Canadian law, Métis peoples have been consigned to a half-existence. This is insulting. They are seen as half-Indian and half-White which amounts to never any more than half-person. This does no justice to the distinct position that the Métis hold in Canadian history (for example, as the founders of the province of Manitoba). This does no justice to the beautiful and distinct cultures of the Métis. The disappearance of Mr. Racine's Métis culture for whatever reason is a small reflection of a larger experience of the Métis as a nation.

The second discussion of the disappearance of Mr. Racine's culture is seen in a comparision of the structure of Canadian law against the structure of Aboriginal law. First Nations are storytelling people. Our stories are more than oral history. Oral history is just one aspect of the stories of Aboriginal people. Stories also contain teachings of both morality and law. Stories as a process are complete. Canadian law also tells stories and the control for the process of storytelling in legal circles is lifted away from those directly involved. The stories heard in court are consequently never complete.

31. Similar reasoning and reliance on the best interests test is followed in *Nelson* v. *Children's Aid Society of Manitoba*, [1975] 5 W.W.R. 45 (Man.C.A.), although no specific reference is made to the children's race (it is totally ignored) in relation to the best interests test.

32. Ironically, the mother's worst fears were realized; conflict with the law was the outcome in this case. This points to the fact that the issues in the "culture versus bonding" debate are greater than they initially appear. Culture without a connection to your First Nation community and place in the universe can alone be insufficient. The issues that are simplistically dealt with as First Nations culture are actually vast and complex. They can not be measured at a moment in a person's life.

33. See, for example, McGillivray 1985.

34. See, for example, Weaver 1981.

35. Mr. Justice Martland took a similar approach in a British Columbia case, *Natural Parents*, which involved the legality of inter-racial adoption. Not only did the Supreme Court rule that these adoptions are permissible, but Mr. Justice Martland actually seemed to suggest that they ought to be valued: "I do not interpret section 91(24) as *manifesting an intention to maintain a segregation of Indians from the rest of the community* in matters of this kind and, accordingly, it is my view that the application of the *Adoption Act* to Indian children will only be prevented if parliament, in the exercise of its powers under this subsection, has legislated in a matter which would preclude application," *Natural Parents* at 164 (emphasis added). This position also amounts to racism. It is important to note that the best interest test as applied in the *Racine* and *Natural Parents* cases affects *all* children, regardless of their racial heritage. The test was developed in two cases which involve First Nations children and the unique circumstances they face. It is possible that a test developed on facts unique to First Nations children could also impact on First Nations children in a negative way, because the factual basis of the test is not shared. The test may, therefore, affect other children negatively as well.

36. It should also be noted the way in which gender and parenting responsibilities are also disappeared. The adoptive father is not mentioned.

37. *McNeil* v. *Superintendent of Family and Child Services*, [1984] 4 C.N.L.R. 41; *S.A.L. and G.I.L.* v. *Legal Aid of Manitoba*, [1982] 6 W.W.R. 260, [1983] 1 C.N.L.R. 157; *Wilson* and *Wilson* v. *Young and Young* (1983), 28 Sask.R. 287, [1984] 4 C.N.L.R. 185.

38. *Tom* v. *Children's Aid Society*, [1982] 1 C.N.L.R. 172.

39. I suspect there is a relationship between the patronizing tone of this judgment and the ideologies of the legal system (White, male and middle-class). The

doctrine of *parens patriae* (the state as father) also contains the common elements of male superiority and protector of the common good.

40. Interestingly, the academic literature does not discuss this issue or the new Indian provisions in detail. Personal experience and informal discussion with Native family court workers indicate that a concern that non-reserve residents are being excluded from the interpretation of these new provisions is valid.

41. These sections read as follows:

> 53(4) Where the court decides that it is necessary to remove the child from the care of the person who had charge of him or her immediately before intervention under this Part, the court shall, before making an order for society or Crown wardship under paragraph 2 or 3 of subsection (1), consider whether it is possible to place the child with a relative, neighbour or other member of the child's community or extended family under paragraph 1 of subsection (1) with the consent of the relative or other person.

> 53(5) Where the child referred to in subsection (4) is an Indian or native person, unless there is a substantial reason for placing the child elsewhere, the court shall place the child with,
> (a) a member of the child's extended family;
> (b) a member of the child's band or native community; or,
> (c) another Indian or native family.

42. In the summer of 1993, there were no reported cases which review the meaning of sections 37(3) and 37(4) of the Act.

43. These articles include: Davies 1994, Goldsmith 1990 (this articles discusses the law in the United States), Kline 1992, 1994a, and 1994b, Pellat 1991, Perry 1990-91, Sinclair *et al.* 1991, and Warry 1991.

44. Often these cases are not reported. It is difficult to determine what exactly is going on in the field without being able to easily access the case law. This is particularly odd in Ontario where there has been new legislation.

45. Leave to appeal was denied by the Supreme Court of Canada on February 10, 1994.

46. For example, in a recent article by Sinclair et al. my child welfare article is referred to as "provocative." I knew when I first found this reference that it was neither complimentary nor an example of good academic method. Provocative is defined in the Oxford Dictionary as "intentionally irritating." This was hardly my purpose in trying to expose the racism inherent in both the minds of judges and other legal child welfare experts. If non-Aboriginal scholars would examine seriously their own biases and cultural preferences as well as how particular worldviews are subtly advanced by courts and laws, then I would be able to stop finger pointing.

47. This is not meant to be a comprehensive discussion of this case. My purpose is solely to demonstrate that things have not improved since the *Racine* case was decided.

48. Except to Karen, Richard, Mel and Tony.

The Roles and Responsibilities of
Aboriginal Women: Reclaiming Justice

CHAPTER 11 WAS ORIGINALLY *"Reclaiming Justice: Aboriginal Women and Justice Initiatives in the 1990's,"* in *Royal Commission on Aboriginal People,* Aboriginal Peoples and the Justice System *(Ottawa: Minister of Supply and Services, 1993), 105-132. It was revised and published as "The Roles and Responsibilities of Aboriginal Women: Reclaiming Justice,"* 56(2) Saskatchewan Law Review *1992, 237-266.*

Locating Aboriginal Thought in Mainstream Academia

S torytelling is the way in which knowledge is shared in traditional Aboriginal relations. I wish to begin this conversation on justice by sharing my story as a Mohawk woman (mother and wife) who accommodates academia on a daily basis as the way in which I support myself and my family. Often we hear the Elders[1] tell us, "This is how I have come to understand it." Through my experiences of both the academic world and the Aboriginal world, this is what I have come to understand about justice[2] from the perspective of one Aboriginal (Mohawk) woman.[3]

Speaking to the Manitoba Aboriginal Justice Inquiry, Elijah Harper said:

> With so much discrimination occurring against our people, it is often amazing how accepting we are of our situation. We know that without tolerance there can be no justice. Without understanding there cannot be justice. Without equality there can be no justice. With justice we can begin to understand each other. With justice we can work and live with each other. Aboriginal people want a judicial system that recognizes the native way of life, our own

values and beliefs, and not the white man's way of life. (Hamilton and Sinclair 1991: vol. 1: 251)

These words summarize, shape and conclude my own thoughts on the matter of Aboriginal justice systems. The concepts of justice, truth, tolerance, understanding and equality are the themes that weave themselves in and out of my thoughts as I consider what justice would have been traditionally[4] to Aboriginal women. These are the concepts that we must recapture in our search for healing.

A fundamental difference between Aboriginal and non-Aboriginal societies is the way in which truth is located. Truth in non-Aboriginal terms is located outside of the self. It is absolute and may be discovered only through years of study in institutions which are sanctioned as sources of learning. In the Aboriginal way,[5] truth is internal to the self. The Creator put each and every one of us here in a complete state of being with our own set of instructions to follow. Truth is discovered through personal examination, not just through systematic study in state-sanctioned institutions. In the Ojibwe language truth is "niwii-debwe." "Truth," however, is not the literal translation. This Ojibwe word more fully means "what is right as I know it" (Hamilton and Sinclair 1991: vol. 1: 41). Leila Fisher, an Elder of the Hoh nation in what is now known as Washington state, tells this story which helps to underscore the importance of both truth and introspection:

"Did you ever wonder how wisdom comes?" Without taking her hands from her weaving or even looking up to see if we're listening, she continues: "There was a man, a postman here on the reservation, who heard some of the Elders talking about receiving objects that bring great power. He didn't know much about such things, but he thought to himself that it would be a wonderful thing if he could receive such an object—which can only be bestowed by the Creator. In particular, he heard from the Elders that the highest such object a person can receive is an eagle feather. He decided that was the one for him. If he could just receive an eagle feather he would have all the power and wisdom and prestige he desired. But he knew he couldn't buy one and he couldn't ask anyone to give him one. It just had to come to him somehow by the Creator's will."

"Day after day he went around looking for an eagle feather. He figured one would come his way if he just kept his eyes open. It got so he thought of nothing else. That eagle feather occupied his thoughts from sunup to sundown. Weeks passed, then months, then years. Every day the postman did his rounds, always looking for that eagle feather—looking just as hard as he could. He paid no attention to his family or friends. He just kept his mind fixed on that eagle feather. But it never seemed to come. He started to grow old, but still no feather. Finally he came to realize that no matter how hard he looked he was no closer to getting the feather than he had been the day he started."

"One day he took a break by the side of the road. He got out of his little jeep mail-carrier and had a talk with the Creator. He said: 'I'm so tired of looking for that eagle feather. Maybe I'm not supposed to get one. I've spent all my life thinking about that feather. I've really hardly given a thought to my family and friends. All I cared about was that feather, and now life has just about passed me by. I've missed out on a lot of good things. Well, I'm giving up my search. I'm going to stop looking for that feather and start living. Maybe I have time enough left to make it up to my family and friends. Forgive me for the way I have conducted my life.'"

"Then—and only then—a great peace came into him. He suddenly felt better inside than he had in all these years. Just as he finished his talk with the Creator and started getting back in his jeep, he was surprised by a shadow passing over him. Holding his hands over his eyes, he looked up into the sky and saw, high above, a great bird flying over. Almost instantly it disappeared. Then he saw something floating down ever so lightly on the breeze—a beautiful tail feather. It was his eagle feather! He realized that the feather had come not a single moment before he had stopped searching and made his peace with the Creator. He finally learned that wisdom comes only when you stop looking for it and start truly living the life the Creator intended for you. That postman is still alive and he's a changed person. People come to him for wisdom now and he shares everything he knows. Even though now he has the power and the prestige he searched for, he no longer cares about such things. He's concerned about others, not himself. So now you know how wisdom comes." (Wall and Arden 1990: 74)

Individuals of Aboriginal ancestry who try to walk in both the academic world and the Aboriginal world are confronted by the profound cultural differences in the ways in which truth, knowledge and wisdom are constructed. The instructions we receive through institutionalized education indicate that we must locate truth and knowledge outside of ourselves. Introspection is not a proper research method. It is improper to footnote the knowledge that my grandmother told me. Yet, more and more frequently, Aboriginal academics are asked to explain our unique cultural ways of being. However, it is expected that the objective style of academic writing ought not to be changed to accommodate the new understandings that Aboriginal academics bring to various disciplines. These two understandings of truth are, perhaps, diametrically opposed. Yet these two ways of knowing co-exist within my experience. My experience is one of negotiating the contradictions. Justice requires that this accommodation not be negotiated solely on an individualized basis but must also be embraced institutionally. This understanding must come to form part of the basis that we recognize knowledge to be built upon.

As I come to the topic which is currently under review in this chapter, my mind is first turned to these questions of construction. It must be recognized that there are few academic sources to refer to in answering the questions that an analysis of Aboriginal justice from the woman's perspective requires.[6] Usually, the negotiations I go through to produce an academic paper are not visible in the final product. However, as we look to the future, little is accomplished when these contradictions are faced only on an individualized level. The contradictions, although confronted on a personal level, are *not* personal inadequacies located within the self, but contradictions that exist between the two cultures. The contradiction exists in the way that knowledge and truth are constructed and sanctioned in each culture. The contradiction is compounded when the knowledge is implemented in the corresponding institutions or belief structures of mainstream life. By failing to publicly label and address this contradiction, it is perpetuated.

A similar contradiction exists when asked to write or speak from the experience of a woman who is Aboriginal. The historic oppression of women and our subsequent powerlessness in mainstream society has been challenged through the creation of bureaucracies, organizations and ministries which focus solely on women's experience.[7] We see the same structure within academia with the creation of women's studies programs and women's courses within other departments, faculties and programs. The problem of exclusion from mainstream thought is not remedied through the creation of programs that hold the potential for women's experience to be marginalized. The conclusion is simple enough. Although many institutions of the dominant society claim to be objective or value free, they actually reflect a male construction of reality. The solutions we advocate must be seen to challenge the male-dominated structure.

Law is a particularly good example of the way in which the male construction of reality is implemented in such a way that the gender specificity of legal relations is vanished. Sherene Razack, drawing on the work of Ann Scales (1989) explains:

> The legal test cases that constitute feminism applied to law in Canada are fundamentally projects of naming, of exposing the world as man-made. Men, Ann Scales writes, have had the power

to organize reality, "to create the world from their own point of view, and then, by a truly remarkable philosophical conjure, were able to elevate that point of view into so-called 'objective reality.'" Women working in law find themselves demystifying that reality and challenging its validity in court, substituting in the process their own description of reality. In law, the issues that preoccupy women, Scales notes, are all issues that emerge out of a male-defined version of female sexuality. Abortion, contraception, sexual harassment, pornography, prostitution, rape, and incest are "struggles with our otherness," that is, struggles born out of the condition of being other than male.[8] (Razack 1990-91: 441)

The construction of woman as "other" must be the fundamental focus of any analysis which hopes to significantly end the oppression of women. When one gender is constructed as "other," then the goal of equality will continue to be elusive.

The examination of the creation of roles of "otherness" must not conclude in the construction of a definition of equality prefaced on sameness. This is equally problematic. Equality when constructed as sameness perpetuates race and gender oppression. Again, an analysis of legal relations illuminates this point:

> There is also a reluctance to record and acknowledge differences when everyone is supposed to be treated the same. In theory, race and sex are irrelevant to being a good lawyer. The "Myth of Equality" is a culturally sanctioned belief that everyone in our society is legally and socially equal and that any differences in their situation are attributable to factors personal to them, such as effort, responsibility, and honesty. This "Myth of Equality" is superimposed on our inherently biased institutions and social systems, hiding from view the pervasive nature of racism and sexism. (Neallani 1992: 151)

The identification of the similarities between race[9] and gender oppression is essential to the development of comprehensive theories of equality and justice which can be applied in a meaningful manner to both Aboriginal women and mainstream individuals.

The same way in which women's programs are marginalized within mainstream institutions is paralleled in the marginalization of Aboriginal Peoples.[10] Over the last two decades, "Native" studies departments and courses have been created in a way which parallels the development of women's studies departments. A second example worthy of note is the criminal justice system. The move to embrace Aboriginal experience within the existing mandate of the Correctional Service of Canada is well-documented in the many reports of recent Aboriginal Justice inquiries.[11] The Canadian correctional system is a further demonstration of the process of marginalization of those individuals who do not occupy mainstream status and/or share a respect for the notions of incarceration and rehabilitation. This process does not require the actors in the system to question the status quo or how systemic constructions of race and culture affect their behavior and/or the institution's structure. Again, the conclusion is simple enough. Although many institutions of the dominant society claim to be objective or value free, they actually reflect a specific cultural (that is, "White"[12]) construction of reality.

My point is *not* to suggest that the development of Aboriginal specific programs or women specific programs is wrong and should be discontinued. To the contrary, these programs are both essential and necessary; particularly in the short term. However, if the goal of women, or Aboriginal Peoples, is to change the structure of society we must also develop new ways of challenging the philosophies and beliefs of the mainstream. To not encourage structural change is to continue to accept the marginalization of any perspective that is not White or male and so on. Structural change is the only way in which meaningful and substantive long-term change can be secured.

The systematic review of the Aboriginal experience of oppression in this country now called Canada is essential to the reclamation project I support.[13] The result of this review must be the creation of a detailed understanding of our oppression and the oppression of others. We must understand exactly how oppressive relations operate and are perpetuated. Language is one such condition.

Language is the mechanism by which we communicate what knowledge is. Language is a powerful tool which reinforces mainstream cultural meanings and insights. Language[14] invisibly incorporates culture into our communications:

> "descriptions of People of Colour include their race, while descriptions of White People do not." For example, one reads: "'A black woman crossed the street,' when, had the woman been white, the sentence would have read, 'A woman crossed the street.'" This use of language reinforces the view that everyone is White unless defined otherwise, that White is the norm, and that People of Colour are outside the norm. (Neallani 1992: 155)

As we develop a knowledge of justice, we must also illuminate the many other manifest ways in which gender, racial and cultural "otherness" is reinforced.

As we approach the question of Aboriginal justice systems, we must take extreme care to challenge existing structures so that the end result is greater than a mere accommodation of Aboriginal people or the creation of a "safe" corner for Aboriginal Peoples. Thus far, the majority of reforms to the existing system of Canadian justice have attempted to change Aboriginal people so we fit that system (while the system structurally maintains the status quo). The challenge to do more than just accommodate the needs of Aboriginal Peoples in the existing justice system is not important to Aboriginal Peoples alone. It is not something to be done just for us. Relegating Aboriginal Peoples to a removed corner of experience also fundamentally denies the mainstream the opportunity to benefit and learn from the culture and ways of the Aboriginal nations. This point cannot be over-emphasized.

The way we shape our aspirations is doubly important to Aboriginal women. If the existing remedial process is not questioned then the result will be to create a safe place for Aboriginal women inside the safe place for Aboriginal Peoples. This will marginalize Aboriginal women twice. This result must not be satisfactory to either Aboriginal Peoples or to the mainstream culture.

In recent years, I have began to assess the meaningfulness of Aboriginal justice initiatives against a two-pronged standard. First, will the conditions of Aboriginal criminal justice "clients" be ameliorated in the short-term? Second, in what way will the long-term needs of Aboriginal communities[15] be positively affected? I see this two-pronged standard as the optimum criterion. We cannot forget the painful realities Aboriginal individuals face today in the criminal justice system any more than we can forget the faces in the sand, the faces of the children yet to come. We must change today's reality of individualized oppression at the same time as we create a vision for the future. Similar approaches have been adopted by the Aboriginal Justice Inquiry of Manitoba and the Law Reform Commission of Canada. Furthermore, to repeat the previous point, both of these Commissions also recognize the contribution to mainstream society that will be lost if Aboriginal experience continues to be denied and/or marginalized and/or merely accommodated.

This chapter proceeds on the assumption that the solution to the over-representation of Aboriginal Peoples in the criminal justice system and the systemic discrimination in that system requires the re-creation of Aboriginal justice systems. It is not just over-representation that characterizes the experience of Aboriginal people within the justice system. This is merely the best known and most spoken to aspect of our involvement. Aboriginal people are also drastically under-represented as people with authority in the Canadian justice system. Few Aboriginal people are police officers, lawyers, judges, prison guards or correctional workers (Hamilton and Sinclair 1991:

249, 409, 620). Aboriginal communities are both over- and under-policed. Over-policing is a partial explanation of the over-representation of Aboriginal people as "clients" of the criminal justice system (595). Under-policing occurs mainly in remote communities where the nearest police detachment may be a day away in good weather (596). Both over- and under-policing contribute to the negative way many Aboriginal people view the police. To suggest that the problem Aboriginal people have with the justice system is one of over-representation alone is a drastic simplification of the situation. Understanding the full scope of the difficulties in respecting this foreign system of justice further substantiates the need for the re-creation and legitimization of Aboriginal social control mechanisms.

The Aboriginal Justice Inquiry of Manitoba also proceeded to this same conclusion after lengthy discussions. The Commissioners state:

> In the face of the current realities confronting Aboriginal people, we believe that it is important to recognize that the greatest potential for the resolution of significant Aboriginal social problems lies in Aboriginal people exercising greater control over their own lives.
>
> The dependency on alcohol, the increasing rates of suicide, homicides and criminal charges, and the high rates of incarceration are problems that we believe can be dealt with best by Aboriginal people themselves.
>
> These social conditions, we believe, are indeed the products of dependency and powerlessness, created by past government actions and felt deeply by the majority of Aboriginal people. This dependency will not disappear, we are convinced, until Aboriginal people are able to re-establish their own sense of identity and exercise a considerable degree of self-determination. (263)

This regeneration of Aboriginal cultures must occur through the healing of both Aboriginal men and Aboriginal women. Justice as the Canadian system of law understands it is too narrowly constructed to allow the opportunity to fully reconstruct Aboriginal social control methods. For this reason, the entire criminal justice debate that has to date occurred in Canada is misleading. It is this justice vision that sees nominal accommodations made within the existing system, such as sentencing circles (the correct Aboriginal term is healing circles), *Indian Act* courts, courtworkers, Aboriginal recruitment initiatives and so on, appear more Aboriginal than they really are. While these ideas might change the experience of the justice system for particular individuals, they do not create a significant or complete amelioration of the experience of injustice that we experience within Canadian justice systems.

"Justice as healing" is a better phrase but the concept may still be incomplete. Healing of individuals alone will not be sufficient. Healing eradicates the affects of the multi-dimensional oppression Aboriginal Peoples have faced. Healing creates a "clean slate," and from this place the new beginning Aboriginal Peoples dream about may be built. Healing approaches only prepare us for the new vision, they are *not* the new vision. Healing is merely a different way of stating the two roads on which our efforts must travel.

The relationships among Aboriginal women and Aboriginal men must also be restored and this may require more than just the healing of individuals. Aboriginal justice discussions which do not focus on women (at the same time that the men are remembered) are also incomplete. In fact, I suspect that an Aboriginal justice system (or project) without women is not Aboriginal at all. There is a story which may help us understand the balance between women and men that we are trying to achieve:

> "Power" in an Indian sense is understood according to a different set of values. In Aboriginal terms, "power" or empowerment is individual and can be equated with self-determination: the right to have control of your life and future, as an individual and as a community. Power is relational but not dichotomous or hierarchical. It is balanced and complimentary. Marie Wilson of the Gitskan Wet'suwet'en Tribal Council helps me here. She has compared the relationship between women and men to the eagle. An eagle soars to unbelievable heights and has tremendous power on two equal wings—one female, one male—carrying the body of life between them. Women and men are balanced parts of the whole, yet they are very different from each other and are not "equal" if equality is defined as being the same. Marie Wilson's metaphor of equality is the contribution of both wings to the flight. "Power" in an Indian sense is understood according to a different set of values. (Stevenson et al. 1993: 164)

Actively pursuing the goals of justice re-created, I believe, is one way of facilitating the regeneration of Aboriginal nations including the healing of the women and men of these many nations.

It is essential not only to regenerate Aboriginal nations from within but also to establish meaningful external relations with the mainstream communities that surround us.[16] Essential to this development is the necessary construction of an analysis of race which is inclusive of the Aboriginal worldview. Frequently, race is constructed merely as biological difference. This grossly over-simplifies the Aboriginal worldview which is also fundamentally influenced by culture, tradition and spirituality. Just as much as I turn myself around to fit my cultural understandings into the English language, I also must undertake a form of intellectual gymnastics to fit myself into the manner in which racism theory has developed. Reliance on the current academic construction of racism may not as completely advance our understanding of the issues that confront our conversations as need be. One analysis of the Marshall Inquiry provides this example:

> In the absence of critical examination of racial beliefs and information, the Inquiry validated the immigrants' view of the *Indian*. It accepted the racial tool of colonialism: the European invention of Aboriginal "reality" and their names for that reality. For example, not once did testimony of non-Mi'kmaq in the Inquiry ever mention the particular tribe of *Indians* to which Junior Marshall belonged. He was always considered an *Indian*, a member of a certain race of people, probably primitive in nature. There was no mention of nationality or ethnicity— only his race. Nationality, like ethnicity, is primarily a subjective phenomenon, a sense of social belonging reinforced by common language, culture, custom, heritage, and shared experience. The difference between being *Indian* and Mi'kmaq is the frontier between racial existence and being human. (Henderson 1992: 39, emphasis in original)

Justice requires us to embrace all humanity without constructions of superiority and inferiority. It is this recognition that must shape our efforts in dealing with issues of race and culture, spirituality and tradition.

Concurrently, the valuing of cross-cultural understanding and racism theory (for lack of better phrases) in a way that is sensitive to gender considerations must also be paramount. The experience of all so-called minority women is not the same. One simple example is worthy of consideration:

> . . . women of colour differ in our races, cultures, class, and our experiences of racism and sexism. A woman of colour of Asian heritage may have experienced membership in a dominant group before coming to Canada. She may be economically wealthy and from a privileged class. Her experiences in Canada may differ from the experiences of a First Nations woman whose people have lived in a White dominated society for generations. Each woman encounters different stereotypes directed towards her. Each has her own strategy for coping with discrimination. (Neallani 1992: 149)

This particular danger in the construction of alternatives may be characterized as the danger of over-inclusiveness—that is, assuming that all individuals who experience "otherness" share the same understandings.

There is one particular way in which the over-inclusiveness of race theory disadvantages Aboriginal aspirations in the field of justice. Many of the so-called racial and cultural minorities who have come to Canada, fled here or have been brought here and are satisfied with the existing structures of Canadian society and in particular with the criminal justice system. Their dissatisfaction stems from the fact that they are not represented in the positions of power, status and influence. Their goals focus around equitable access to the existing structures and positions. For Aboriginal Peoples, this is not seen as a full or final solution. At most it is seen as a step along the way. We do not want into the existing system in greater numbers, we want *out!* Wanting in would only amount to supporting the indiginization of existing systems. Aboriginal aspirations isolate us from the "mainstream" of anti-racism collectives.[17]

Before developing this discussion in a way which focuses on Aboriginal women and justice, one further comment about education is required. The relationship between Aboriginal Peoples and the education system must also be understood as having been about the oppression of Aboriginal Peoples. In many ways this oppression remains central to the Aboriginal experience of educational institutions today. For example, the removal of Aboriginal children from their homes and their placement in residential schools was one of the paramount factors in the oppression of Aboriginal languages and cultures. As a result, education alone, and especially academia, cannot be seen to be *the* solution (as once perceived) and remains to be one of the central problems. The solution to the justice conundrum does not lie in better research or better researchers, but within Aboriginal communities themselves. We must rely on the knowledge of the people of the many Aboriginal communities, both reserve and off-reserve (including rural, urban or settlement experiences), if we expect meaningful progress to be made. We must rely on our ability to deconstruct a colonial history. Especially, we must rely upon the Elders and their wisdom.

Moving Justice Forward

In 1992 Aboriginal Peoples celebrated 500 years of resistance to colonial oppression. Understanding the context of resistance is very important to understanding justice on Aboriginal terms. To understand that Aboriginal Peoples are resisting is to understand that Aboriginal Peoples have been reacting to powerful colonial forces outside of themselves. To resist, means to push away. To resist means to never be in control of your own life or the destiny of your community. To resist means to be ever focused on the past and the roots of our oppression. It means living a life of re-action (challenging backlash) as opposed to action and empowerment. Dreams for the future remain illusive.

226

Looking to the criminal justice system, which houses so many of our people, reform must include the rejection of the very basis on which the non-Aboriginal system is constructed. This system turns on the value of punishment, in other words, coercion. It is coercion that binds both the individuals in mainstream society, as well as the institutions, in a seemingly cohesive pattern. James Youngblood 'Sakej' Henderson is a Chickasaw man who married into the Mi'kmaq family. This is his legal analysis of the role coercion plays in mainstream society:

> The generality of the criminal laws and formal equality before the law are two principles that reflect the artificial nature of an immigrant state. It is a voluntary association of individuals from various circumstances around the globe. To equalize individuals' social circumstances and perpetual struggle for their interest in comfort and honour, all individuals are viewed and treated by the law as fundamentally equal.
>
> The general criminal laws enacted by the federal parliament are viewed as somehow above the antagonism of private interests. The rules are imperatives of the state. They are commands of an artificial political order over individuals, who have no inherent social or cultural order. By acts of a national institution the contending private interests are reconciled; rather than embody any factional interest in Canadian society, an impersonal criminal justice is established.
>
> Given the fact that the criminal laws are an artificial compromise between various interests in Canadian society, the greater is the importance of force and punishment as the bond among individuals to guide human conduct. *Coercive enforcement takes the place of a natural community of culture. It is seen as the best way to guarantee order.* (1992: 35-36, emphasis added)

Can the same be said for Aboriginal social order? Aboriginal people have maintained both a sense of community and culture that is related to the natural order. The conclusion is logical. The criminal justice options available for guaranteeing order (obviously a value in both cultures) are not limited within Aboriginal nations in the same manner that they are limited within mainstream society. The central question which must be answered is also simple. Should Aboriginal Peoples be forced to forego these opportunities because they are no longer available to mainstream individuals and institutions?

This analysis of Sakej Henderson is contextualized in his discussion of the Marshall Inquiry. He notes:

> If the law appliers in Nova Scotia could justify their actions to the
> Commissioners, the concept of the uniform application of the law
> would be upheld. If not, the uniform application could be rejected
> as a sham. If the law appliers cannot rationally justify their decisions
> according to established procedures, then those to whom the criminal
> law is applied are subjected to arbitrary exercise of local power.
> Legal justice becomes transparent; no decisions can be said to be
> uniformly applied. (36)

The findings of the Marshall Inquiry are well known. Justice was not done;
an innocent Mi'kmaq man was convicted of a murder he did not commit. For
many Aboriginal Peoples, the Marshall Inquiry only affirmed what we
already knew—justice is not applied uniformly in Canada. This is substantiated
by the real life experiences of too many Aboriginal individuals at the hands
of the criminal justice system. It is, again, minimally demonstrated through
our over-representation in that system.

If the principles of uniformity and coercion which preface the operation
of criminal law in Canada are inappropriate in their application to Aboriginal
individuals, then the end result must be that the entire system of criminal law
will fail Aboriginal nations (notwithstanding that some individuals who are
Aboriginal still advocate the reliance on that system). Yet many mainstream
individuals continue to refuse to confront this obvious conclusion. If the
principles are wrong, then the system they support must also be misinformed.
Reform is, from the Aboriginal perspective, seen to be not only essential but
obvious. The failure to recognize and create a climate of commitment in
which the inappropriateness of the application of mainstream values to
Aboriginal Peoples will be addressed. The result is seen in the necessity of
Aboriginal people who continue to resist the dominant culture and its
institutions. A climate of resistance cannot foster the development of
equality or justice.

When this climate of resistance is recognized as the overwhelming force
in Aboriginal Peoples' lives, then we must accept that justice will remain
an elusive goal. To have justice, means to be in control of one's life and
relations in terms of either individuals or communities. To address justice,
we must therefore address the realities of colonial oppression and the forces
which create the situation that Aboriginal Peoples are not able to be central
actors (as opposed to the re-actors) in our own lives. Aboriginal men and
Aboriginal women as groups experience this colonial oppression in different
ways. I believe the end result to be the same—the denial of the basic right
to be in control of your own life.

The experience of Aboriginal women, as that of "double disadvantage"[18]
exposes the consequences of resistance in even more fundamental terms, if

only because it is more extreme and therefore more obvious. The goal that we set for ourselves should be to eliminate the disadvantage that Aboriginal women face because it is more startling than the experience of either race or gender alone. Eliminating this disadvantage is the greatest of the challenges that face Aboriginal people. By confronting the disadvantage that women face as both women and as Aboriginal, we will also be confronting the discrimination, disadvantage, oppression and dependency faced by our fathers, uncles, brothers, sons and husbands. We must also accept that in some circumstances it is no longer the descendants of the European settlers that oppress us, but it is Aboriginal men in our communities who now fulfill this role. In particular, we have the *Indian Act,* the Indian Affairs bureaucracy and residential schools to blame for this reality, but any form of blaming will not solve the problem.

It is not enough to recognize that Aboriginal Peoples must be afforded the opportunity to be actors in their own lives. It is not enough to reject resistance and reject compartmentalized justice. All Aboriginal Peoples have been influenced by colonial oppression, dependency and powerlessness—obviously to varying degrees. The first step must be to recognize that we must unlearn our own individual as well as our community responses that are based on the philosophy of resistance.[19] Only then, when we are able to think and see with de-colonized minds and hearts, can progress be honestly made.

The words of Oren Lyons, a member of the Haudenosaunee Confederacy, inspire my own thoughts on this matter:

> Sovereignty—it's a political word. It's not a legal word. Sovereignty is the act. Sovereignty is the do. You act. You don't ask. There is no limitation on sovereignty. You are not semi-sovereign. You are not a little sovereign. You either are or you aren't. It's simple. (cited in Hill 1992: 175)

Healing is the pathway. Aboriginal action is the answer.

Within a Legal Paradigm: Aboriginal Women and Feminism

Feminist[20] academics have challenged the way in which experience has been separated from knowledge in mainstream social institutions. This feminist challenge has benefited many individuals and collectives who share the robes of "otherness" with women. Standpoint theory[21] exposes the fact that knowledge is socially constructed. The location of the "knower" is as important as the understanding that is put forth. This principle has a further application:

"outsiders," those who are excluded from dominant systems of knowledge, are "able to see patterns of belief or behavior that are hard for those immersed in the culture to detect." (Harding 1992: 7)

It is the status of "otherness" or "outsider" and the corresponding consequences where the feminist mind and the perspective of Aboriginal women is shared. This shared reality does not amount to a shared totality of experience such that the "commonality of all women" becomes a fact. The experience of Aboriginal women is minimally[22] based on an experience of "otherness" that is layered and involves both race and culture, as well as gender. However it has also been part of Aboriginal culture to pick up the good things and simply walk by those things that will harm our people. It is within this teaching that feminism must be placed.

Much energy within the feminist praxis has been devoted to understanding the way in which patriarchy is reproduced in modern society. For example, criminal law is seen to reinforce patriarchy in the following way:

> It is essential to understand that Western law, of which Canadian criminal law is a part, has been constructed out of male experience. Law is both a support for and a means of exercising patriarchal domination. One of the problems that feminists confront is that patriarchal dominance has existed for so long that male experience under patriarchy is perceived as the "norm." Thus concepts which have a particular importance in law such as "bias," "neutrality," "objectivity," "reasonableness," and "common-sense," are all interpreted from within a masculinist social construction of reality. When feminists question this masculinist experience, they are immediately perceived as "biased," "non-objective," "subjective," "unreasonable," and "irrational." (Russell 1989: 552)

Although I do not want to disturb the conclusion of many renowned feminists regarding their experience of patriarchy and the legal system, I do wish to question the totality of this approach as a solution when it is applied to Aboriginal women.

As indicated, an Aboriginal woman's experience of mainstream criminal justice as an experience of "otherness" based on gender, it is also an experience of "otherness" based on both culture and race. Experiencing the criminal justice system as masculinist is not more profound in the experience of Aboriginal women. In fact, it is next to impossible to separate the experience I have as woman from the experience I have as Mohawk. It is not just Mohawk women[23] who have rejected the totality of feminist analysis.[24] A Cree colleague, Winona Stevenson, states:

I do not call myself a feminist. I believe in the power of Indigenous women and the power of all women. I believe that while feminists and Indigenous women have a lot in common, they are in separate movements. Feminism defines sexual oppression as the Big Ugly. The Indigenous Women's movement sees colonization and racial oppression as the Big Uglies. Issues of sexual oppression are seldom articulated separately because they are part of the Bigger Uglies. Sexual oppression was, and is, one part of the colonization of Indigenous peoples.

I want to understand why feminists continue to believe in the universality of male dominance, the universality of sisterhood, and why they strive so hard to convert Aboriginal women. I want feminists to know why many Aboriginal women do not identify as feminists. I perceive two parallel but distinct movements, but there ought to be a place where we can meet to share, learn, and offer honest support without trying to convert each other.

Many Aboriginal women are aware of this basic contradiction which exists between their experience and the constructs of feminist thought. This contradiction does not foreclose the sharing of our experience with the feminist movement any more than it forecloses the borrowing of feminist analysis to inform our own consciousness. However, caution must be exercised before any complete embracing of feminist thought or feminist analysis occurs. The consequences of the feminist analytical structure contains serious barriers for the scope of social change defined as desirable from the Aboriginal perspective.

It is worth noting that the history of the feminist movement is a history which has been informed by Aboriginal women's experience. American feminists in the 1880s, such as Elizabeth Cady Stanton and Matilda Joslyn Gage, drew on their exposure to Aboriginal experience prior to the Seneca Falls Convention.[25] In particular, they studied the position of women within the Iroquois Confederacy (I would say the Haudenosaunee) (Wagner 1992: 115). To separate Aboriginal history from feminist history is to re-write the past. In particular, early American feminists were influenced by the political power and ownership of property maintained by the women of the Haudenosaunee. To fully reject feminism, means to reject part of my own Mohawk history[26] and the influence of my grandmothers. It is important for both Aboriginal women and feminists to reclaim our histories and to note that our histories are, in fact, shared. It is equally important to see how parts of this shared history have been erased.

More recent history does expose the reality that Aboriginal women and other racial minority women have frequently been written out of both the history and action of feminist undertakings (Wagner 1992: 115). In studying the Women's Legal Education and Action Fund (LEAF),[27] and the involvement in litigating so-called women's issues, Sherene Razack concludes:

> Along the path to a more inclusive feminist theory and practice, it is tempting to reduce the theoretical and practical tasks at hand to merely "adding" on layers of oppression by grafting racism on to sexism, as understood by white women . . ..
>
> If whiteness remains unproblematized, that is if white privilege remains unexamined, and feminist analysis continues to "universalize otherness" so that sexism and racism are not seen as interlocking systems of domination, there is little chance that women of colour will be able to ask "what is true for us?" There is still less chance that minority women will be in a position to reshape their answers into forms acceptable in court. . . .when sexuality is identified as central to women's oppression, as it is in cases involving rape, there is little room left for understanding the experience of women equally oppressed by racism and, I would add, little space for understanding how sexuality itself is constructed along racist lines.[28] (Razack 1990-91: 454-455 (footnotes omitted)).

Feminist thought can inform attempts to understand Aboriginal women's reality. But, feminism must be seen as only one tool which may or may not accurately inform our developing understanding.

A second example of the way in which feminist praxis may invalidate Aboriginal women's thought is found in the work of Zuleyma Tang Halpin (cited in Razack 1990-91: 445). Halpin suggests that there is a relationship between the domination of women and the domination of nature by a patriarchal structure, such that women and nature are both seen as "other." Nature (and all spirit beings except humans) are seen to be inferior to the human condition. Thus, the belief is that man[29] can control nature. I will not fully dispute the validity of this conclusion here, but I would suggest when man (or woman) can keep the sun from coming up nature is under control! However, the cultural relationship between nature and humans in an Aboriginal construct is vastly different from the way it is viewed in mainstream thought. Harmony with nature and with natural law is essential to the Aboriginal perspective. Oren Lyons explains how this natural worldview informs all aspects of Aboriginal thought:

> What are aboriginal rights? They are the law of the Creator. That is why we are here; he put us in this land. He did not put the white people here; he put us here with our families, and by that I mean the

bears, the deer, and the other animals. We are the aboriginal people and we have the right to look after all life on this earth. We share land in common, not only among ourselves but with the animals and everything that lives in our land. It is our responsibility.[30] (1985: 19)

Aboriginal philosophies do not share the belief that people are superior to all other life. There is no natural hierarchy of domination in Aboriginal worldviews. Halpin assumes that domination of women (and other life) is a natural construct in patriarchal society. Only when it is recognized that belief in domination is not a universal characteristic can the position of Aboriginal women be understood. Aboriginal women presently live in a patriarchal society but do not share this tradition with other women from other cultural or national groups. This is a particular form of oppression that Aboriginal women survive. Until all the contradictions and differences are expressed, then it is the oppressed view of the world that is vanished; the consequences of difference and contradiction will be disproportionately carried by Aboriginal women.

The way in which issues are first named and then sanctioned as important is also a necessary consideration when applying feminist thought to Aboriginal women's realities. Feminist[31] accounts have documented and criticized the way in which rape laws have protected the "sexual property" of a husband in his wife. An examination of child custody laws exposes that prior to the nineteenth century, fathers were almost always awarded custody of their children as children were also seen to be the property of the man (Backhouse 1987). The following quotation illuminates the way in which the law condoned (and many would suggest still condones) the husband's "right" to batter his wife:

> Where they were forced to confront such cases, the judges searched scrupulously for particulars that would justify a husband's violent response. Many probed for evidence about the battered wife's behavior or character, speculating that her shortcomings might "excuse considerable severity" on the part of her husband. Ruling that it was all a question of degree, they meticulously weighed the amount and nature of the violence. Before a court would "sanction her leaving her husband's roof," the law laid "upon the wife the necessity of bearing some indignities, and even some personal violence." "Danger to life, limb or health" was necessary to "entitle the wife to relief." (Backhouse 1991: 176)

The history of law is very much a loud history of sanctioning women's oppression and violence against her.

It is now time to recognize that Aboriginal women do not share with Canadian women the history of legally sanctioned violence against women. The laws of our people sanctioned only respect for women. Perhaps this fact makes it more easy to understand why Canadian law has so fully attacked traditional Aboriginal systems and why Aboriginal Peoples have such little faith in the dominant system of laws.

Recognizing that Aboriginal women do not share the same history of legally sanctioned violence against women also results in a number of other more specific recognitions. For example, it cannot be (and should not be) concluded or assumed that Aboriginal women will construct a response to rape, battering and other instances of abuse, incest, child welfare laws and abortion in the same way that the mainstream feminist movement has. Nor can it be assumed that the dispute resolution mechanisms that Aboriginal women will advance will look the same as those advanced by the mainstream women's movement. All of these are presumptions which must be questioned first, prior to any assumptions being made about the general applicability of the solutions.

Another example should clarify any confusion regarding the seriousness of this discussion around consequences. In the child welfare field, feminists have studied the impact of parental custody proceedings on women's lives.[32] In particular, the way in which domestic violence is relevant to these disputes is exposed. For most Aboriginal people, disputes over the custody of children are not actualized as disputes between parents. Rather, the two parties are the parents and the state: father and mother "fight" against the state to maintain custody. The mother, if involved in a situation of domestic violence cannot expose it because her right to custody of her children is dependent on the man who batters her. She and the batterer are *one* party in the court proceedings. If she does tell, it is used against her to demonstrate that the home is not a safe one. Feminist analysis of children's law, because of the choices made to focus narrowly on custody battles, has yet to examine the special disadvantage that Aboriginal women face within the legal system. Failing to examine the situation, in fact, perpetuates it.

Some Aboriginal women have turned to the feminist or women's movement to seek solace in their (common) oppression. The implications of this choice have some devastating effects on Aboriginal constructions of reality. Many, but not all, Aboriginal women reject the rigours of feminism as the full solution to the problems that Aboriginal women face in both the dominant society and within our own communities. One further consequence of relying on feminist analysis without first searching the landscape for the crevices is found in the way in which rights are conceived. In the constitutional debates, the media emphasized the alleged chasm which exists between Aboriginal men and women as exemplified by the position on individual and collective rights. The traditional understanding that has been shared with me indicates that this construction is a false one. Individual rights exist within collective rights and the rights of the collective exist in the individual. Any hierarchical ordering (that is, giving a preference to either the individual or the collective nature of rights) of either notion will fundamentally violate the culture of Aboriginal Peoples. It must also be remembered, especially by Aboriginal individuals, that the roots of our oppression lie in our collective loss of memory.[33]

It is not enough to understand the historical roots of Aboriginal oppression. It is also necessary to understand how surviving oppression impacts on our lives. Through both my studies and my struggle to understand, I have begun to see that law is one of the central sources of the oppression of Aboriginal women. I have also begun to understand how this impacts on my life. There are several particular examples of law and legal practices which turn the social relations of Haudenosaunee (Iroquois) women completely upside down. These particular examples are easily identified and should not be seen to be a complete construction of all the ways in which our Aboriginal realities are turned inside out—an important consequence of oppression. As already noted, at the time of European contact, it was the European fathers who had custody of their children (perhaps this is more accurately expressed as ownership). Writing in the late 1800s, Matilda Gage notes:

> If for any causes the Iroquois husband and wife separated the wife took with her all the property she had brought into the wigwam, the children also accompanied their mother, whose right to them was recognized as supreme.[34] (cited in Wagner 1992: 122)

For the Haudenosaunee, the children followed the mother's line. It was the right of the children to be with their mother. The selected quotation shows that Haudenosaunee women also had control over their personal property.[35]

Since the early 1900s the historical relationship between Aboriginal women and the feminist movement has been disappeared from the mainstay of feminist discourse. Today, the relationship between many Aboriginal women and the feminist movement is strained, if not fully estranged. Recovering our shared history is perhaps one way in which feminists and Aboriginal women can begin again to respectfully share our experiences, dreams and challenges—in a space that respects both culture and gender.

In conclusion, then, feminism is one source of analysis that Aboriginal women may be able to borrow from in our search for our own answers. In the end, however, the answers that are developed must be our own. Working in co-operation with other collectives will ensure that the knowledge that is developed by Aboriginal women will be shared across collectives in a positive way.

What is Known about Traditional Justice Systems and the Role of First Nations Women

> Indian people must wake up! They are asleep! . . . Part of this waking up means replacing women to their rightful place in society. It's been less than one hundred years that men lost touch with reality. There's no power or medicine that has all force unless it's balanced. The woman must be there also, but she has been left out! When we still had our culture, we had the balance. The woman made ceremonies, and she was recognized as being united with the moon, the earth, and all the forces on it. Men have taken over. Most feel threatened by holy women. They must stop and remember, remember the loving power of their grandmothers and mothers.
> *Rose Auger* (Meili 1991:25)

This chapter began with a recognition that little documentation and discourse exists within mainstream academic understanding about the ways in which justice was traditionally constructed by Aboriginal Peoples. This is true for First Nations[36] generally, but it is even more true for First Nations women. Most historic accounts are polluted by beliefs that First Nation societies were absolutely inferior to European societies. The historic material is also undulated with European perceptions of the inferiority of women. One example, from the archival materials in the New York State Library, provides all the illumination that is necessary:

> Women are admitted to the Council fire and have the liberty of speaking, which is sometimes used; when the nature of the Education of this tribe is considered, the difference of the instruction of the girls and boys is so small, the sources of knowledge are so inconsiderable that I see no reason why a Woman with strong natural sense should not acquit herself in the Council with general Satisfaction. . . . (Johnston 1964: 28-29)

This individual sees the Haudenosaunee as so very inferior that it is no surprise that the women can be seen as equally inferior! This is a very telling description which advises us on just how little status the European woman had. It must be emphasized that this diminished view on the status and contributions of women is *not* the view of the Longhouse people.[37] In fact, they would be quite insulted by the comment.

This historic construction of both women and First Nations as inferior to the European settlers has been carried forward through time and is the root of some distressing consequences for First Nations today. The consequences are even more harsh for First Nations women:

Women in our society live under a constant threat of violence. The death of Betty Osborne was a brutal expression of that violence. She fell victim to vicious stereotypes born of ignorance and aggression when she was picked up by four drunken men looking for sex. Her attackers seemed to be operating on the assumption that Aboriginal women were promiscuous and open to enticement through alcohol or violence. It is evident that the men who abducted Osborne believed that young Aboriginal women were objects with no human value beyond sexual gratification. . . .

It is intolerable that our society holds women, and Aboriginal women in particular, in position of such low esteem. Violence against women has been thought for too long to be a private affair. Assaults on women have not been treated with the seriousness which they deserve. Betty Osborne was one of the victims of this despicable attitude towards women. . . .

There is one fundamental fact: her murder was a racist and sexist act. Betty Osborne would be alive today had she not been an Aboriginal woman. (Hamilton and Sinclair 1991: vol. 11: 52)

The construction of First Nations as inferior cannot be viewed solely as a historic construction that we have moved beyond. Although no longer expressly accepted, this construction of First Nations as inferior still influences our legal relationships in subtle ways today. This is the legacy of colonialism. All of the ways in which the historic belief of European superiority infiltrates our present reality must be discovered, exposed and clearly rejected.

The history of the criminal justice system must also be carefully scrutinized. Its relationship to Aboriginal People must be understood to be a relationship of violence. The criminal justice system, the police and other authorities by their omissions have perpetuated and perhaps even encouraged the violence[38] that First Nations and particularly First Nations women have endured. The death of Helen Betty Osborne is but one example. Any initiative constructed in the future must take into direct account the histories, both personal and collective, that First Nations women have faced. This is a principle which must guide the construction of future justice initiatives. First Nations do not trust that the existing justice system can in fact deliver justice to our people. (Re)gaining the trust of Aboriginal Peoples must become a guiding principle of future justice related efforts.

Of particular interest to First Nations women is the fact that many historical accounts of the ways of our people note that violence and abuse against women or children was not tolerated in our societies.[39] In fact, there were strong cultural taboos against such behavior which were enforced by the women's family members.

> . . . the wife never becomes entirely under the control of her
> husband. Her kindred have a prior right, and can use that right to
> separate her from him or to protect her from him, should he maltreat
> her. The brother who would not rally to the help of his sister would
> become a by-word among his clan. Not only will he protect her at
> the risk of his life from insult and injury, but he will seek help for
> her when she is sick and suffering. . . .[40]

This realization must bring us back to the earlier assertion that from the First
Nations perspective the root of our oppression is in collective memory loss.
The men must be re-educated about what their responsibilities are in our
efforts to abolish the experience of violence against women in our communities.
Of necessity, this re-education should be occurring within our aspirations
to take control over our own relations of justice. However, it is interesting
to note that if the men of our communities at this time reconstructed their
traditional responsibilities they would likely be vulnerable to the imposition
of current Canadian law which prohibits the "taking of law into one's own
hands." The criminal laws of the dominant system have played an express
role in the collective loss of memory of our men.[41]

When I am trying to understand traditional ways of being, I have found
that learning the word in my own language and the literal interpretation
facilitates my own understanding of the matter in question. When I first
queried about the word for justice in Ojibwe, I was told "ti-baq-nee-qwa-
win."[42] When literally translated, it means, "to come before a system for
something that has already been done wrong." The reference to "a system"
is a reference to the Euro-Canadian system of law. It became obvious that
this Ojibwe word was used to describe justice after the period of contact with
European society's justice system. During our conversation, the grandmother
repeated many times to me that there really is no word for justice in the
Ojibwe language. I found our conversation interesting because it was most
obvious the effect on the people and the language that contact had. The
reference point for this word in the Ojibwe language was a system not their
own.

Intrigued by what I had learned about Ojibwe, I began to ask other
people who spoke their language how to say justice. Professor Leroy Little
Bear of the Native American Studies Department at the University of
Lethbridge and a citizen of the Blackfoot nation, also affirmed that there was
no word in his language for justice. "Justice is not a concept but a process,"
he stated. Chief George Guerin of the Musqueam First Nation, a member of
the Salish people, also confirmed that they too had no word for justice. And
in Mohawk, the closest word that we have for justice is one that means "it
is fitting."[43] Several of the people that I spoke to found humour in my

question. This indicated to me the importance of the information I had come upon.

For me, recognizing the impact contact had on the Ojibwe word for justice as well as the discussions with other traditional language speakers, was a profound reminder of the nature of the work of regenerating traditional justice mechanisms in our communities. We are attempting to recover a concept for which there is no word in our own languages! This realization must make us suspicious about our desire to focus on that concept, justice. Justice for me has become a concept which is not my own, but that we have begun to borrow from another's way. This must not be taken to mean that Aboriginal systems are less fair or less well-developed than non-Aboriginal systems.

The principle of respect must guide our efforts to reclaim traditional mechanisms of dispute resolution. Respect must be manifest in several ways. We must respect the uniqueness of Aboriginal ways of being, but must equally respect the separate responsibilities of women and men. We must also respect the realization that decolonization is both a painful and long process.

This realization leads to some conclusions about the involvement of First Nations individuals in the current criminal justice system. A First Nations person does not understand that system. In the First Nations system, you do not admit guilt, but you admit honesty. "I have done wrong." This understanding must be connected to the realization that coercion and punishment are not the "glue" that holds the First Nations system of dispute resolution together:

> In the Mi'kmaq worldview, individual behavior faithfully accommodates collective culture; there is a firm consensus of proper respect of inherent dignities. The mechanism by which individual passions are prevented from wreaking havoc on society is deference to shared values, reinforced by family opinion and rewarded with honour and respect. Order in society presupposes and evokes order in the soul. Order is a matter of kinship, education, and personal self-control. Every family is equal and every Mi'kmaq has an equal right to be heard and heeded by others. Coercive institutions are generally absent, if not vigorously opposed. Aggressiveness is considered wrongful and contrary to human dignity. (Denny 1992: 103)

The first understanding that Kjikeptin Alex Denny shares with us is the need to accept that the current system is non-sensical from a First Nations perspective. This realization is the realization upon which decolonized thought will come to rest. Second, we are provided with some of the reasons why options exist in Aboriginal communities that are not as easily available to mainstream citizens. If more options exist for Aboriginal communities, then bringing crime into control in our communities ought be attainable. The truth is that crime in our communities should never have gotten so out of control.

When I asked Shirley O'Connor, the Ojibwe grandmother I had been speaking to, if her understanding of justice was based on gender, my question made little sense to her. However, when I asked her if there was a difference between how men and women would understand the concept of justice in a traditional sense, then she was easily able to respond.[44] She told me to go and ask a grandfather and see what they would say.[45] When pressed, Shirley thought that a man's answer would in fact be different. A man's perspective, she thought, would focus around what happened in the bush. Justice was the offering you made when you took an animal's life. For Shirley, the women's view of justice is the respect that women receive because they are women. The conclusion is that justice initiatives must respect experiences—the totality of an individuals experience—not just incidents or alleged offences. This comes back to a principle difference in the systems of justice. Further, the experiences of women and men cannot be presumed to be the same.

We know that First Nations social relations, including relations of justice, were and continue to be holistic. This means a variety of things. First Nations recognize that our relations and institutions must address the well-being of individuals in a complete way. This means that the body, mind and spirit all must be well to have a healthy individual.[46] Communities cannot be healthy if the individuals which comprise those communities are not healthy. Within recent years, First Nations have also been recognizing that to have a healthy body, mind and spirit may not necessarily be enough. The emotional well-being of individuals has also gained prominence in the teaching of Elders on holistic ways of being.[47] Perhaps this new emphasis on the emotional realm did not require a great deal of attention in historic societies because First Nations were not surviving oppression and abuse. It is the emotional well-being of women, children *and men*[48] that is most significantly affected by physical and sexual violence in the home and in the streets.

It is also well-documented that the structure of First Nations societies was based on kinship systems. If justice, or the settlement of disputes, was based on kinship—that is familial relations—then obviously women were integrally involved in these systems. Alex Denny, Kjikeptin,[49] of the Mi'kmaq Nation provides:

> The Mi'kmaq did not have any adjudicative institution, no inquisitional system, no specialized professional elite, because they did not conceive of "public" wrongs. There were only private wrongs, and families themselves were the courts. This remains our vision of a fair and equitable system. (1992: 104)

Historical records also indicate that women had many different responsibilities in First Nations societies. In Iroquois tribes, the government established by the clans was firmly controlled by the women, who enjoyed the right to select and even depose chiefs, and had competence in such matters as land allotment, supervision of field labour, the care of the treasury, the ordering of feasts and *the settlement of disputes* (Noon 1949: 49, emphasis added). The concept of kinship relations is an important key in understanding traditional justice mechanisms and establishing those relations (or the equivalent structures which operate on the same premises and values) is necessary to restore women's respected position in First Nations society.

What were the mechanisms of dispute resolution in First Nations societies? Again, I turned to Shirley O'Connor who shared her understanding with me. Justice starts from childhood.[50] Children are taught about respect, honesty and the truth life. This is taught to the child by way of example and by lecture, that is, the telling of legends. The teaching stressed to the child is that he or she must always be mindful of doing what is right. "So this generation will know and will understand," are the words of Shirley's own grandparents to her. "Justice was a part of everyday living and how you were good to yourself. Every individual knew why this was beneficial both spiritually and emotionally." This is where we must begin to understand what justice is in a First Nations sense.

When a "wrong-doing" had occurred, the Ojibwe treated males and females in different ways. When the "wrong-doer" was male, male members of the extended family would speak to him. If he did not listen to these men then eventually he would be taken to a very old grandmother.[51] At that time, everyone in the community knew what this action meant, being spoken to by that old woman. Shirley questioned: "How many men today still respect and understand this traditional way of being? How many of our men even remember?"

The grandmother would give the man the entire history and all the teachings on why it is that we must respect each other. It seems quite important to emphasize that the "offence" did not lie in the incident itself but in the lack of *respect* that had been displayed for self and community. The grandmother will begin by explaining why we respect all living things. She talks about why we respect our bodies. And finally, she will tell him all about the things that are men's and why they happen (such as when the young man's voice changed). Nothing will be said about the so-called wrong-doing. What is important to teach, or perhaps re-emphasize to the man, is the reason why he is on this earth. The grandmother is so kind. She has no resentment or anger. Always that grandmother assumes that the man has not learned certain things in his life and it is her responsibility to teach him now.[52] Eventually the man is humiliated. He understands. When the man walks away it is his choice on how he will fix things. He may fast or just meditate in a quiet place. He is not required to confess to any person, but he could talk to the Creator or a tree or a plant or a spirit. It is the job of all the other living things to take away the "garbage" that the man has been carrying around with him.

If the "wrong-doer" is a woman, then the process is slightly different. It may be her grandmother by kinship and/or mother who speak to her first. Because women are very close to their grandmothers and mothers, maybe this will not help, particularly if the "wrong-doing" is serious. Her great aunties may be called upon to speak to her in this situation.[53] The woman who speaks to the female "wrong-doer" will give the woman the teachings that are required. A woman who has done wrong may also end up sitting before a grandmother from the community. This grandmother is the oldest woman in the community. It will be a woman who no longer can conceive children. Such a woman is believed to have the ultimate "power." Woman is the only one who is the giver of life. Once a woman has entered her advanced years (that is past menopause), she has almost walked a full circle. She can now turn around and look at life, her own but also at where you have come from. Disciplining is therefore the responsibility of the grandmothers. It is a greater responsibility than the responsibility that parents have to discipline. It is not punishing, this kind of discipline, but nurturing. To the Ojibwe, "justice is teaching about life."[54]

Justice must be seen to be a process not a concept, and particularly not a concept that is once removed from the process of dispute resolution as it is currently known in Canadian law. One final story will expand on this point. During a conference on justice held in 1986, the participants play acted an informal dispute resolution mechanism involving a store that was vandalized in the belief that they were mimicking a non-adversarial process that was akin to the First Nations system of dispute resolution. This is a very common misunderstanding—if a system is non-adversarial it is close to being Aboriginal. In the conclusion of the session, Charlie Fisher, an Ojibwe man from Whitedog, was asked if the exercise bore resemblance to what might have occurred in traditional times in his community. The strength of his resounding "no" jarred the participants. As a result, Mr. Fisher reconstructed the exercise:

He began by getting rid of the chairs and tables; everyone sat on the floor in a circle, as equals. He then asked for two other people to act as "Representing Elders," one each for the boy and the store manager. As he continued, it became clear that our little experiment in non-adversarial mediation was flawed in virtually every respect. In Charlie's version, the boy and the store manager never spoke in the presence of the panel of Elders. There was no discussion whatever about the break-in, the damage, the feelings of the disputants, or what might be done to set matters straight. There was no talk of compensation or restitution, much less the actual imposition of such measures.

Once we understood what was not going to take place, we had only one question left: "Why, then, is there a panel at all?"

Charlie Fisher tried to answer us in this way. The duty of each Representing Elder, he explained, was not to speak for the young man or the store manager, but to counsel them in private. That counseling was intended to help each person "rid himself of his bad feelings." Such counseling would continue until the Elder was satisfied that "the person's spirit had been cleansed and made whole again." When the panel convened, an Elder could signify that such cleansing had taken place by touching the ceremonial pipe. The panel would continue to meet until both Elders signified. At that point, the pipe would be lit and passed to all. As far as the community was concerned, that would be the end of the matter. Whether the two disputants later arranged recompense of some sort was entirely up to them. Passing the pipe signified, as Charlie phrased it, that each had been "restored to the community and to himself."[55]

After considering Charlie's story and listening to Shirley, I wondered if perhaps, approaching this paper through the concept of justice was in itself an error. I take seriously that there is no word in many First Nation languages to express this concept, justice.

Alex Denny stated that: "Harmony, not justice, is the ideal" (1992: 104). What Aboriginal women as a people have lost over the last five hundred years is our ability to live in harmony with each other. Aboriginal women have survived oppression, colonization and abuse. Now we seek recovery. Recovery and healing will only come when we learn to walk in balance again, with the men, with the leaders, with the children, with the Elders, and with the many nations that have come to this land. For me, seeking harmony is striving to reach a higher standard than mere justice.

Notes

1. When the words of Elders and grandmothers are cited in this paper their nations and clans will also be referenced where possible. This is *not* a way of credentialing these well-respected individuals. In fact any such attempt would be a grave insult. I offer this information for the reader, in order to assist them in understanding and organizing the information that is presented. It is one way of addressing the false homogeneity that seems to exist when the term Aboriginal Peoples is used.

2. Although my original intention was to focus solely on justice within the criminal law paradigm, this has not been possible, at least in the introduction of this paper. I believe that this is a reflection of the way in which justice is constructed in the Aboriginal worldview. The focus on criminal justice will develop as the paper proceeds.

3. My experience of the culture to which I was born has often been an experience of negation, as I was raised in cities away from the Mohawk people. I am also influenced in my understandings as a result of my parentage, one Mohawk and one White. Over the years, I have come to respect that I was put down in the middle and this is where my work is. I have also "married into" a different nation. My understandings now also reflect the teachings my Cree husband and his people share with me.

4. A word of caution is necessary regarding my use of the word traditional. This word is frequently misinterpreted in the mainstream discourse. It does *not* mean a desire to return through the years to some historic way of life. Aboriginal traditions and cultures are neither static nor frozen in time. It is not a backward-looking desire. Traditional ways have not been lost as some would assert, but the right to have recognized, respected and to exercise these distinct ways of being have been overtly and covertly oppressed. Traditional perspectives include the view that the past and all its experiences inform the present reality.

5. Although I frequently speak of a single Aboriginal way, this is misleading. Aboriginal Peoples are not homogeneous. We are recognized in law as the "Indian, Inuit and Métis." Even within these three legal references there exists great diversity based on our experience and membership in specific nations, our place of residency (including north/south, reserve, settlement, rural, urban), our gendered understandings, and so on.

6. This is partially a result of the covert and overt exclusion of Aboriginal people from educational institutions. For example, as of July 1, 1992 there are only three Aboriginal people who have tenure-track teaching appointments in Canadian law schools. There are several others who have "special" positions relating to Native Law programs in several faculties and at least two others teaching on contract. Of the three tenure-track professors, all three were only appointed in July 1989. This is a very recent occurrence, and the void in the academic writing of Aboriginal Peoples (note, not writing *on*) must be seen in light of this realization. I would be remiss if I did not also point out that of the three, we are all women (Ojibwe, Cree and Mohawk).

7. I am *not* suggesting that these developments are *not* necessary or valuable. They are just incomplete as they do not challenge the existing structure or foundation of the institution.

8. I am clearly not suggesting that the current construction of sexuality is the central aspect of the way in which Aboriginal women view their gender oppression. This topic will be fully canvassed later in the chapter.

9. This is not to suggest that racial oppression is a single experience. It vastly varies based on the individual's cultural and national identity.

10. Again, I am *not* suggesting that these developments in "Native" programming and departments have been unnecessary or serve no purpose. They are just incomplete in that they do not fully challenge the dominant structures. The marginalization of "Native" studies is also a real danger. Such marginalization fits very neatly into the historical construct of European superiority. I also recognize that the creation of departments of "Native" studies is effective in that it can foster an environment where Aboriginal Peoples feel safe. I also fully support the creation of an Aboriginal Law School.

11. For a discussion of the many justice inquiries from a woman's perspective please see Monture-Okanee 1992.

12. Just as Aboriginal cultures are not homogeneous, neither are European cultures. We must keep in the backs of our minds the specificities of the Canadian reality.

13. As part of my personal commitment to "unlearn" colonization, I refuse to think of this land as Canada, Ontario, Quebec and so on. When I travel I think in terms of who's territory I am visiting—the Cree, the Algonquin, the Dene and so on.

14. Obviously, the reference to language here is a specific reference to the English language. This specificity should be express. The relationship between language and culture is not unitary. For Aboriginal Peoples, I believe, we experience both English and French in similar ways. Both are the languages of our colonization. However, there is also a relationship of domination between English and French. Within the francophone experience there are also relationships of dominance between residences of Quebec and Acadian or Franco-Ontarians, or Franco-Manitobans, or the Métis. For a fuller discussion of the way in which language operates see Monture-Okanee 1993.

15. I use the phrase, community, to refer to any collection of Aboriginal people, from a small and remote reserve to those living in major urban centres.

16. In the absence of *true* Canadian political will to change this relationship, then Aboriginal energy is best spent in our own communities.

17. I want to thank Susan Zimmerman for sharing with me the insights she gained while working on the Law Reform Commission of Canada projects regarding Aboriginal Peoples, Visible Minorities and the criminal law. Her insights have helped me understand and verbalize my own experiences.

18. I am not fond of this term because it does not embrace the reality that I have experienced. In this society, being Mohawk and being women is not disadvantage that can be measured by adding one to the other. It is disadvantage that is wound within disadvantage.

   Sherene Razack proposes, "if male domination is the prism through which gender oppression is viewed, race and class enter the picture as background scenery" (1990-91: 441). Serious methodological problems arise when the multifaceted forms of oppression are presented in an additive and/or hierarchical form.

19. This has been, perhaps, the most difficult lesson in understanding the politics

of resistance that I have personally had to face. I believed that if I just struggled hard enough up someone else's ladder of success, studied hard in university for years, then one day mainstream society would accept this Mohawk woman as an equal. This has not been my experience of either academia or mainstream society. In many ways, I lead a very privileged life (based on so-called socio-economic variables) and this has been very difficult to reconcile against the experiences of discrimination that I still face. What I now understand is that I do have a limited amount of control regarding my personal circumstances (or the individual experience of oppression), but I still remain powerless to eradicate the effects of systemic oppression of First Nations people.

20. Although I will discuss feminism as though it is a single unified theory, this is a simplification. The subtleties of feminist thought are beyond the scope of this paper.

21. Standpoint theory is articulated by (and continues to be developed) in the work of the following authors: Alcoff 1989; Harding 1989, 1991; Harstock 1987; Smith 1987.

22. Aboriginal women's experience may also be compounded by class, disability and sexual orientation.

23. For a more complete discussion, please refer to Kane and Maracle 1989.

24. This recognition should *not* be constructed as a suggestion that Aboriginal women share a commonality of experience based on our culture and/or gender. Our experiences are not homogeneous and are filtered by our experiences of our national identities, residence, northern versus southern geography, education and so on.

25. The first women's rights convention.

26. The Mohawk are one of the six nations which comprise the Haudenosaunee Confederacy.

27. LEAF is the most visible Canadian women's organization that is involved in litigating women's issues before the courts.

28. If unfamiliar with any notion of difference in the way sexuality is constructed, the reader should examine the murder of Helen Betty Osborne as examined in Volume II of Hamilton and Sinclair 1991.

29. Gender specificity is intended.

30. It should be noted that in Aboriginal languages there is no gender referencing. The word for Creator is both he and she. Only when we pick up the colonizers language does a perversion of our culture occur. Some Elders, such as Dr. Art Solomon, consciously chose to use the word she to describe the Creator to make noticeable the gender discrimination as well as to restore the balance.

31. This is not to suggest that a single cohesive theory of feminism has been articulated. See for instance Boyle 1991: 273.

32. See for example Boyd 1987: 168.

33. Paula Gunn Allen (1986: 213-214) originally speaks of this need to remember. This idea of collective memory loss is also discussed by Sally Roesch Wagner (1990: 223).

34. Please note that my people lived in longhouses and not wigwams.

35. This relationship also extended to realty, although it would be a mistake to characterize the Aboriginal view of the relationship to land as one of ownership. For further discussion see Brown 1990: 182-198.

36. At this point in time my discussion is to become, unfortunately, more focused. This is reflected in my purposive change in language from Aboriginal Peoples to First Nations. I use the term First Nations to refer to the people who the government of Canada would refer to as "Indians." I, however, refuse to adopt the on-reserve/off-reserve dichotomy artificially created by the federal government. I also do not embrace the distinction of status/non-status. How a human being can have no status is a construction that my mind is not able to comprehend. In earlier articles, I have used the term First Nations to include the Métis and the Inuit; that however, is not my intention here. I think it is worthwhile to point out that the general usage of the term First Nations has become more specialized over time, perhaps more specialized than is my intent, to refer primarily to "Indian bands."

     In the course of writing this chapter I have been forced to come to terms with just how particularized my understanding about traditional justice relations is. My understanding does more accurately reflect what First Nations understand.

     Although I do not wish to shirk my personal responsibilities for the exclusion of Métis and Inuit that I have just made, I do believe that there are some structural justifications for this exclusion. The Métis trace their history to "nine months after the arrival of the first European man in this country." First Nations trace their histories to "time immemorial." The Inuit also trace their histories to "time immemorial"; however, their experience is unique in their experience of the north. Therefore, the process used to properly trace the traditional relations of justice of each of these distinct peoples must necessarily be different. I set the Métis and the Inuit apart in an attempt to do justice to their distinct ways of being.

37. This is another way of referring to the Haudenosaunee.

38. For a full discussion please refer to Sugar and Fox 1989.

39. For a discussion please refer to Green 1992: 24-26.

40. These are the words of Alice Fletcher who wrote in the late 1800s as cited in Wagner 1992: 125.

41. I would recommend that further research be undertaken in this area. For example, I am of the firm belief that one of the reasons why violence against women and children was seen to be a crime among the Haudenosaunee was that women played a central role in the definition and administration of justice in our communities. I know of no current or historic academic source that fully substantiates this position. See also the preliminary discussion in Monture and Turpel 1991: 1-39.

42. This understanding was shared with me by Shirley O'Connor. Ms. O'Connor is a grandmother and is from the Lac Souel reserve in Northern Ontario. She is Ojibwe. Currently employed as a counselor in the child welfare field, Ms. O'Connor now resides in Sioux Lookout.

     Any error in recording or understanding the teaching Ms. O'Connor shared with me is my own.

43. Elder Ernie Benedict, Akwesasne, shared this information with me.

44. This is an important comment on research methods and the nature of the pitfalls when Aboriginal people are the objects of research.

45. Shirley was not trying to avoid my question. The structure of gender relationships

in traditional Aboriginal societies does not mirror the gender relations as we understand them today. It is wrong for a women to address men's understanding as we have never experienced life from their point of view.

46. This is a very common traditional teaching, one of the first I learned after I sought out the red road. It is more fully discussed in Hamilton and Sinclair 1991, vol. 1: 19.

47. Although it was several years ago, I believe the first person I heard share this teaching in a workshop that I attended was Edna Manitowba. Edna is of the Bear Clan, Ojibwe Nation. She is a member of the Medewin Society.

48. The perspective of many traditional First Nations women does not allow for the condemnation of the men who are the abusers in their communities. This is quite complicated to understand. It is based on the mistrust Aboriginal Peoples have of the justice system as it presently exists. It also partially arises, I believe, from the different conceptualization of justice within First Nations communities. It is also sourced in a different gender construction. A detailed discussion is found in Hamilton and Sinclair 1991, vol. 1: 475-485.

49. This Mi'kmaq word indicates that he is the Grand Captain, Grand Council of the Mi'kmaq Nation.

50. This reminds me of the day my son Blake, aged two, was presented with an eagle feather. We were at a celebration and he was dancing pow-wow. The Elders were all smiling that such a young man knew all the right moves to the sneak-up dance. When presenting the feather for his dancing, the Elder explained that what the little boy had been teaching was the true law.

51. This is not the man's grandmother by blood relation. The name grandmother is assigned to the old women of the community and the grandmother in this instance will usually be the oldest woman in the community. She is the court of last resort—so to speak.

52. This is very different from the Canadian justice system. The Ojibwe system does not place any value on the individual wrong-doer's intent or purpose. If an assumption is to be made, it will be assumed that the person does not understand the way in which he or she is expected to behave.

53. It is important to note that unlike the male wrong-doer, the men of the extended family do *not* speak to the woman. Shirley also explained to me that the woman will never be sent to speak to a grandfather.

54. I am indebted to Shirley O'Connor for trusting me with her culture and her insights into the way in which justice is constructed within the Ojibwe community traditionally.

55. I have respectfully borrowed this story from Rupert Ross (1992: 8-9). I would also add that Mr. Ross is a non-Aboriginal, legally educated man. The understanding that he has developed, although not always perfect or exact, gives me hope and inspiration for our collective futures.

12

Myths and Revolution: Thoughts on Moving Justice Forward in Aboriginal Communities

AN EARLIER VERSION OF CHAPTER 12 was published as "Aboriginal Peoples and Canadian Criminal Justice: Myths and Revolution," in Richard Gosse, James Youngblood Henderson and Roger Carter, Continuing Poundmaker and Riel's Quest: Presentations Made at a Conference on Aboriginal Peoples and Justice. (Saskatoon: Purich Publishing, 1994).

I am going to stand because that was the way I was taught to do things. I would like to begin by saying I am very honoured to be in this territory, the territory of the Cree. This is the territory of Treaty Six. It is also a home to citizens of the Métis nation. This territory has come to be known as both Saskatoon and Saskatchewan, but that is not how I understand where I am.

I never name beforehand the talks that I am asked to give because the way I was brought up I was taught you speak from your heart with your mind. You have to double understand all things. I never really know what I am going to say as I am sitting down there waiting to come up here. I cheated this time because I am a little bit nervous because issues of criminal justice are so important to me. I have written down some things that I want to cover.

I want to make it clear that I am not going to speak about Inuit or Métis women. I have no expertise in either of these two topics. I certainly have no authority to speak on behalf of Métis or Inuit women. They have never asked me to speak for them. They are quite capable of speaking for themselves. I cannot speak for all "Indian" women either. I am, I suppose, in the minds of some people, an "Indian" woman. I am registered under the *Indian Act* and am registered on the band list at Six Nations. However, in my mind I am Haudenosaunee.[1] At the same time, I also recognize that I have had the great honour of marrying into the Cree nation and into Treaty Six. I understand that my marriage creates a new set of responsibilities and relationships to another nation of people. Even though I now reside among the Cree, I am Mohawk and that is one of the ways I understand my world. What I am going to talk to you today about are my own Mohawk woman thoughts, not so much on self-government, but on what justice is.

Self-government is a very misused term. Justice is perhaps easier to understand. If we look hard at the oppression of Aboriginal people in this country we will see that all of the oppression we have faced—from residential schools to section 12(1)(b) of the *Indian Act* (1970), from the removal of our children through child welfare practices to the exemption of the *Indian Act* from the purview of the federal human rights legislation (*Canadian Human Rights Act*, R.S.C., 1985, c.H-6, s.67), from the prohibitions against our ceremonies[2] to the ban against lawyers representing us (*Indian Act*, R.S.C., 1927, s. 141)—all share in common one fact. All the oppression of Aboriginal Peoples in Canada has operated with the assistance and the formal sanction of the law. The Canadian legal system is at the heart of what we must reject as Aboriginal nations and as Aboriginal individuals.

Although I have never experienced the mainstream system of law as a just system but only as an instrument of my oppression, I still believe that there ought to exist a relationship between law and justice. As law is so central to the oppression of Aboriginal Peoples in Canada, self-government alone will not correct the problems we face in our communities. We will still have relationships with the rest of Canada, and Canadian laws will continue to touch on Aboriginal lives. To speak of separate Aboriginal justice systems only simplifies the discussion without accomplishing anything.

When I was thinking about what I was going to say this morning I looked at the conference theme. I thought "Getting It Together"—now that is kind of "kicky"—I like that. What does this mean? What does this mean in real terms to me? What does it mean to get it together or preferably to have it together. Well, I think in order to get it together, the very first thing we have to deal with is truth. What is the truth about who I am? This is the most truth—who I am—that I can ever know. That is why I started where I started, affirming the knowledge that I am a Mohawk woman. What is the truth about who you are and what is the truth about that which brings us into this room together? All of us, independent of our tribal affiliations or status as a member of the "dominant" society must learn to think about ourselves in a decolonized way.

Standing in the way of both Aboriginal and non-Aboriginal Peoples when we try to think in a decolonized way are a number of myths about the history of both this country and of Aboriginal Peoples. The first thing that we collectively must do is to dispel the myths that surround us. These myths perpetuate the conversations that we have about Aboriginal justice in

Canada. The myths distort the conversations about justice, and our justice relationships continue to be dysfunctional. This discussion about dispelling myths is not a complete discussion. The myths and the manner in which they are perpetuated vary from region to region in this country. This discussion about myths dispels only the most obvious ones, and more work and thought in this area is required. Talking about myths on which this country has been built should be seen as a soft way to examine the impact of colonialism on the lives of Aboriginal people as well as Canadians.

I first want to say that there is a myth about how difficult this task is. One of my Elders taught me that in its vast complexity it is profoundly simple.[3] It is as simple as I am and I am responsible. I understand my responsibilities to myself, to the Cree man that I married, to the children that we have made and brought into this world through the gift that I have as woman. I understand my responsibilities to my new relations in the Cree territory; to Mother Earth on whom we walk and who nurtures all life; to Father Sky; to Brother Sun; and to Grandmother Moon who watches over the women. It is just that simple. We are not trying to do a very hard thing. When we get to truly sharing an understanding we will see that it is in fact quite simple.

The second myth to be dispelled involves the question of government power or jurisdiction. When Aboriginal people assert jurisdiction in matters of so-called criminal justice (which is not by any means how I conceive what justice is), we hear in response that there is a single system of criminal laws in Canada. Non-Aboriginal people fear the results of Aboriginal Peoples asserting jurisdiction over criminal law matters.[4] What should be heard is the simple plea of Aboriginal Peoples to have both the resources and the control to address the many problems that our communities now face. People must stop fearing the possible creation of many Aboriginal criminal codes. What Aboriginal people seek is the acceptance that there can be more than one valid and legitimate way to address disputes and wrong-doings. Aboriginal Peoples do not wish to displace anyone else's right to be governed by the legitimate and properly consented to laws of their nation. To do such a thing would amount to becoming oppressors ourselves. Our challenge is not a challenge to your right to be in your own unique way, but a simple desire to follow our own ways. The creation of written criminal codes that merely mimic the dominant system's solution of social order is not what I am talking about when I talk about Aboriginal justice systems. This idea of too many criminal codes is also a myth that is perpetuated by those who have been unable to understand that there are many paths to follow to arrive at a just society.

In reality, there are already many criminal law authorities in Canada. Yes, Canada has a single federal criminal code. Canada also has a number of other federal statutes that create a vast number of offences. The federal criminal code also passes certain authority over to the provinces although this authority is not always expressly stated. We had one example this morning, gaming. There are other areas of provincial jurisdiction over offences such as the control of traffic and highways. The administration of justice, that is to say the organization of the courts and the appointment of judges, is shared between federal and provincial authorities with provinces occupying the centre of this sphere. There exists both federal and provincial authority for policing. Canadians do not complain loudly about the separate criminal law jurisdiction held by the military. The Canadian system of justice is a very complicated system. I do not believe that word, unitary, describes it at all.

Canadians do not question the general workability of the civil and common law traditions in this country. Why is the recognition of a third tradition of law such an impossible and unworkable one? To suggest that there is a single, unitary system of criminal justice in the first place in Canada is to perpetuate a dangerous myth which acts to support only the existing, status quo arrangements. At the same time, this assertion of an existing unitary system forecloses the discussion about Aboriginal justice systems in a premature way.

The next step in our journey is to consider the myth that was dispelled when the *Charter*[5] became a significant part of the supreme law of this land. The *Charter* has revolutionized the practice of criminal law, including the manner in which people are incarcerated in Canada. It has turned the entire legal system upside down and inside out. To provide but one example, I was reading in *The Globe and Mail* yesterday on the plane that Gerald Gall, an esteemed professor of law at the University of Alberta, was suggesting that in his next text on law he is going to comment on the fact that the courts are no longer necessarily open courts in Canada.[6] More and more judges are granting bans on publication of court proceedings. This prohibits for a time, the media's ability to disseminate information about particular criminal trials. Canadian people have had their ability to know what is happening in the courts infringed. This denies the ancient legal principle that individuals shall receive a full, fair and *public* hearing. It also challenges the value attached to the notion of deterrence, which is one of the justifications for the imposition of the criminal sanction, because others cannot be deterred if they do not know of those who are charged, the charges and the punishments imposed. The *Charter* has turned what were age-accepted truths in Canadian law around on their heads. Criminal law has been "revolutionized" since 1982. Yet, the system of criminal justice in Canada still remains intact.

From my Mohawk point of view, with the entrenchment of the *Charter*, Canadians have now begun to respect, or perhaps it is only initial acceptance, a principle of legal revolution. In my mind then, there should be no problem with a little bit of Aboriginal revolution. It is not going to hurt things or change things or shake up anything so badly that the country is bound to come apart at its seams. In fact, the Canadian criminal justice system has so clearly failed to provide justice to Aboriginal Peoples that it is hard to imagine a situation where Aboriginal justice systems would not be an overall improvement. Even if Aboriginal people stumble and fall on this path to self-government (a self-government that includes Aboriginal justice systems) then lessons will be learned and success will be one step closer.

It has taken a lot of Aboriginal energy to move the debate on self-government the short distance it has come in the last hundred years. This energy is required at the community level as there is much healing work to be done. I want to get on with the business of healing as opposed to merely being able to protect Aboriginal citizens and our nations from further harm. There are some simple ways in which non-Aboriginal people could assist us in having the time and space to work in our communities. For example, Aboriginal Peoples frequently have their motivations questioned when we assert our rights. This takes a lot of energy. I think it is now time that the tables were turned and we question the motivations of those who staunchly refuse to agree to the positive changes Aboriginal Peoples seek. Non-Aboriginal people could be of great assistance if they assisted us in turning the conversation around so that Canada is required to be accountable for the wrongs that it has perpetuated. Vested self-interest in maintaining status quo power relations on the part of individuals, institutions and the country as a whole must be factored into the discussions of the creation of Aboriginal justice systems.

Non-Aboriginal people frequently ask me if they have a place in this new justice order that Aboriginal people are advocating. I certainly do not think that non-Aboriginal people can or should run Aboriginal justice projects. But this is not to say that they have no place. As the new relationship that Aboriginal people require is developed, this question of place can be more easily answered. At the developmental stage, I am concerned that the involvement of non-Aboriginal people as the key actors in Aboriginal justice projects will have serious and negative consequences. What needs to be provided by non-Aboriginal people is an articulation of their role rather than a repackaging of Aboriginal thought. To do otherwise is to appropriate both Aboriginal experience and Aboriginal writing. This particular appropriation is dangerous as the appropriation is masked behind standard Canadian liberalism (equality as sameness for all). It is masked under a false and misleading understanding of Aboriginal Peoples that is gained solely from academic readings and no lived experience. You cannot quote from an article that I have written in the same way that you can quote from a piece by a non-Aboriginal person. It is time non-Aboriginal people began to take seriously the issues of their appropriations of Aboriginal thought; afterall, it's colonialism dressed up 1990s.

The next myth also qualifies as a major personal aggravation. There is no such thing as an Aboriginal court. Courts are, by their very nature, adversarial. This was not the historic process whereby disputes and disturbances in our communities were resolved. I am not saying there is no such thing as Aboriginal jurisdiction over matters of justice. I firmly believe this jurisdiction exists. All I am saying is that I am not willing to run only one justice conversation with you, particularly when that conversation always ends with the establishment of small pilot projects, diversion initiatives, sentencing circles and the possibility of someday, Aboriginal courts. I am not willing to assume that is all of what we need to be talking about. Although sentencing circles, diversion projects and Aboriginal justice personnel within the mainstream system are all goals worthy of support in the short term, they require nominal energy, nominal commitment and nominal resources from the existing system. However, these kinds of initiatives are both inadequate and insufficient if the goal of our joint efforts is to ameliorate the existing oppression and discrimination that Aboriginal people face. At least in my Mohawk woman's view an indigenized criminal justice system is not what we are talking about.

I want to offer one example by way of explanation. We know that at least in one instance in Canada an Aboriginal person was convicted of a crime they did not commit and we also know that the fact that Donald Marshall Jr. was a "Native person" was causal in this wrongful conviction (Hickman et al. 1989). The Marshall Inquiry report documents, albeit not by using the word racism, that the results of the trial and subsequent appeals of Donald Marshall Jr. were shaped by the courts' bias. In fact, the Marshall Inquiry concluded that Donald Marshall Jr. was wronged by every part of the justice system he came into contact with. We can choose to believe that this example is an anomaly. I know that this is not the truth. As a result of the history between Aboriginal people and the courts, many Aboriginal people do not see Canadian courts as dispensers of justice. This means that Aboriginal people most frequently do not perceive Canadian courts as courts of justice but rather as tools of colonialism and oppression.

Personal acquaintance with a number of Aboriginal prisoners in Canada leads me to the conclusion that many of them are wrongfully convicted. Not all of the individuals are fully innocent of the criminal acts for which they were convicted, but the racism of the justice system has impacted harshly on both their sentences and the seriousness of their charges. The fact that they are not "innocent" does not mean that no legal wrong has occurred. All of these individuals in my view are "wrongfully convicted" in a moral sense of that phrase. There exists no legal remedy for a racist trial (which by the way can only have one outcome—a racist one). If we are content to accept only the parameters that the mainstream system is willing to provide (such as the *Charter* or diversion or sentencing circles) then we will never be able to clearly focus on prevention and the recovery of our own ways of doing justice. Many Aboriginal people are in need of our support and our creative remedial ideas. There are past, present and future wrongs which need righting as well as preventing. Ideas or institutions are not good simply because they have been around for a long time. Perhaps we need to fully change the dialogue by injecting some new language and rejecting some old ideas.

Language is one of the biggest challenges that confronts me when I try to image what an Aboriginal justice process would be. I have problems using the words that justice systems and legal systems use because they mask the true relationship between Aboriginal law and the Aboriginal community. This is to say that the words do not literally translate back and forth between Indian languages and English. One example is the fact that words such as guilt, integral to the criminal trial process, do not have exact Aboriginal translations.

Whenever I am struggling to understand tradition (that is to say who I am), I always try to reclaim the meaning of the words in my own language. This is important to me as a method of understanding and I mention it often. In the Mohawk language when we say law, it does not really translate directly to the "Great Law of Peace," as many of us have been told. What it really means is "the way to live most nicely together."[7] That is what law means to my Mohawk mind. When I think about courts, when I think about police, when I think about people's experiences at law school, or maybe constitutional negotiation—to really bait you—are these the experiences of law that reflect living nicely together? The Mohawk standard is the standard that I carry with me and compare my experiences against. Living nicely together is an onerous standard. Aboriginal law is not inferior to Canadian law. In many ways it is a more onerous system.

There is another newer idea that must be firmly rejected. The suggestion that alternative dispute resolution practices mirror Aboriginal reality is not a truth. Alternatives are merely that, small add-ons to the existing system—which stands ready with the full force of its adversarial and punishment-oriented values if the "nice" solution does not work.[8] Aboriginal people and Aboriginal nations have been marginalized for long enough. I do not like or think appropriate the comparison between Aboriginal ways of resolving disputes and the movement known as alternative dispute resolution (sometimes fondly called ADR).

My initial response to the comparison of Aboriginal experience with the goals of alternative dispute resolutions was actually pleasure. This joy was not long lived. The way in which disputes were (and sometimes are) resolved in Aboriginal communities does not correspond to any process that I have any knowledge about that exists within the current system. Diane LeResche provides this insightful description of social control mechanisms in Aboriginal communities:

> Indirect social control methods are prevalent and usually make distasteful interventions by anyone outside the family unnecessary. At its core, Native American peacemaking is inherently spiritual; it speaks to the connectedness of all things; it focuses on unity, harmony, on balancing the spiritual, intellectual, emotional, and physical dimensions of a community of people. A peacemaking process tends to be viewed as a "guiding process," a relationship healing journey to assist people in returning to harmony. Peacemaking is capable of healing hurts and wounds. It brings peace through good feelings, not through fear. Peacemaking involves deep listening, not defending, arguing, forcing. It includes the widest circle of people concerned, each having a voice if they wish, not just the immediate "parties" and their representatives. Elders are frequently asked to be present. The gathering of all concerned tends to be public. Peacemakers seek solutions relevant to each situation, using accumulated tribal wisdom. They tell stories that impart the expected behaviors and beliefs by which people should live.[9] (LeResche 1993: 321)

Peacemaking, not alternative dispute resolution, is an English word that captures the essence of Aboriginal systems of social order. Peacemaking is a complex process and is unique because the roles of policing, adjudicating and corrections are not necessarily fragmented.

Peacemaking is both family-based and spiritual. An "offender" in the Navajo system is often described, "He acts as if he had no relatives" (Bluehouse and Zion 1993: 331). These two values bring a system of peacemaking into direct conflict with the values of western dispute resolution where objectivity and neutrality are omnipotent. Underlying any superficial resemblance between alternative dispute resolution and Aboriginal systems of dispute resolution are fundamental and often contradictory value systems. These differences are often masked under attempts to explain the Aboriginal system of dispute resolution in terms that the mainstream system can easily understand. The result is dangerous and takes us further away from our goals.

It is not just non-Aboriginal people that fall into this language trap. It is the same trap that was the source of my initial pleasure at the inclusion of the Aboriginal ways in alternative dispute resolution discussions. Aboriginal justice must be seen to be a process, not a concept or an institution. Too frequently when conversations occur about Aboriginal justice systems we all begin by imagining Aboriginal police officers, courts or tribunals, Aboriginal jails filled with Aboriginal staff and inmates. This is *not* an Aboriginal justice system. I think it is misleading to talk about Aboriginal justice systems. I fear that it is also dangerous to have this discussion. Dangerous because indigenizing the existing system has been tried and has not yet provided a solution to the drastic over-representation of Aboriginal people in the Canadian system. Indigenization may alleviate some of the pain and confusion that a person who is brought before the Canadian system experiences, but it is only a partial solution. I have never been very happy with less than all.

I worry too that some people will interpret what I am saying as an admission that Aboriginal Peoples and our systems of law were less advanced than non-Aboriginal Peoples or that we did not have a process of justice. This is not what I am saying, hinting or suggesting. Consider for a moment the draining cost of criminal justice on the Canadian pocket. Aboriginal people did not have a system of jails. We did not have jails because we did not need jails. We did not have a justice system or systems as we know them today. This does not mean we did not have systems and processes that guaranteed social order. Our system of law would also be a cost effective adoption to the Canadian experience. We had systems of law that were very successful and efficient. Consider some facts about the Canadian system of justice in a different way. If it costs up to $90,000 to keep one inmate in a maximum security federal penitentiary for one year.[10] Imagine the savings that would accrue to all Canadians if even 10 percent of Aboriginal federal offenders could be released and stay released. Aboriginal people's desire to regain some of the control over our systems of law and order should not been seen as a threat to the greater Canadian social order. They should be understood as aspirations that will benefit the entire country.

The path that I am advocating is a path on which revolution is possible. It is not going to be any easy path for Aboriginal people to walk.[11] It is no secret that many of our communities are very troubled. We only need to think of the youth suicide rates; the rampant alcohol, drug and substance abuse; the over-incarceration; the impact of child welfare systems and residential schools; political abuses and misappropriation; and the abuse of Aboriginal women and of our children. Existing systems of Canadian law are both implicit and complicit in this reality. Existing law is not the solution. Tradition is the solution. Recovering our distinct ways of being is the solution. That recognition is merely a philosophical statement and bringing it down to the daily experience of all people in Aboriginal communities is a monumental task. We need to have the space to have the conversation about solutions at the community level rather than having to engage in a lofty discussion at the political level about our legal rights. The myth that legal rights are the solution also troubles me.

As we turn to tradition, we must recognize that Aboriginal social systems did not historically have to deal with the grave social ills that we presently face in our communities. Romanticizing systems of Aboriginal social control will not help us. For example, many historical records indicate that the abuse of women in many Aboriginal societies was almost non-existent at the time of contact. We cannot look to the past to find the mechanisms to address concerns such as abuse, because many of the mechanisms did not exist. The mechanisms did not exist because they were not needed. What we can reclaim is the values that created a system where the abuses did not occur. We can recover our own system of law, law that has at its centre the family and our kinship relations. We must be generous with ourselves and kind as well, as we discover again how to live again as healthy and disciplined individuals. We must know that the dominant system of government will also be kind and generous to us as we heal from five hundred years of oppression. We must be patient with each other as we learn to live in a decolonized way. This means that we, as Aboriginal individuals, must stop accepting the myth of White superiority and begin advocating truly Aboriginal responses. This means looking further than the mere creation of so-called Aboriginal or tribal courts. It means rejecting the *Indian Act* regime and all of the foreign system of relating to each other that was imposed.

The whole presumption in the mainstream system is that we need law because there inevitably and invariably will be disputes among people that are not resolvable. The mainstream system is based on the presumption that there will be conflict and we need a system of coercion to correct that conflict. That is obviously not my Mohawk woman's view of what law is. Law is about retaining, teaching and maintaining good relationships. To come to this conversation about getting Aboriginal justice together, as soon as we start talking courts and we start talking constitution and we start talking policing, we are defeating an Aboriginal construction of justice. The most important part of the dialogue which needs to take place is lost. We must start by recovering our Aboriginal notions of justice. As I understand this concept, it embraces a knowledge of who I am, an understanding of my responsibilities which are both individual and collective, and only then a sense of what is fitting, right or fair.

The more reading and the more listening I do the more I notice how much this conversation about Aboriginal justice is becoming solely about the mainstream system accommodating us. I do not want to be accommodated. It is truly an offensive suggestion. Offensive because in the long run I expect it will not make even a little bit of difference for the experiences my children will have. I want to be able to live my life with the faith that my children will live their lives in the way of our law. That is the way to live most nicely together. What we need to look at is whose decision has it been to have a conversation about accommodation of individuals and about accommodating the existing justice system. The truth about what has changed in the last decade is that all the reforms that have taken place in justice have expected Aboriginal people to do the changing. This is wrong because the problem with justice is a problem that exists within the justice system and not within Aboriginal people. Those people who have jumped into the conversation in the middle need to stop and have the honesty, the integrity and the kindness to walk back and understand what Aboriginal people mean when we say justice.[12]

Noel Lyon suggests that to persist in looking for ways to adopt the dominant society's criminal laws and processes to Aboriginal people perpetuates a very destructive breach of the fiduciary duty that is owed to Aboriginal Peoples by the Canadian governments (1992: 311). The idea of a fiduciary relationship will not be familiar to everyone. It is not a complicated idea but neither is the legal meaning precise.[13] The duty owed to Aboriginal Peoples is a unique one. It is like no other duty owed in law. It is the duty that is owed by a person to another over whom they have power. Common examples of the relationship would be doctor/patient or teacher/student. In the case of Aboriginal Peoples, the duty owed by government arises out of our historic occupation of the land and the notion that the Crown must always act honourably.[14] It seems to me that the concept of fiduciary duty or relationship is the key to moving the justice dialogue forward in a good way. Judging government action against the notion of a unique fiduciary relationship seems progressive in that it forces the disempowerment of Aboriginal Peoples to the front and centre of the conversation. If the standard remains to be mere accommodation not only is it potentially dangerous it fails to focus the conversation on the power that certain people have to define— power that is based on the untrue belief in European (White) superiority. The additional value of constructing the Aboriginal justice debate around the fiduciary concept is the fact that monetary damages are available if the standard owed to Aboriginal people has been breached.

The fact that mere accommodation has become the standard that Canada is willing to embrace in the face of overwhelming documentation of the wrongful treatment of Aboriginal people at the hands of the criminal justice system is a disturbing one. The accommodations made to date have had little impact on the rates of incarceration of Aboriginal People over the last decade. In fact, the rates of over-representation continue to increase despite the reforms implemented to date. It is also my suspicion that the standard of mere accommodation is illegal and unconstitutional. It fails to give meaning to the "solemn promises" made is section 35(1) of the *Constitution Act, 1982.* Mere accommodation is a breach of the Crown's fiduciary obligation which requires the state to act in the best interests of Aboriginal people.

I have two messages to share now that the myths that disturb me the most have been exposed as untruths. I have a message for Aboriginal people and I think this message was also delivered to you last night. I am going to do it in a little different way. We are here as the original peoples; there is no doubt in my mind that we will continue to be here as the original peoples. There is no doubt in my mind that we have every right, every jurisdiction, moral, legal or otherwise, to assert and be who we are. Do not wait for anybody to pat you on the head and say do it before you pick up your responsibilities. When we have it together, we will do it. Go home, pick up your responsibilities and do it now. In particular, when you know of abuses—from political corruption to the abuse of women and children— occurring within your community or within your own family, do not turn the other way. Remember our law is family law. Exercise your responsibilities. Do not trust in a colonial justice system to solve those problems. Escaping the Canadian criminal justice system can be as simple as *not* picking up the telephone to call the police if some harm has been done to you. This option involves thinking through what are good Aboriginal responses at the community level to wrong-doing.

There is another challenge I want to share with Aboriginal people. It was more than a decade ago that I first started volunteering in the federal prisons with the Native Brotherhood and Sisterhood groups. If I have learned anything across these years, it is this simple truth. Our people can "do the time." This should really come as no surprise. A wing of Stoney Mountain Penitentiary was built for the rebels of the 1885 Rebellion. Then there are the memories of Big Bear and Poundmaker and the five dancers from Thunderchild convicted for their ceremonial activities in 1897.[15] Our people have been doing time for more than one hundred years now. The use of the criminal law sanction against Aboriginal people is not a new phenomenon.

As a law graduate who is interested in prisons, I have learned how to get Aboriginal people out. I have learned the parole system and there are other lawyers who are real experts at parole. Too many times, however, my heart has been broken when the phone rings and the person who worked so hard to secure their release is calling me for bail money. As a result of this heartbreak, for the last year I have been struggling with a question. How do we keep our people out?

Keeping Aboriginal people out of prison has two aspects. There is no long-term sense in emptying prisons to only fill them up again. While we are busy emptying the prisons, we must also ensure that we are turning off the tap. Most importantly, we must keep our young people from ever becoming involved in the criminal justice system. Aboriginal youth need options and opportunities. Keeping Aboriginal people from ever entering the criminal justice system will require the support and creativity of the Aboriginal community.

Keeping our people out is an important question because until we know the answer to this question we do not know anything about how to reform the existing system. In particular, we do not know how to program effectively. I know of many studies that examine what factors make a person a danger to society and therefore not an acceptable parole risk. These studies have proven to be inapplicable to Aboriginal inmates. I do not know of any study that examines successful releases from prison. There is no body of knowledge that identifies what helps an Aboriginal person readjusting to society after release. This is astounding. Keeping Aboriginal people from returning to prison once released is a question that must be examined with the full involvement of Aboriginal communities. Many communities are not prepared to accept people back after they have offended. This is easy to understand for anyone who knows the consequences of oppression and colonialism. Aboriginal people have lost, at a general level, our ability to trust and forgive. This is the most important reason why non-Aboriginal people do not have a central role to play in the healing that must occur in Aboriginal communities.

Sitting in a circle at the Native Law Centre in January of 1994, a small group of Aboriginal people met to discuss issues of justice.[16] During our two days of discussions, an Inuit man asked the only member of our circle who had survived the Canadian prison system what would have helped him.[17] I think the answer given astounded many of us. We were told that it is simple things that make the difference, like a letter from home letting you know that you are cared about. In ten years, this man had few if any letters from home. The answer given initially surprised me but it makes so much sense to me now that I have thought about it. The answer was about caring. If we know that Aboriginal law was always family law then logically it is a system of social control based on caring.

I also have a message to deliver to Canada and Canadians.[18] As far as I am concerned the question is not Aboriginal justice systems or not. It is merely a question of when. Aboriginal justice systems are already happening. They will occur and there will have to be some form of reconciliation of the jurisdiction questions. We, the original people, will continue to make Aboriginal justice occur. It is merely a question of how long is it going to take. How long will the Aboriginal people of this country be forced to wait? How much will we be forced to suffer to be able to go back to that place where we live most nicely together? How much more pain and oppression will there be? Canada and Canadians have a unique role to play in only the question of *when* Aboriginal justice systems will fully be recognized. Canada and Canadians only have the power to delay or facilitate. No matter how long it takes, Aboriginal people will reclaim and recover.

For non-Aboriginal people, I also want you to have the opportunity to understand what self-government means to me. It is very simple. When we say it in my language it means I or we (depending on the context) are responsible. It boggles my mind to think that all of this constitutional debate, the number of conferences, the amount of federal money and federal energy spent trying to figure out what Aboriginal people want is merely the struggle to accept that we want to be responsible as Peoples. At the centre of our demands is one simple thing. I want and I need and I have the right to live as a responsible person in the way that the Creator made me, as a Mohawk woman. That is the only right I need. When I have the right to live in my territory as a Mohawk woman then I will have justice.[19] I am disturbed by what we see in self-government, the kind of self-government where we are merely granted the authority of administering our own misery. This is not self-government as I understand it. Self-government requires the significant letting go of Canadian government power over the lives of Aboriginal citizens. I do not doubt that the release of power (or learning to be decolonized) is a difficult thing.

So what does all of this mean? Well I told you I was not going to talk about women. I fibbed, because we come right back to women. Women are at the heart of it. Women are at the centre of it. The way that women are treated, not only within Aboriginal nations but within this country and any other one you want to choose, for me is the ultimate test of whether a country is democratic, is free, is just. Well, within these territories which have come to be known as Canada, I think we are failing miserably. We know about the abuses that are going on and let's not just look at Aboriginal territories. The truth is that the abuse is not worse in Aboriginal communities, it may be more focused upon and more easily documented, but it is not worse than in the rest of the country. That assertion is also a myth. The truth is that if rape occurs, if battering occurs, if any form of violence is present, if so-called women's work is devalued, all women are harmed and live with the knowledge that each of us are potential victims. The abuse of women is not an activity that is quantifiable as better or worse.

Women's involvement in justice work is not just a measure or standard of success of justice initiatives, the Aboriginal women's role is much more central and essential. There is one message I have heard so many times in trying to figure out what justice is. I have heard the old people say, "It was grandmother who made the laws, it was grandfather who enforced them." So when talks occur among political leaders about the administration of justice or constitutional rights for self-government you are not talking to the right people because you are not talking to the women. It was the women who had a fundamental role in making laws in our communities. I cannot stress enough that the answer lies with the women *of the communities*. I do not have much long-term use for national organizations, be they organizations of chiefs or women. These forms of organization are not Aboriginal. These organizations mimic non-Aboriginal forms of organization. We need to organize ourselves within our communities and worry less about national political venues. Involving women in a full, complete and respectful way in this process, be they Aboriginal or not, will again revolutionize what we think of law and justice. I do not believe that justice can even exist without women's central participation in all aspects of that system. Women are the doorway through which all life passes.

What I have come to understand is that justice is not a legal problem. It is a human problem. It is a women's problem and a men's problem. Every challenge and criticism that the legal system now faces, and there are many, is rooted in this reality. We have to carry that with us in both our minds and our hearts because if we do not, we do not have it together.

Notes

1. This is the word in my language that expresses my membership in the Six Nations Confederacy (as the English expressed it) or the Iroquois (in the French expression). We are the Oneida, Onondaga, Tuscrora, Seneca, Mohawk and Cayuga nations.

2. *Indian Act*, R.S.C. 1886, c. 43, s. 114. In 1951, this prohibition (in revised form) was repealed. *Indian Act*, S.C. 1951, c. 29.

3. I pay my respects to Dr. Art Solomon for his vision and the gift he made to me when he shared this teaching.

4. I do not mean to create simple dichotomies of Aboriginal and not. In fact, the phrase Aboriginal is a legal fiction. We are in truth, many nations with many ways of being. I struggle in a language that is not my own.

5. I am not suggesting that the *Charter* is a solution to Aboriginal Peoples' trouble with Canadian law. In fact, I am worried that the application of the *Charter* will just create another layer of legal oppression over Aboriginal concerns. I am merely pointing out a contradiction.

6. This by no means suggests that I have any particular opinion on this matter.

7. I am again grateful to my Mohawk friend, Tom Porter, of the territory of Akwesasne, for sharing this information with me.

8. For a detailed discussion, please refer to Monture-OKanee 1994: 131-140.

9. It is impossible to cultivate a true understanding of peacemaking from reading a single paragraph no matter how accurately and eloquently the reading expresses the process.

10. The costs of incarceration are just a small fraction of the costs to run the Canadian justice system. There are police, courts, lawyers and so on. Canadian justice finances are not available in such a way that the cost per person from arrest to the end of sentence can be compiled. ·

11. I will leave it to non-Aboriginal people to express their difficulties at moving out of the way to allow Aboriginal people to have the space to create our path.

12. A lot of this difficulty arises out of the fact that the conversation takes place in English or French only. It is not carried on in the language of Aboriginal people but in one of the two languages of our colonization. Part of the process of colonization is inherent in both of these languages. Those with the privilege of having either of those languages reflect their cultural reality do not see the contradictions that arise for those of us who are continually forced to negotiate, converse and discuss in a second and foreign language.

13. See for example, Bartlett 1989, McMurty and Pratt 1986, Pratt 1991.

14. *R.* v Sparrow, [1990] 3 *C.N.L.R.* 160-188 at page 178 and 181.

15. I am grateful to Professor Constance Backhouse who shared this research with me. Oddly, I have not been able to locate any reported cases for prosecutions under the provisions in the *Indian Act* which outlawed ceremonies such as the Sundance and Potlatch.

16. This talking circle was funded by the Royal Commission on Aboriginal Peoples.

17. The participant was Darrell Tart, a Saskatchewan Cree from Sandy Lake. In a recent conversation he told me that I could share his name with you, despite the fact that it exposes that he has a record. Darrell is like my brother. His courage and wisdom is a source of inspiration to me.

18. Aboriginal people who do not have any wish to follow our ways in the area of criminal justice are also Canadian. I have been taught that as Mohawk citizens we have a choice about whether we walk the Mohawk way or the Canadian way. My choice is obvious. This is also reflected in the treaties we have signed, such as the Treaty of Fort Albany (also more appropriately known as the "Two Row Wampum").

19. This is one of the reasons that I so strongly identify with my Mohawk citizenship and heritage. It is my understanding of the teaching about rights and responsibilities, patiently shared with me by several Elders in my community when I sought their support during my struggles in law school—struggles which once coalesced around issues of rights.

References

Aboud, Ray. 1986. "A Death in Kansas," *Saturday Night Magazine* (April): 28-39.

Adams, Howard. 1975. *Prison of Grass: Canada from the Native Point of View*. Toronto: General Publishing.

Alcoff, Linda. 1989. "Cultural Feminism versus Poststructuralism: the Identity Crisis in Feminist Theory." In Malson.

Allen, Paula Gunn. 1986. *The Sacred Hoop: Recovering the Feminine in American Indian Traditions*. Boston: Beacon Press.

Asch, Michael. 1984. *Home and Native Land: Aboriginal Rights and the Canadian Constitution*. Toronto: Methuen.

Backhouse, Constance. 1987. "Nineteenth Century Judicial Attitudes Toward Child Custody, Rape, and Prostitution." In Martin and Mahoney.

———. 1991. *Petticoats and Prejudice: Women and Law in Nineteenth-Century Canada*. Toronto: Women's Press.

———. 1990. "Women Faculty at the University of Western Ontario: Reflections on the Employment Equity Award." In *Canadian Journal of Women and the Law* 4, 1.

Baines, Bev. 1981. "Women, Human Rights and the Constitution." In *Women and the Constitution in Canada*. Edited by Audrey Doerr and Micheline Carrier. Ottawa: Canadian Advisory Council on the Status of Women.

Barman, Jeane, Yvonne Hebert and Don McCaskill, eds. 1986. *Indian Education in Canada: Volume 1, The Legacy*. Vancouver: University of British Columbia Press.

———. 1987. *Indian Education in Canada: Volume 2, The Challenge*. Vancouver: University of British Columbia Press.

Barreiro, Jose, ed. 1992. *Indian Roots of American Democracy*. New York: Akweikon Press.

Bartlett, Richard H. 1989. "The Fiduciary Obligation of The Crown to the Indians." *Saskatchewan Law Review* 53: 301-325.

Bluehouse, Philmer, and James W. Zion. 1993. "Hozhooji Naat'aanii: The Navajo Justice and Harmony Ceremony." In *Mediation Quarterly* 10, 4 ("Editorial" Special Issue): 327-337.

Boldt, Menno, and J. Anthony Long. 1985. *The Quest for Justice: Aboriginal Peoples and Aboriginal Rights*. University of Toronto Press.

Boyd, Susan. 1987. "Child Custody and Working Mothers." In Martin and Mahoney.

Boyle, Christine. 1986. "Teaching Law as if Women Really Mattered, or, What About the Washrooms." *Canadian Journal of Women and the Law* 2, 1: 96.

———. 1991. "A Feminist Approach to Criminal Defences." In *Canadian Perspectives on Legal Theory*. Edited by Richard F. Devlin. Toronto: Emond Montgomery.

Brodsky, Gwen, and Shelagh Day. 1989. *Canadian Equality Rights for Women: One Step Forward or Two Steps Back?* Ottawa: Canadian Advisory Council on the Status of Women.

Brown, Judith K. 1990. "Economic Organization and the Position of Women Among the Iroquois." In Spittal.

Brown, M. 1989. Native Law Centre Memorandum, University of Saskatchewan.

Canada. 1991. *Shaping Canada's Future Together*. Ottawa.

Canada, Government of. 1960. "Statement of the Government of Canada on Indian Policy." Ottawa.

Canada, Government of. 1990.*Creating Choices: Report on the Task Force on Federally Sentenced Women*. Ottawa.

Canadian Bar Association. 1988.*Aboriginal Rights in Canada: An Agenda for Action*. Ottawa.

Carasco, Emily. 1986. "Canadian Native Children: Have Child Welfare Laws Broken the Circle?" *Canadian Journal of Family Law* 5, 111.

Cardinal, Harold. 1969. *The Unjust Society: The Tragedy of Canada's Indians*. Edmonton: M.G. Hurtig Publishers.

Carter, Roger. 1980. "University of Saskatchewan Program of Legal Studies for Native People." *Canadian Community Law Journal* 4, 28.

Coates, Robert. 1989. "Lost in a Sea of White." *Canadian Lawyer*. October, pp. 27-29.

Comeau, Pauline. 1993. *Elijah: No Ordinary Hero*. Vancouver: Douglas & McIntyre.

Correctional Law Review. 1988. *Correctional Issues Affecting Native People*. Working Paper No. 7. Ottawa: Solicitor General.

Cox, Marilyn, and Wally Fox-Decent. 1993. *Children First, Our Responsibility: Report of the First Nation's Child and Family Task Force*. Winnipeg: First Nation's Child and Family Task Force.

Davies, Christe. 1994. "Racial and Cultural Issues in Custody Disputes." *Canadian Family Law Quarterly* 1-31.

Deloria, Sam. 1974. "Legal Education and Native People." *Saskatchewan Law Review* 38: 22-39.

Denny, Kjikeptin Alex. 1992. "Beyond the Marshall Inquiry: An Alternative Mi'kmaq Worldview and Justice System." In Mannette.

Dworkin, Ronald. 1977. *Taking Rights Seriously*. Cambridge: Harvard University Press.

Feldthusen, Bruce. 1990. "The Gender Wars: 'Where the Boys Are.'" *Canadian Journal of Women and the Law* 4, 1: 66-95.

Finn, Geraldine. ed. 1993. *Limited Edition: Voices of Women, Voices of Feminism*. Halifax: Fernwood Publishing.

First Nations Circle on the Constitution. 1992. *To the Source: Commissioner's Report*. (Chief Macwoot at the Elders' Assembly). Ottawa: Assembly of First Nations.

Freire, Paulo. 1970. *Pedagogy of the Oppressed*. New York: Continuum.

Frideres, James S. 1983.*Native People in Canada: Contemporary Conflicts*. Scarborough: Prentice Hall Canada.

————. 1988. *Native Peoples in Canada: Contemporary Conflicts*, 3rd edition. Scarborough: Prentice Hall.

Frum, David. 1994. "Native Law Program part of affirmative action lie." *Financial Post*, Oct. 15-17, editorial.

Garnier, Karie. 1990. *Our Elders Speak: A Tribute to Native Elders*. White Rock, BC: Karie Garnier.

Gavigan, Shelley A.M. 1988. "Law, Gender and Ideology." In *Legal Theory Meets Legal Practice*. Edited by Anne F. Bayefsky. Edmonton: Academic Printing and Publishing.

Goldsmith, Donna J. 1990. "Individual versus Collective Rights: The Indian Child Welfare Act, 1990." *Harvard Women's Law Journal* 1-12.

Green, Rayna. 1992. *Women in American Indian Society*. New York: Chelsea House Publishers.

Greschner, Donna. 1992. "Aboriginal Women, the Constitution and Criminal Justice." Special Edition, *University of British Columbia Law Review*, 338-359.

Gunn Allen, Paula. 1986. *The Sacred Hoop: Recovering the Feminine in American Indian Traditions*. Boston: Beacon Press.

Hagan, John. 1977. *The Disreputable Pleasures*. Toronto: McGraw-Hill Ryerson.

Haig-Brown, Celia. 1988. *Resistance and Renewal: Surviving the Indian Residential School*. Vancouver: Tillacum Library.

Hamilton, A.C., and C.M. Sinclair. 1991. *Report of the Aboriginal Justice Inquiry of Manitoba: The Justice System and Aboriginal People*. Winnipeg: Queen's Printer.

Hammersmith, Bernice. 1992. "Aboriginal Women and Self-Government." In *Nation to Nation: Aboriginal Sovereignty and the Future of Canada*. Edited by Diane Engelstad and John Bird. Concord: Anansi.

Harding, Sandra. 1989. "The Instability of Analytical Categories of Feminist Theory." In Malson.

————. 1991. *Whose Science? Whose Knowledge? Thinking From Women's Lives*. Ithaca: Cornell University Press.

Harding, Susan. 1992. "Starting Thought." Cited in "Equity and the University: Learning from Women's Experience." *Canadian Journal of Women and the Law* 5: 5-36.

Harstock, Nancy C.M. 1987. "The Feminist Standpoint: Developing Ground for a Specifically Feminist Historical Materialism." In *Feminism and Methodology* . Edited by Sandra G. Harding. Unversity of Toronto Press.

Hawthorne, H.B. 1966. *A Survey of the Contemporary Indians of Canada*. Ottawa: Indian Affairs and Northern Development.

Haycock, Ronald G. 1972. *The Image of the Indian*. Waterloo Lutheran University Monograph Series.

Henderson, James Youngblood 'Sakej'. 1992. "The Marshall Inquiry: A View of the Legal Consciousness." In Mannette.

Hepworth, H. Phillip. 1980. *Foster Care in Canada*. Ottawa: Canadian Council on Social Development.

Hickman, T. Alexander, Lawrence A. Poitras and Gregory T. Evans. 1989. *Royal Commission on the Donald Marshall Jr. Prosecution*. Halifax: Province Nova Scotia.

Hill, Jessica. 1983. *Remove the Child and The Circle is Broken*. Thunder Bay: Ontario Native Women's Association.

Hill, Richard. 1992. "Oral Memory of the Haudenosaunee: Views of the Two Row Wampum." In Barreiro.

Hogg, Peter W. 1985. *Constitutional Law of Canada*. Toronto: Carswell.

hooks, bell. 1981. *Ain't I Woman: Black Women and Feminism*. Boston: South End Press.

Jackson, Margaret. 1994. "Aboriginal Women and Self-Government." In *Aboriginal Self-Government in Canada: Current Trends and Issues*. Edited by John H. Hylton. Saskatoon: Purich.

Jackson, Michael. 1988. *Locking Up Natives in Canada*. Toronto: Canadian Bar Association.

James, David R. 1987. "Legal Structures for Organizing Indian Child Welfare Resources." *Canadian Native Law Reporter* 2: 1-20.

Jamieson, Kathleen. 1978. *Indian Women and the Law in Canada: Citizens Minus*. Ottawa: Advisory Council on the Status of Women.

Johnson, Patrick. 1982. "The Crisis of Native Child Welfare." *Native People and the Justice System in Canada*. CLAB.

————. 1983. *Native Children and the Child Welfare System*. Toronto: James Lorimer and Company.

Johnston, Charles M. ed. 1964. *The Valley of the Six Nations: A Collection of Documents on the Indian Lands of the Grand River*. University of Toronto Press.

Johnston, Darlene M. 1986. "The Quest of the Six Nations Confederacy for Self-Determination." *University of Toronto Faculty of Law Review* 44, 1: 2-32.

Jolly, Stan. 1983. *Anicinabe Debtors Prison*. Toronto: Ontario Native Council on Justice.

Kaiser, H. Archibald. 1992. "The *Criminal Code of Canada*: A Review Based on the Minister's Reference." In Special Edition, *University of British Columbia Law Review*, 41-146.

Kallen, Evelyn. 1982. *Ethnicity and Human Rights in Canada*. Toronto: Gage Educational Publishing Company.

Kane, Marlyn (Osennontion) and Sylvia Maracle (Skonaganleh:ra). 1989. "Our World." *Canadian Woman Studies*, 10, 2 and 3. (Summer/Fall): 7-19.

Kirkness, Verna. 1987-88. "Emerging Native Women." *Canadian Journal of Women and the Law* 2, 2: 408-415.

Kline, Marlee. 1989. "Race, Racism and Feminist Legal Theory." *Harvard Women's Law Journal*, 12 (Spring): 115-150.

Kline, Marlee. 1992. "Child Welfare Law: 'Best Interest of the Child' Ideology and First Nations." *Osgoode Hall Law Journal* 30,2: 1-50.

Kline, Marlee. 1994a. "The Colour of Law: Ideological Representations of First Nations in Legal Discourses." *Social and Legal Studies* 3:451-476.

Kline, Marlee. 1994b. "Complicating the Ideology of Motherhood: Child Welfare Law and First Nations Women." *Queen's Law Journal* 18:306-342.

Knockwood, Isabelle. 1992. *Out of the Depths: The Experiences of Mi'kmaw Children at the Indian Residential School at Shubenacadie, Nova Scotia*. Lockeport, NS: Roseway Publishing.

Krosenbrink-Gelissen, Lilianne E. 1991. *Sexual Equality as an Aboriginal Right: The Native Women's Association of Canada and the Constitutional Process on Aboriginal Matters, 1982-1987*. Germany: Breitenbach Publishers.

Lahey, Kathleen A. 1987. "Feminist Theories of (In)Equality." In *Equality and Judicial Neutrality*. Edited by Sheilah L. Martin and Kathleen E. Mahoney. Toronto: Carswell.

LaPrairie, Carol Pitcher. 1983. "Native Juveniles in Court: Some Preliminary Observations." In *Deviant Designations: Crime, Law and Deviance in Canada*. Edited by Thomas

Fleming and L.A. Lisano. Toronto: Butterworths.

LeResche, Diane. 1993. "Native American Perspectives on Peacemaking." In *Mediation Quarterly* 10, 4 ("Editorial," Special Issue): 321-324.

Little Bear, Leroy. 1976. "A Concept of Native Title." In *CASNAP Bulletin*, December, p. 58-62.

Livesey, Bruce. 1994. "Learning Blocks: Aboriginals and Law School." *Canadian Lawyer*. November.

Longboat, Diane. 1987. "First Nations Control of Education: The Path to Our Survival as Nations." In Jean Barman et al.

Lorde, Audre. 1983. "The Master's Tools Will Never Dismantle the Master's House." In *The Bridge Called My Back: Writings by Radical Women of Colour*. Edited by Cherrie Moraga and Gloria Anzaldua. New York: Kitchen Table Women of Colour Press.

Lyon, Noel. 1988 "An Essay in Constitutional Interpretation." *Osgoode Hall Law Journal* 26: 95-126.

————. 1992. "A Perspective on the Application of the Criminal Code to Aboriginal Peoples in Light of the Judgment of the Supreme Court of Canada in R. v. Sparrow." *University of British Columbia Law Review* (Special Edition): 306-312.

Lyons, Oren. 1985. "Traditional Native Philosophies Relating to Aboriginal Rights." In *The Quest for Justice: Aboriginal Peoples and Aboriginal Rights*. Edited by Menno Boldt and J. Anthony Long. University of Toronto Press.

————. 1986. "Spirituality, Equality and Natural Law." In *Pathways to Self-Determination: Canadian Indians and the Canadian State*. Edited by Leroy Little Bear, Menno Boldt and J. Anthony Long. University of Toronto Press, p. 5-13.

MacDonald, John A. 1983. "The Spallumcheen Indian Band By-Law and Its Potential Impact on Native Indian Child Welfare Policy in British Columbia." *Canadian Journal of Family Law* 1: 75-95.

————. 1985. "Child Welfare and the Native Indian Peoples of Canada." *Windsor Yearbook of Access to Justice* 5: 284-305.

MacKay A. Wayne, et al. 1989. "Breaking Barriers: Report on the Task Force on Access for Black and Native People." Submitted to Dr. H.C. Clark, President of Dalhousie University on September 21.

MacKinnon, Peter, and Peter Rhodes. 1974. "The First Canadian Program of Legal Studies for Native People" *Saskatchewan Law Review* 38, 40.

Malson, Micheline R., ed. 1989. *Feminist Theory in Practice and Process*. University of Chicago Press.

Mandamin, Leonard, Dennis Callihoo, Albert Angus and Marion Buller. 1992. "The Criminal Code and Aboriginal People." In Special Edition, *University of British Columbia Law Review*, 5-39.

Mandell, Louise. 1987. "Native Culture on Trial." In *Equality and Judicial Neutrality*. Edited by Sheila L. Martin and Kathleen E. Mahoney. Toronto: Carswell.

Manette, Joy. 1992. *Elusive Justice: Beyond the Marshall Inquiry*. Halifax: Fernwood.

Maracle, Lee. 1988. *I am Woman*. North Vancouver: Write On Press.

Martin, Sheilah L., and Kathleen E. Mahoney, eds. 1987. *Equality and Judicial Neutrality*. Toronto: Carswell.

Mathes, Valerie Sherer. 1990. "Nineteenth Century Women and Reform: The Women's National Indian Association." *American Indian Quarterly* XIV, 1: 1-18.

Matsudi, Mari. 1988. "Affirmative Action and Legal Knowledge: Planting Seeds in Plowed-Up Ground." *Harvard Women's Law Journal* 11: 1-17.

————. 1989. "When the First Quail Calls: Multiple Consciousness as Jurisprudential Method." *Women's Rights Law Reporter* 11: 7.

McGillivray, Ann. 1985. "Transracial Adoption and the Status Indian Child." *Canadian Journal of Family Law* 4: 437-467.

McIntyre, Sheila. 1987-88. "Gender Bias within the Law School: 'The Memo' and Its Impact." 2(1) *Canadian Journal of Women and the Law*, 2, 2: 362-407.

McMurty, W.R., and Alan Pratt. 1986. "Indians and the Fiduciary Concept, Self-Government and the Constitution: *Guerin* in Perspective." *Canadian Native Law Reporter* 19: 19-46.

McNeil, Kent. 1984. *Indian Child Welfare—Whose Responsibility*. Saskatoon: Legal Information Service, University of Saskatchewan Native Law Centre.

————. 1989. *Common Law Aboriginal Title*. Oxford: Clarendon Press.

Meili, Diane. 1991. *Those Who Know: Profiles of Alberta's Native Elders*. Edmonton: NeWest Press.

Mercer, Dean Peter P, Faculty of Law, University of Western Ontario. Letter, February 8, 1990.

Mohawk, John. 1987. Keynote Address given at the Race Relations Conference at the Can-Am Indian Friendship Centre, Windsor, Ontario, December. Copies of the address are on file with the author.

Montour, Martha. 1987. "Iroquois Women's Rights with Respect to Matrimonial Property on Indian Reserves." 4 C.N.L.R. 3.

Monture, Patricia A. 1987. "A Vicious Circle: Child Welfare and First Nations." *Canadian Journal of Women and the Law*, 3, 1: 1-17.

————. 1993. "I Know My Name: A First Nation's woman speaks." In *Limited Edition: Voices of Women, Voices of Feminism*. Edited by Geraldine Finn. Halifax: Fernwood Publishing.

————, and Mary Ellen Turpel. 1991. "Aboriginal Peoples and Canadian Criminal Law: Rethinking Justice." *Aboriginal Peoples and the Criminal Law: Report 34*. Ottawa: Law Reform Commission of Canada.

Monture-Okanee, Patricia A. 1992. "Discussion Paper: Aboriginal Women and the Justice System." Unpublished manuscript prepared for the Royal Commission on Aboriginal Peoples.

————. 1992b. "The Violence We Women Do: A First Nations View" *Contemporary Challenges: Conference Proceedings of Contemporary Women's Movement in Canada and the United States* . Edited by Backhouse and Flaherty. Montreal: Queen's-McGill Press. 191-200.

————. 1993. "Ka-Nin-Geh-Heh-Gah-E-Sa-Nonh-Yah-Gah" (French translation). *Canadian Journal of Women and the Law* 6, 1: 119-123.

————. 1994. "Alternative Dispute Resolution: A Bridge to Aboriginal Experience?" In *Qualifications for Dispute Resolution: Perspectives on the Debate*. Edited by Catherine Morris and Andrew Pirie. Victoria: Uvic Institute for Dispute Resolution.

Nahwegahbow, David, and Darlene Johnson. 1989. "Presentation to the Standing Committee on Aboriginal Affairs Regarding the Post-Secondary Education Assistance Program by the Indigenous Bar Association." *Canadian Native Law Reporter*, 3: 16-26.

Native Women's Association of Canada. 1986a. *Guide to Bill C-31: An Explanation of the 1985 Amendments to the Indian Act.* Ottawa.

Native Women's Association of Canada. 1986b. *A First Nation Citizenship Code.* Ottawa.

Neallani, Shelina. 1992. "Women of Colour in the Legal Profession: Facing the Familiar Barriers of Race and Sex." *Canadian Journal of Women and the Law* 5: 148-165.

Newell, William B. (Ta-io-wah-ron-ha-gai). 1965. *Crime and Justice Among the Iroquois Nations.* Montreal: Caughnawaga Historical Society.

Noon, J.A. 1949. *Law and Government of the Grand River Iroquois.* New York: The Viking Fund.

Nova Scotia. 1989. *Royal Commission on the Donald Marshall, Jr., Prosecution, Volume 1: Findings and Recommendations*, Chief Justice T. Alexander Hickman (Chairman), Associate Chief Justice Lawrence A. Poitras and the Honourable Mr. Gregory T. Evans. (Province of Nova Scotia: December 1989).

O'Brien, Mary, and Sheila McIntyre. 1986. "Patriarchal Hegemony and Legal Education" *Canadian Journal of Women and the Law* 2, 1: 69.

Ontario Ministry of Community and Social Services. 1985. *Tentative Policies for Indian Provisions of the Child and Family Services Act, Parts i-ix..* Toronto.

————. 1988. *Amendments Proposed to the Indian and Native Sections in the Child and Family Services Act, 1984.* Toronto.

Ontario Native Women's Association. 1987. *Bill C-31 Information Package .* Thunder Bay.

Ontario Native Women's Association. 1989. *Breaking the Cycle of Aboriginal Family Violence: A Proposal for Change.* Thunder Bay.

Pellat, A.S. 1991. *An International Review of Child Welfare Policy and Practice in Relation to Aboriginal People.* Canadian Institute for Law and the Family: Calgary.

Pentney, William. 1988. "The Rights of the Aboriginal People of Canada and the Constitution Act, 1988." *University of British Columbia Law Review* 22.

Perry, T.L. 1990-91. "Race and Child Placement: The Best Interests Test and the Costs of Discretion." *Journal of Family Law* 29,1:51-127.

Pickard, Toni. 1989. "Lament on the Rhetoric of Pain." In *Newsletter of the Conference on Critical Legal Studies*, November: 44.

Ponting, J. Rick, and Roger Gibbins. 1980. *Out of Irrelevance: A Sociopolitical Introduction to Indian Affairs in Canada.* Toronto: Butterworths.

Pratt, Alan. 1991. "Aboriginal Self-Government and the Crown's Fiduciary Duty: Squaring the Circle or Completing the Circle?" *National Journal of Constitutional Law* 2: 163-195.

Purich, Donald J. 1987. "Affirmative Action in Canadian Law Schools: The Native Student in Law School." *Saskatchewan Law Review* 51,79.

Ramsey, Henry Jr. 1980. "Affirmative Action at American Bar Association Approved Law Schools." *Journal of Legal Education* 30, 4-5.

Razack, Sherene. 1990-91. "Speaking for Ourselves: Feminist Jurisprudence and Minority Women." *Canadian Journal of Women and the Law* 4: 440-458.

Roesch Wagner, Sally. 1990. "The Root of Oppression is the Loss of Memory: The Iroquois and the Early Feminist Vision." In Spittal.

Ross, Rupert. 1992. *Dancing with a Ghost: Exploring Indian Reality.* Markham: Octopus Publishing Group.

Russell, Marguerite. 1989. "A Feminist Analysis of the Criminal Trial Process." *Canadian Journal of Women and the Law* 3: 552-568.

Ryser, Rudolph C. 1984. "Nation-States, Indigenous Nations, and the Great Lie." In *Pathways to Self-Determination: Canadian Indians and the Canadian State.* Edited by Leroy Little Bear, Menno Boldt, and J. Anthony Long. University of Toronto Press.

Sanders, Douglas. 1975. "Indian Women: A Brief History of their Roles and Rights." *McGill Law Journal* 21, 4: 656-672.

Scales, Anne. 1989. "Militarism, Male Dominance and Law: Feminist Jurisprudence as Oxymoron?" *Harvard Women's Law Journal* 12: 25-73.

Scott, Joan W. 1988. "Deconstructing Equality—Versus—Difference: Or, The Uses of Poststructuralist Theory for Feminism." *Feminist Studies*, 14, 1. (Spring): 33-50.

Silman, Janet, ed. 1987. *Enough is Enough.* Toronto: Women's Press.

Sinclair, Associate Chief Judge Murray of the Provincial Court of Manitoba. 1990. Presentation to the Western Workshop sponsored by the Western Judicial Education Centre, Lake Louise, Alberta, May 14.

Sinclair, Judge Murray, Donna Phillips and Nicholas Bala. 1991. "Aboriginal Child Welfare in Canada." In *Canadian Child Welfare Law: Children, Families and the State.* Edited by Nicholas Bala, Joseph P. Hornick and Robin Vogl. Thompson Educational Publishing: Toronto.

Slattery, Brian. 1984. "The Hidden Constitution: Aboriginal Rights in Canada." *American Journal of Comparative Law* 32, 361.

———. 1987. "Understanding Aboriginal Rights." *Canadian Bar Review* 66.

Smith, Dorothy. 1987. *The Everyday World as Problematic: A Feminist Sociology.* University of Toronto Press.

Solomon, Art. 1990. *Songs for the People: Teachings on the Natural Way.* Toronto: NC Press.

———. 1994. *Eating Bitterness: A Vision Beyond Prison Walls.* Toronto: NC Press.

Spittal, W.G., ed. 1990. *Iroquois Women: An Anthology.* Ohsweken: Iroquois Reprints.

St. Lewis, Joanne, Director Employment Equity Programme, University of Ottawa. Letter, February 2, 1990.

Statistics Canada (Aboriginal Peoples Output Program). 1989. *A Data Book on Canada's Aboriginal Population from the 1986 Census of Canada.* Ottawa: Supply and Services Canada.

Stevenson, Winona, Rhonda Johnson and Donna Greschner. 1993. "Peekiskwetan." *Canadian Journal of Women and the Law* 6,1: 153-173.

Strickland, Rennard. 1974. "An Essay: Take us by the Hand: Challenges of Becoming an Indian Lawyer." *American Indian Law Review* II, 2.

Sugar, Fran, and Lana Fox. 1989. "Nistum Peyako Se'ht'wawin Iskwewak: Breaking Chains." *Canadian Journal Women & the Law* 3: 465-482.

Tarnopolosky, Walter S. 1968. "The Iron Hand in the Velvet Glove: Administration and Enforcement of Human Rights Legislation in Canada." *Canadian Bar Review* 46: 565.

Task Force on Federally Sentenced Women. 1990. *Creating Choices: Report of the Task Force on Federally Sentenced Women.* Ottawa: Solicitor General.

The Lawyers Weekly. 1994. "Native students exemption sparks debate at U. of A." November 11: 4.

Thomas, Yvonne and Joacob. 1986. *The Constitution of the Confederacy of the Peacemaker*. Mimeographed volume.

Thompson, Ruth. 1988. "The University of Saskatchewan Native Law Centre." *Dalhousie Law Journal* II, 2 (March): 712-720.

Turpel, Mary Ellen. 1989-90. "Aboriginal Peoples and the Canadian Charter: Interpretive Monopolies, Cultural Differences." *Canadian Human Rights Yearbook* 6,3 pp. 3-45.

———. 1991a. "Aboriginal Peoples and the Canadian Charter: Interpretive Monopolies, Cultural Differences." In *Canadian Perspectives on Legal Theory*. Edited by Richard F. Devlin. Toronto: Emond Montgomery, p. 503-538.

———. 1991b. "Home/Land." 32(1) *Canadian Journal of Family Law*, 17-40.

———, and P.A. Monture. 1990. "Ode to Elijah: Reflections of Two First Nations Women on the Rekindling of Spirit at the Wake for the Meech Lake Accord." 15 *Queen's Law Journal* 345-359.

United Nations. 1948. U.N. Document A/811.

———. 1959. U.N. General Assembly Resolution 1386 (XIV), 14 G.A.

Viskelety, Beatrice. 1987. *Proving Discrimination in Canada*. Toronto: Carswell.

Waddams, S.M. 1987.*The Introduction to the Study of Law*. Third Edition. Toronto: Carswells.

Wagner, Sally Roesch. 1990. "The Root of Oppression is the Loss of Memory: The Iroquois and the Early Feminist Vision." In Spittal.

———. 1992. "The Iroquois Influence on Women's Rights." In Barreiro.

Walker, Lenore E. 1979. *The Battered Woman*. New York: Harper Books.

Wall, Steve, and Harvey Arden. 1990. *Wisdomkeepers: Meetings with Native American Spiritual Elders*. Hillsboro: Beyond Words Publishing.

Warry, Wayne. 1991. "Ontario's First People." In *Children, Families and Public Policy in the 90s*. Thompson Educational Publishing: Toronto.

Waubageshig, ed. 1970. *The Only Good Indian*. Toronto: New Press.

Weatherford, Jack. 1988. *Indian Givers: How the Indians of the Americas Transformed the World*. New York: Fascett Columbine.

Weaver, Sally M. 1981. *The Hidden Agenda*. University of Toronto Press.

White, Pamela M. 1985. *Native Women: A Statistical Overview*. Ottawa: Social Trends Analysis Directorate and Native Citizens Directorate.

Williams, Patricia J. 1991. *The Alchemy of Race and Rights: Diary of a Law Professor*. Cambridge: Harvard University Press.

Wuttunee, William I.C. 1971. *Ruffled Feathers: Indians in Canadian Society*. Calgary: Bell Books.

York, Geoffrey. 1990. *The Disposed: Life and Death in Native Canada*. Boston: Little Brown.

Related titles from Fernwood Publishing

POLITICS ON THE MARGINS
Restructuring and the Canadian Women's Movement
Janine Brodie York
This book explores the evolution of the Canadian women's movement, especially during the turbulent politics of the 1980s, and the cultural and political foundations of the emerging neo-liberal order. It shows how these foundations are bringing about profound and disturbing changes in state form and governing practices, for example, closed doors to elected officials, repeated funding cuts, the disappearance of women in social policy documents and the now popular allegation that organized feminists are unrepresentative of Canadian women. Brodie concludes that the women's movement is uniquely placed to build a new social consensus about the appropriate boundaries among the state, the economy and the home and to provide an ethical alternative to neo-liberalism's market-driven political philosophy.
120pp Paper ISBN 1 895686 47 4 $11.95 (From the Fernwood *Basics* series)

UNDRESSING THE CANADIAN STATE
The Politics of Pornography from Hicklin to Butler
Kirsten K. Johnson
This book examines whether the Canadian state's interest in maintaining the long-term legitimacy of current social relations has prompted a co-opting response to Canadian feminists' critique of pornography. Specifically, Johnson questions whether a feminist interest in promoting insurgent social change—by altering the nature of the state's approach to pornography—has been co-opted by the landmark decision brought down by the Supreme Court in 1992 (R. v. Butler). She argues—from a socialist feminist perspective— that pornography is an institution of an imperialist-capitalist and hetero-patriarchal society.
112p Paper ISBN 1 895686 48 2 $11.95 (From the Fernwood *Basics* series)

BECOMING AN ALLY
Breaking the Cycle of Oppression
Anne Bishop
This book is a dialogue—by a white, lesbian feminist who co-leads with a Black colleague a workshop on racism—about the answers to questions on the nature of oppression: where does it come from, has it always been with us, what can we do to change it, what does individual healing have to do with struggles for social justice, why do members of the same oppressed group fight each other, why do some who experience oppression develop a life-long commitment to fighting oppression, while others turn around and become oppressors themselves?
137pp Paper ISBN 1 895686 39 3 $13.95

ECOFEMINISM
Maria Mies and Vandana Shiva
Mies and Shiva write a powerful critique of the ideas of the Enlightenment, which measured civilization in terms of the domination of Nature. They argue that feminism should see linkages between patriarchal oppression and the destruction of Nature in the name of profit and progress. Through examining issues such as the growth of new reproductive technologies, "development," indigenous knowledge, globalization, the concepts of freedom and self-determination, the authors provide a vision of a different value system.
288pp Paper ISBN 1 895686 28 8 $25.95

FEMINISM AND THE POLITICS OF DIFFERENCE
Sneja Gunew and Anna Yeatman eds.
Increasingly "Western" feminism is being challenged to confront the multiple characters of domination and exploitation, usually conceived of as gender, class, race, and ethnicity. This innovative and timely collection reveals exciting contemporary theorising; raising and exploring the problems posed by identity politics and the possibilities for non-exclusive cultural and gendered positions.
254pp Paper ISBN 1 895686 27 X $19.95

NAMES, NUMBERS, AND NORTHERN POLICY
Inuit, Project Surname, and the Politics of Identity
Valerie Alia
Names are the cornerstones of cultures. They identify individuals, represent life, express and embody power. When power is unequal and people are colonized at one level or another, naming is manipulated from the outside. In the Canadian North, the most blatant example of this manipulation is the long history of interference by visitors with the ways Inuit named themselves and their land.
120pp Paper ISBN 1 895686 31 8 $11.95 (From the Fernwood *Basics* series)

LIMITED EDITION
Voices of Women, Voices of Feminism
Geraldine Finn ed.
This book is an introductory text and reader for use in Women's Studies. Feminist activists, teachers, students of Women's Studies, and women in the paid and unpaid labour force speak about their own experiences of feminism and the difference it has made in their public and private lives.
399pp   Paper   ISBN 1 895686 13 X $26.95

MAID IN THE MARKET
Women's Paid Domestic Labour
Sedef Arat-Koç and Wenona Giles   eds.
Chapters on domestic workers, chambermaids, daycare workers, the retail sector, the fast food industry, and home and office cleaners demonstrate that the work of reproduction in capitalist society is subordinated and devalued in the marketplace as well as at home.
160pp   Paper   ISBN 1 895686 35 0 $14.95

ELUSIVE JUSTICE
Beyond the Marshall Inquiry
Joy Manette ed.
The essays in this volume reveal how, even in this latest inquiry, the traditions, wisdom, customs and culture of the Mi'kmaq people were almost completely ignored.
110pp   Paper   ISBN 1 895686 02 4 $11.95   (From the Fernwood *Basics* series)

ISSUMATUQ
Learning from the Traditional Healing Wisdom of the Canadian Inuit
Kit Minor
Kit Minor helps us to understand what and how we can learn from the traditional helping wisdom of the Canadian Inuit. Through the develpment of a *culture-specific* design the author shows us how Inuit people, in a working relationship with members of the dominant culture, can continue to define and decide on appropriate helping skills.
112pp   Paper   ISBN 2 896586 05 9 $11.95   (From the Fernwood *Basics* series)